Sacrifice and Delight in the Mystical Theologies

of Anna Maria van Schurman and Madame Jeanne Guyon

STUDIES IN SPIRITUALITY AND THEOLOGY

Lawrence Cunningham, Bernard McGinn, and David Tracy

SERIES EDITORS

SACRIFICE *and* DELIGHT

in the

MYSTICAL THEOLOGIES

of Anna Maria van Schurman *and*

Madame Jeanne Guyon

BO KAREN LEE

University of Notre Dame Press

Notre Dame, Indiana

Library of Congress Cataloging-in-Publication Data

Lee, Bo Karen, 1971–
Sacrifice and delight in the mystical theologies
of Anna Maria van Schurman and
Madame Jeanne Guyon / Bo Karen Lee.
pages cm. — (Studies in spirituality and theology)
Includes bibliographical references and index.
ISBN 0-268-03391-9 (pbk. : alk. paper)
1. Mysticism. 2. Quietism. 3. Schurman,
Anna Maria van, 1607–1678. 4. Guyon,
Jeanne Marie Bouvier de La Motte,
1648–1717. I. Title.
BV5082.3.L44 2014
248.2'209252—dc23
2014028630

This book is dedicated to

my parents, Jong and Sunny Lee,

who joyously pour out their lives for God and others.

They embody beautifully the substance of this book.

Contents

Acknowledgments

This book began to take shape in me long before I became a student of theology. My parents and their life of ministry were the original inspiration. In them, I witnessed the beauty of a surrendered life, a life fully devoted to serving God even at apparent cost to themselves. They, however, never spoke of sacrifice and instead considered themselves most blessed. Now in their silver years, they exude a "joy unspeakable" and continue to love God and others tirelessly. They embody the best of Anna Maria van Schurman and Jeanne Guyon. If not for my parents, I would not have had the courage to write on the uncomfortable subject of self-denial.

Indeed, I took up that very subject for my doctoral dissertation, an earlier rendition of this monograph. I am thankful to my mentors at Princeton Theological Seminary who encouraged me to pursue the thesis. Ellen Charry, who instilled in me a love of theology when she taught that theology can lead to greater love for God, was a gracious guide and support throughout the dissertation phase. Thanks go also to Stacy Johnson, who introduced me to Anna Maria van Schurman in the first place, and to James Deming, who asked me important historical questions about the early modern period.

More immediately, I am grateful for the support of Bernard Mc-Ginn, who took the time to read my work and believed in it, even when I was a young, stumbling scholar. I first had the privilege of learning from him in 2002 at the University of Chicago, where his seminars helped me to understand the broader sweep of Christian mysticism during the medieval and early modern periods and enabled me to begin exploring the themes of this project. This past year, he was a steady guide through the "Generations in Dialogue" program, sponsored by the Institute for Advanced Catholic Studies. His keen eye and sage advice mean more to me than I can express. I am also grateful to Princeton Theological Seminary for its support of junior faculty, granting a sabbatical year to focus on our scholarship. Dean James Kay especially encouraged me in the completion of this book project, and I remain in his debt for his insightful counsel. The Collegeville Institute for Ecumenical and Cultural Research provided a beautiful place to work during my sabbatical year, as well as an opportunity to test some of my ideas. The John Templeton Award for Theological Promise also opened avenues for international conversation around the themes of this book, which helped to refine my thought. I thank Michael Welker and Peter Lampe for their support and the John Templeton Foundation for its generous grant.

During the past year, my five-year-old nephew Jonathan was diagnosed with cancer, and my family and I experienced the most difficult season of our lives. Months later, my brother-in-law was also diagnosed with cancer. Thankfully, both are now healthy and well. But during a time when writing became challenging, God's tender mercies and the loving support of friends buoyed me. I thank Sr. Josephine Aparo and Sr. Mary Gintella at the Morning Star House of Prayer, who offered me a prayerful shelter to heal from some of the year's travails. I also want to acknowledge my pastors and small group at the Washington Crossing United Methodist Church, and my friends from Princeton Seminary and Princeton University, for their prayers and steady encouragement. Some read portions of my manuscript and offered thoughtful feedback: Jessica Lowe, Laura Thelander, Arthur Murray, Greg Lee, Mary Carlson, and my dear sister Eunny. I also thank Joy Arroyo, Jennifer DiRicco, Harry Yoon, and Sharon Kim, for engaging my ideas, as well as Joyce Irwin, Janet Martin, and Josephine Dru, for their Latin expertise.

Finally, I owe an enormous debt of love to my family. My sister Shinna and her husband Don provided encouragement and advice over the years, as well as countless prayers; their children Jonathan, Anna, and Gabrielle give constant delight. Their faith in the midst of trials continues to inspire me. And my sister Eunny has been a dear, faithful friend through every season of life. Her loyalty and kindness, together with her husband Justin's, are inestimable gifts to me. I am deeply blessed to have been surrounded by the rich support of family, mentors, and friends, who helped to carry me through the entire process of completing this project.

I thank Brill Academic Publishers and the journal *Franciscanum* (Universidad de San Buenaventura) for allowing me to reuse published material. Portions of chapters 2 and 3 appeared in my essay "'I Wish to Be Nothing': The Role of Self-Denial in the Mystical Theology of Anna Maria van Schurman," in *Women, Gender, and Radical Religion in Early Modern Europe,* ed. Sylvia Brown (Leiden: Brill, 2007), 189–216, and various portions of the book appeared in summary form in my "Sacrifice and Desire: The Rhetoric of Self-Denial in the Mystical Theologies of Anna Maria van Schurman and Madame Jeanne Guyon," *Franciscanum* 51, no. 151 (2009): 207–39.

Preface

Self-denial can ruin a person. During my doctoral program in theology, I read account after account of women abused in the name of Christianity. Annie Imbens's book *Christianity and Incest*, was particularly painful to read. Imbens demonstrated how fathers, appealing to Jesus's self-denial as a model for "good Christians," forced their daughters into unspeakable acts. Her case studies came from the Dutch Reformed Church but can extend to other contexts; my own friend from the midwestern United States was abused by her father, a prominent church elder who forced her into submission with all the weight of the church's teachings. The theology of self-denial was tragically manipulated. It seemed obvious that a stronger sense of self was needed to bolster the defenses of female victims.

When I encountered Madame Jeanne Guyon's seventeenth-century writings, her biblical commentaries seemed to contain an unhealthy preoccupation with the notion of self-annihilation, which furthered my misgivings about the church's teaching on self-denial. However, as I continued to read more deeply, a strange beauty emerged. Guyon drew power from her particular theology; indeed, it allowed her to overcome cruel hardships, including persecution from the church and royal court, and inhumane imprisonments. Her theological and spiritual framework provided resources with which she could confront the ecclesial and political structures of her day. Guyon's writings have inspired many notable thinkers across multiple continents. Her enduring influence is astonishing given that she was a condemned figure in the Catholic Church.

I was surprised to find a similar pattern in Anna Maria van Schurman's theology in seventeenth-century Holland: her reflections on self-denial promised a deep inner strength, peace, and even joy. According to van Schurman, self-denial, when understood and practiced properly, enlarges rather than diminishes the individual. Indeed, we see a gradual transformation of tone in van Schurman's own writings—from that of acquiescent female to self-possessed leader in her circle and beyond.

These women and their texts, oddly enough, resonated in my mind with an emerging movement within feminism today. This generation of scholars promotes a feminism that does not seek to mimic that which it resists. In other words, this brand of feminism does not seek power as the primary good, necessary to redress previous imbalances of power. Rather, it embraces counterintuitive avenues by which an individual might be strengthened and made whole.[1]

In many ways, these two women of seventeenth-century Europe promoted a similarly counterintuitive journey. But they were even more radical in their formulation of how one may find true freedom. They argued that self-denial or, more appropriately, self-surrender *toward* God was not only the path to finding one's true self but also the secret to the deepest enjoyment possible in God. This coupling of self-denial with enjoyment is surprising and deserves to be explored. Both van Schurman and Guyon claim that they experienced self-denial as the source of an "unspeakable joy which the world does not know."[2] Their bold writings, theologies, and lives have shaped many people and movements, making them significant figures in the history of the church. They have become so precisely through this curious theology—a theology that promotes the deepest enjoyment of God, even through sacrificial surrender.

I

Reclaiming the Enjoyment of God: *Desiderium* and Sacrifice

Christians of various centuries considered the enjoyment of God to be the preeminent goal of humanity. As early as the fourth century, Augustine argued that God was the *summum bonum* of life and, as such, should be enjoyed exclusively.[1] As the "highest good," God was to be the object of humanity's desire and enjoyment (*fruitio*), while created things were to be used (*usus*) as a means toward the greater enjoyment of that good.[2] By implication, then, one of the central tasks of theology was to facilitate the enjoyment of God; likewise, it was imperative that the theologian cultivate his or her own delight in God. Not only was one's study to be pleasurable, but the object of one's study was to become the supreme source of joy.[3]

　　Subsequent generations of theologians, however, did not universally recognize the preeminence of this theme. While various authors attempted to recover its primacy, the emphasis in the "schools" of the medieval period, for example, shifted to other goals.[4] Augustine himself may have contributed to the subsequent waning of his vision when he concluded that the human capacity to enjoy the *summum bonum* during this life is but partial.[5] Despite his own longing (*desiderium*), he averred that the consummation of enjoyment awaited a different time, a different "city," when one was finally united with God. One had to look toward the "end without end" to experience unbounded delight; God would be the "bliss" only of that eternal city where "we shall see and our hearts rejoice."[6]

The height of joy was thus relegated to the realm of the eschatological. The desire for God, while it tended toward union with the object of desire, was thwarted by the vicissitudes of finite existence. Humanity's lot was simply to glimpse that final beauty, and this limitation fueled yet frustrated that yearning. Life on earth would be marked by toil and loss—a shadow of the blessed life to come.

Within the mystical tradition, however, a vibrant strand emerged that promoted the idea that, contrary to Augustine, union with God could be achieved in this life and *desiderium* fulfilled.[7] For example, commentaries on the *Song of Songs* proliferated during the medieval period, encouraging readers to seek deeper intimacy with the Divine.[8] These commentators agreed with Augustine that union with God would be enjoyed in its fullest measure at the final beatific vision, but they insisted that eschatological incursions of celestial bliss into this present life were both possible and desirable. Given certain conditions, a yearning for God could result in complete, unhindered enjoyment of God, that is, union with God during this life.[9] Some authors went so far as to trace careful steps—spiritual itineraries—by which the seeker might reach this goal.[10]

During the Reformation conflict of the sixteenth century, again the theme of *fruitio Deo* (the enjoyment of God) slipped into the background.[11] Theologians devoted their energies to disputing issues such as salvation, justification, faith, and the nature of grace. Polemic fervor only increased in the following century as Protestants sought to delineate categories, crafting their self-identity over and against other camps both within and without the Protestant world.[12]

Despite strident debates during the post-Reformation era of the church, select Catholic and Protestant thinkers reclaimed Augustine's imperative to enjoy God and developed it further. While the impetus is not clearly established, it is unmistakable that it returned with renewed force in disparate pockets of the church. The French school of spirituality, for example, emphasized the "sweetness of Christ," and Catholic mystical treatises detailed the soul's journey toward delectable union with God.[13] On the Reformed side, the Westminster Shorter Catechism of the 1640s heralded the claim that the "chief end of [humanity] is to glorify God and to enjoy [God] forever."[14] Though Calvin did not develop this theme, he hinted at it in his *Institutes*,[15] and those within the provenance of the Reformed Church would have been familiar with the language of both Calvin and the Creeds.

Anna Maria van Schurman (1607–78), the most renowned female theologian of seventeenth-century Holland, was among those who recovered this Augustinian strand. Adhering to the Reformed Creeds, she believed that "the chief end for which [humanity] was created is to . . . enjoy [God] forever."[16] To the discomfort of her readers, however, she prescribed means toward that end that departed from the typical categories of Reformed orthodoxy. Though van Schurman retained the core of her theological background, she added layers of thought arguably inherited from the Catholic mystical tradition, yielding a mixture of ideas that provoked suspicion.

Elsewhere in Europe, a similar blending of ideas emerged in the spiritual writings of another female theologian. Madame Jeanne Guyon (1648–1717), a French Catholic who would not have had obvious access to the writings of her Protestant neighbors, began to employ language strikingly similar to that of the Westminster Shorter Catechism. In the *Moyen court et très facile de faire oraison* ("A short and very easy method of prayer," 1685), she argued that "the end for which we were created is to enjoy God from this life on."[17] She wrote that finding pleasure in God is the "height of happiness and the end for which we were created" (le comble de la félicité et la fin pour laquelle nous avons été créés).[18]

Both van Schurman and Guyon would have inherited this idea ultimately from Augustine. The ideal of "enjoying God" in this life took on various permutations, however, after Augustine.[19] One might argue that it was forgotten in significant portions of the church during the seventeenth century and was no longer considered a supreme virtue, despite the nominal attention that both Reformed and Catholic theologians paid to it.[20] This seems true of van Schurman and Guyon's immediate contexts in particular. As Martin Prozesky has convincingly argued, even major strands of Dutch Pietism stressed morality over the enjoyment of God.[21] And Guyon's inherited Catholicism, dominated by the formidable Bishop Jacques-Benigne Bossuet, hardly focused on finding one's "pleasure" in God. There were exceptions to this rule, as in the case of Bérulle and the French school of spirituality, as well as in the writings of St. Francis de Sales. Nevertheless, Bossuet's leadership influenced much of the theological tenor of his day in France and beyond.[22]

This book examines the work of these two women who made the enjoyment of God central to their thought. Both van Schurman and Guyon, standing in divergent theological camps, inherited and expanded this notion and added surprising permutations of their own. Not only was their emphasis on the possibility of achieving union with God on earth a source of controversy, but the road that they mapped for their readers was a difficult one: they uncovered a significant cost to finding enjoyment in God. The demands that they imposed on the follower of Christ seemed so excessive and harsh that their teachings appeared pathological to some observers. Indeed, they called for nothing less than complete self-denial (in the case of van Schurman) and self-annihilation (in the case of Guyon) from those who longed to enjoy the highest good.

A RADICAL SURRENDER: ENJOYMENT'S SHADOW SIDE

Van Schurman and Guyon argued indefatigably that the "chief end of humanity" was to "enjoy God" both "in this life" and forever. This enjoyment, however, came at great cost. If the highest call was to find one's pleasure in the *summum bonum*, they argued together with Augustine that one consequently had to forsake "lesser" pleasures as an end in themselves. Inferior joys offered a mere facade and proved a barrier to the purest pleasure available in God. Ridding oneself of false joys required self-abnegation.

But van Schurman and Guyon went further. Departing from Augustine, they argued that union with God was possible on this earth through this process of purification. The trouble with this claim was not that they extended a strong form of *fruitio Deo* to the temporal; the mystics of the medieval period had already introduced that idea. Rather, it was that they regarded union with God as impossible apart from self-sacrifice. A thoroughgoing denial or annihilation of the self was required for the greatest pleasure in God to be experienced. Put another way, the uprooting of inferior joys required deep, painful purgation. The accent in their writings fell uncomfortably on the arduous nature of the path that leads toward union, even as they purported to celebrate the goal.

An emphasis on self-denial, of course, already had a long history in Christian theology and spirituality.[23] What makes van Schurman and Guyon unique is the way in which they coupled self-denial with pleasure. They intensified the denial as well as the pleasure.[24]

Though van Schurman and Guyon described this journey toward God in painstaking detail, they were careful to affirm that the drive toward self-denial (for van Schurman), or self-annihilation (for Guyon), is an innate longing of the soul to become more intimate with the object of desire. In other words, the soul's desire—its delight—is what motivates and sustains self-denial. Just as union with God is impossible apart from self-denial, the theme of self-abandonment becomes unintelligible apart from the desire for God. Desire (or enjoyment) and denial are thus mutually illuminating.

From this perspective, the "sacrifice" of the self becomes an oblation of love, a self-giving that is voluntary and delightful. Van Schurman and Guyon conclude that in pouring out its love the self is not diminished but rather enriched and enlarged.[25] This yearning for God becomes the driving pulse behind a radical loss of self, as dying to self leaves more room for God to "fill" the whole of self. Only then can the soul come to know and enjoy God in intimate union. Self-denial therefore becomes the secret to a more profound joy. As we shall see, Guyon and van Schurman's understanding of desire and delight provides a key insight into their theology of sacrifice. Self-denial—as opposed to self-hatred or self-effacement—is for them ultimately life-giving.

One of the purposes of this book is to uncover this neglected facet of van Schurman and Guyon's writings. In general, their theological treatises have not been adequately explored and deserve further study. More specifically, their reflections on self-denial must be brought to the foreground and analyzed even though they elicit considerable discomfort, or perhaps precisely because they do so. Their radical emphasis on self-denial may serve to counterbalance the love of comfort and consumption that marks our culture, and even our faith.

REDISCOVERING FORGOTTEN FIGURES IN THE HISTORY OF THE CHURCH

Although scholarly interest in female mystics has grown in recent decades, research on seventeenth-century female mystics and theologians is still lacking. Various surveys on women and gender in early modern Europe have appeared, but minimal attention is paid to women's spirituality.[26] Work on van Schurman's and Guyon's thought and spirituality in particular is scarce. The novelties in van Schurman and Guyon's writings raised the ire of their contemporaries and caused them to be disowned by their respective religious institutions. They fell out of favor with their theological superiors and the gatekeepers of history.

My hope is that these writers will emerge as the creative, energetic thinkers that they were. The "shroud of ignominy and mystery surrounding Madame Guyon" may have lifted, as Bruneau remarks,[27] but only in part. And the recent translations of a few of van Schurman's works are only the first steps to recovering her thought. A veil continues to obscure van Schurman's theology especially for English readers, as her most important work, *Eukleria* ("The better choice," or "Good fortune"), has not yet been translated into English from the original Latin.[28] A rich storehouse of theological material originating from these two remarkable figures has yet to be mined.[29]

Anna Maria van Schurman

Even among the often overlooked women of the seventeenth century, van Schurman especially has suffered scholarly neglect.[30] Her name began to reenter Dutch historical memory more widely on the four-hundredth anniversary of her birth in 2007,[31] but van Schurman's theology remains inaccessible to those who have no working knowledge of Latin, German, or Dutch.

The meager reception of van Schurman's work in the chronicles of church history is especially surprising when one notes the exceptional status she held as a luminary throughout Europe in her own time. Indeed, van Schurman was arguably the most remarkable female scholar of her generation. She rose to prominence among the leaders of the Dutch Reformed Church, and her fame reached far beyond the Reformed world. Lauded as the "tenth muse," the "brightest star" among the educated women of Europe, van Schurman was the pride of royalty, theologians, and poets alike.[32]

Born in 1607 in Cologne, Anna Maria was the third of four children of Frederik van Schurman and Eva von Harff, devout Calvinists. Instructed by a home tutor in matters of the faith, van Schurman recounts that she was able to "read German accurately" and "recite part of the catechism from memory" by the age of three.[33] Her father took great pains to ensure the education of his children. While testing his sons in Latin, he discovered that their younger sister's proficiency far surpassed theirs. From that time on, Frederik initiated Anna Maria in the study of classics, and she readily mastered the philosophy of Seneca, as well as the poetry of Homer and Virgil, among others.

In 1622, this young woman's erudition caught the attention of the renowned Dutch poet Jacob Cats. Her early composition of a poem in his honor gained his admiration, and she, in turn, became the object of his praise. A few years later, others would write elaborate encomia for her. Not only did van Schurman outshine her older brothers in linguistic facility, she outshone all of Utrecht (where she had moved with her widowed mother at the age of nineteen), even when it meant defying customary educational norms. She became the first woman admitted to study at the University of Utrecht and received the special honor of commemorating the university's opening with her own Latin composition in 1636. (It was not until 1872 that another woman would be allowed to study at the university level in all of the Netherlands.)[34]

Aspiring to become a sophisticated biblical exegete, van Schurman mastered over twelve languages and compiled the first Ethiopic grammar.[35] She exercised an uncanny command of Hebrew, Greek, Arabic, Aramaic, and Syriac and wrote treatises in Latin and French; she also composed poems in her native Dutch tongue.[36] Her appetite for knowledge was unbounded and her reputation crossed geographic lines. Van Schurman's renown became more widespread with the publication of her *Dissertatio, de Ingenio Muliebris ad Doctrinam, et meliores Litteras aptitudine* ("A treatise regarding the fitness of the female mind for the study of the arts and sciences") in 1641, and elaborate praise poems continued to be written in admiration of this "marvel of nature." Indeed, to "have been in Utrecht without having seen Mademoiselle de Schurman was like having been to Paris without having seen the king."[37]

However, upon joining a controversial new Pietist movement in the 1660s, van Schurman quickly fell out of favor. Devoting herself to a new spirituality, van Schurman integrated themes from mystical literature.[38] She taught a more extreme form of self-denial than her contemporaries, requiring full surrender to God at the start of the Christian journey. At the same time, her theology promised a deep enjoyment of God in this life, making "union with God" the supreme goal of theology. Though she retained her theological commitments to Calvinism, van Schurman expanded her categories, embracing the thought and spirituality of both nascent Pietism and Catholic mysticism.[39] Self-denial became her central theme,[40] and her life motto, "My love has been crucified," found consistent expression throughout her theological writings in various ways.[41]

Madame Jeanne Guyon

Madame Guyon's reception among her contemporaries followed a similar trajectory. She initially rose to prominence in the courts of Madame de Maintenon, the second wife of King Louis XIV. Serving as her spiritual counselor, she won the respect of nobles and clerics of the court. Nonetheless, her "unconventional" teachings on the interior life, first found in her *Short and Very Easy Method of Prayer*, elicited suspicion, even hostility. Chief among her critics was the indomitable Bossuet.[42]

Religious authorities were on the alert against novelty, and Guyon became a prime target. This period was marked by highly charged dispute between Catholics and Protestants, as well as the clamping down of intra-Catholic orthodoxy, and Guyon was faulted for teaching a form of prayer that sounded both too Protestant and too Quietist. With regard to the former, she was accused of denigrating outward prayers and good works and was thought to promote the doctrine of "justification by faith alone."[43] Furthermore, her writings sounded dangerously similar to the Quietist teachings of Miguel de Molinos, condemned by Pope Innocent XI in 1687 (two years after she penned *Moyen court*). After harsh interrogations in 1694, Guyon was locked away in Vincennes by Louis XIV in 1695, then imprisoned in the Bastille until 1703, and finally kept under house arrest in Blois until her death in 1717.[44]

Despite Guyon's notoriety, her background would not have suggested such a dramatic life. Born to a wealthy family in Montargis, France, and a young girl of frail constitution, Guyon was shuttled around from convent to convent until she married a wealthy neighbor at the age of sixteen. She describes in her *Vie* (*Autobiography*) a rather unhappy union with Jacques, twenty-two years her senior.[45] Trapped in the company of her ailing husband and overbearing mother-in-law, Guyon writes that she was unable to find refuge except in God.[46] Often withdrawing into prayer, she endured the increasing taunts of her mother-in-law until her husband's death in

1676 freed her, now twenty-eight, from her constrained life. It was after this that she felt called to spread her teachings on the interior life. Guyon then found a valuable confessor in Father François La Combe and advanced further in her life of prayer.

Leaving her home, Guyon enjoyed an itinerant ministry throughout Geneva, Turin, and Grenoble, where she guided others in the spiritual life, often in small gatherings. These gatherings inspired her to write for her friends. *Les torrents spirituels* ("The spiritual torrents") appeared in 1682 and her *Short and Very Easy Method of Prayer* a few years later. Guyon's works were not intended for wide circulation, but the latter book came under official scrutiny shortly after the Quietist controversy erupted in Rome. Louis XIV had also revoked the Edict of Nantes, thereby limiting religious freedom. *A Short and Very Easy Method of Prayer* was placed on the *Index of Prohibited Books* in 1688, and her books were burned throughout various cities in France. Though her writings had made her a controversial figure, Guyon became friendly with Madame de Maintenon in 1688 and became her spiritual guide. She also became François Fénelon's trusted friend and inspired his thought throughout his career as royal tutor and eventual archbishop of Cambrai. When her work officially came to trial in 1694, Bossuet won the day in seeing her teachings overthrown, and the majority of Catholic authorities disowned her. Guyon would experience the loss of favor with the court, great "persecution," and various imprisonments.

In the past twenty years, Guyon has received increasing attention on various fronts with the burgeoning of scholarly research on female mysticism. Her contributions to literature and politics have been examined, as well as her personal courage in the face of severe opposition. The historical circumstances surrounding the Quietist controversy of the seventeenth century have also been analyzed, and Guyon's name freed of much of the libel to which it was once subjected. As a result, the energy of Guyon's life has contributed to various streams of feminism. She is slowly becoming a force to be reckoned with in the "modern world."[47]

Guyon's theological work, however, has received less attention in both French and English-speaking contexts.[48] A prolific writer and avid student of the scriptures (a rarity in her day—especially as a Catholic woman), Guyon produced over twenty biblical commentaries and fifteen treatises, as well as a three-volume work, *Justifications* (yet to be translated into English), that provides a 1,200-page theological defense of her work as orthodox. Neglect of these works prevails and may be due in part to the discomfort that many of her writings evoke.[49] Indeed, her thought caused grave consternation among the Catholics of her day and continues to provoke readers today.

Sacrifice, suffering, submission—these themes relentlessly mark Guyon's thought. She teaches that to enjoy the intimate presence of the Divine the soul *must* "lay itself on the altar of sacrifice," undergo acute afflictions, and submit itself entirely to the "good pleasure" of God.[50] But what is "good" about suffering? Guyon goes so far as to claim that the soul must allow itself "to be totally surmounted and destroyed by the operations of love" if it desires to enter the fullness of the Divine.[51] She explains: "God wishes to reduce you to littleness, and poverty of spirit . . . to disarrange you—to destroy self."[52] Because of this pervasive language of self-annihilation, some commentators have diagnosed her thought as violent, masochistic, and pathological.[53]

Guyon's writings are indeed problematic. Not only do they offend modern sensibilities, they earned her the title of "heretic" and "madwoman" in her own day. Interestingly, the Protestant world reclaimed and rehabilitated Guyon's thought during her own time,[54] and her loyal (Protestant) followers surrounded her at her deathbed. That we have a large body of her writings today is due to the efforts of Pierre Poiret, a French Protestant publisher who admired and carefully preserved her work.[55] Guyon's influence on John Wesley, the early Quakers, Nicolas Zinzendorf, Watchman Nee, Søren Kierkegaard, and Arthur Schopenhauer, among others, has also been established.[56]

Central Texts

Before one can criticize the problematic nature of "self-abnegation" in both van Schurman and Guyon's writings, one needs to understand the movement and intricacies of their thought. Their language also needs to be placed in its appropriate context. Guyon's usage of the word *sacrifice* or *annihilation*, for example, is multivalent, yet it continues to be interpreted primarily with a negative lens. She is deemed psychotic or masochistic, or this "strange" aspect of her work is neglected.

From within her own theological framework, however, Guyon explains why she believes that "in faithfulness God afflicted [her]"[57] and why the soul has to experience an anguish that culminates in "death." She writes with conviction that "all the graces of the Christian spring from [this] death of self."[58] Van Schurman likewise claimed that there could be no "true Christianity" apart from self-denial, "except one that is counterfeit [*fucatus*]."[59] What, then, were the theological sources and implications of such a claim?[60]

This volume will examine van Schurman's theology of self-denial alongside Guyon's rhetoric of annihilation. For van Schurman, the *Eukleria*, her most mature work published in 1673, sheds the most light on the theme of self-denial.[61] This treatise is van Schurman's comprehensive summary of her theology by way of a systematic defense of the decisions she made in her intellectual trajectory. A series of important, yet unpublished, letters that van Schurman exchanged in 1673–75 with Johann Jakob Schütz, one of the founders of Lutheran Pietism, will add further insight.[62] These letters clarified some of the questions that arose from her treatise and together with the *Eukleria* arguably helped shape the genesis of Spener's German Pietism.[63]

In language beyond Calvin's, van Schurman argues that *self-denial* is the only means by which an individual can gain "inmost knowledge of God" (*intima notitia Dei*); this kind of knowledge is the secret to enjoying God and ultimately attaining union with God. Apart from a radical denial of the self, knowledge of God remains sterile and lifeless. Van Schurman thus describes the journey of the soul as it learns to lay itself on the "altar" and die to its own desires and will. At the end of this difficult surrender, intimate knowledge and joyous union are the promised goal.

Using more vivid and extreme imagery, Guyon details the "annihilation" of the soul requisite for truly knowing and enjoying

God in order to become united with God. Particularly in her *Commentaire au Cantique des cantiques de Salomon* ("Commentary on the Song of Songs," 1688), Guyon describes different levels of "union" with God and explains that fullness of joy can come only after a painful, decisive death. For Guyon, true joy is impossible without suffering.

Like van Schurman, Guyon was concerned with the question of spiritual itinerary. Intimate knowledge of God may be the goal, but she was concerned to address *how* one reaches that goal. Among all her writings, Guyon's *Commentary* elucidates this itinerary in greatest detail and provides the fullest explanation of her theology of self-annihilation. Guyon avers that this particular work was especially "inspired" of God. Indeed, her *Commentary* has gathered a surprisingly wide readership through the centuries, across different continents.[64]

A SURPRISING CONVERGENCE

Van Schurman and Guyon reach a rather unexpected point of convergence in their writings, despite their different theological commitments and divergent starting points. Both go to great lengths to explain that the highest good of humanity is to enjoy God: as God is the greatest good, enjoying God is humanity's greatest pleasure. More strikingly, however, van Schurman and Guyon share an emphasis on analyzing the difficult path one must follow to arrive at this end, not only in the next life but here and now. Surprisingly, the spiritual itineraries that they recommend are remarkably similar.

Perhaps one ought not to be surprised. In Calvin's *Institutes*, for example, the theme of self-denial and "picking up one's cross" becomes prominent and sounds rather similar to Guyon's own rhetoric.[65] One of my aims, then, will be to discern whether "self-denial" means the same thing in both Reformed Pietist (Labadist) and Quietist Catholic thought, as specifically evidenced by van Schurman and Guyon's writings.[66] Interesting differences may emerge, and we will need to be careful not to make too much of apparent similarities.

In an era of heightened polemic—and even religious warfare— van Schurman and Guyon demonstrated courage in crossing boundaries. Their transgressions of conventional codes served to free them from the constraints placed upon women, or simply upon those (men and women alike) who expressed "new" ideas. This cross-fertilization of ideas will be one of the subjects of the concluding chapter.[67] The point of convergence between Madame Guyon and Anna Maria van Schurman is a telling one, suggesting that the themes of self-sacrifice and *fruitio Deo* were vital in seventeenth-century Christian thought, even if in isolated pockets, both Catholic and Protestant. Amid the important corrections that have been made by feminist theologians in recent decades (corrections that rightly challenge the abuse of such themes), the call of Christ to "deny oneself" joyfully and "pick up one's cross" can be neglected.[68] Much will remain lost if we fail to retrieve these core and indispensable themes—albeit with careful attention to their excesses and abuses—for contemporary theology.

2

"I Wish to Be Nothing": Self-Denial
in Anna Maria van Schurman's *Eukleria*

Then Jesus told his disciples, "If any want to become my followers,
let them deny themselves and take up their cross and follow me."
—Matthew 16:24

Throughout the history of Christianity, the call of Christ to deny the self has inspired his disciples to acts of great sacrifice—from martyrdoms to rigorous forms of asceticism. The power of this appeal to self-denial is especially evident in the writings of Anna Maria van Schurman, seventeenth-century Europe's "star of Utrecht." She went so far as to identify self-denial as the lifespring of Christianity, without which true Christianity cannot exist, "except one that is counterfeit [*fucatus*]."[1] According to van Schurman, self-denial was not a *goal* or destination for mature believers alone, as others were wont to claim. Self denial was rather a *prerequisite* for all who desired even to begin the Christian journey. While self-denial was not by any means a novel concept, the priority that she attached to it was surprising to her contemporaries.

For van Schurman, the final purpose of self-denial was union with Christ. This goal would be unattainable without self-denial, through which one was emptied of the self and thus made ready for union with Christ. Even before the goal was to be reached, however, van Schurman yearned for a kind of knowledge that she would label "the one thing necessary." This *unum necessarium* was an "intimate" or "inmost" knowledge of God (*intima notitia Dei*), and this too was inaccessible apart from a radical denial of the self. Self-denial, then, would be the engine behind an intimate knowledge of God that would, in turn, lead ultimately to union with Christ.

While self-denial was supremely desirable, it proved impossible for van Schurman. Self-denial, she discovered, would not be achieved by sheer effort; rather, it would be the by-product of another process. Only a greater, more pleasurable gain would provide the impetus to motivate (and ultimately enable) her to deny herself, as if by sheer coincidence. Faithful to the creeds of the Reformed Church, van Schurman held that "the chief end of [humanity] is to . . . enjoy [God] forever."[2] This desire to "enjoy God" would become the secret to self-denial; it would also lead the seeker, ultimately, toward union with Christ. When enjoyment of God became the individual's supreme desire, self-denial would inevitably occur. Likewise, a greater self-denial resulted in a sweeter enjoyment of God. Rather than debilitate the soul, self-denial granted deep pleasure and delight to the soul that had learned to deny itself *for the sake of* a greater good. It found both its source and its fruit, its impetus and its reward, in the greater enjoyment of God.

Other theologians in the Dutch Reformed Church of van Schurman's time took issue with her emphasis on self-denial. They argued that it was a "mark of perfection" for mature Christians and feared that its primacy in her writings might oppress or discourage the everyday Christian.[3] Against their doubts, van Schurman contended that self-denial need not be a daunting or restrictive imperative. Rather, it had the power to enlarge and enrich every individual. Indeed, this was the case in van Schurman's own experience. Although the established elite in both the academy and the church would deny her for her choices, and she also had to deny her former loves, van Schurman held to her convictions and found her theological voice.

A stronger sense of self emerged, by the very *means* of her self-denial. She became a key spokesperson for the Labadists, a newly emerging Pietistic movement of her day led by Jean de Labadie. She was also a forerunner of German Pietism, as her writings arguably shaped this important movement from its outset.[4] At the end of the day, van Schurman emerged as a poised and confident leader. Her emphasis on self-denial served not to weaken but to liberate and strengthen her.

To understand van Schurman's argument, one needs to uncover the development in her thought. A dramatic shift marks her theological pursuits and indicates the contours of, and the reasoning behind, her spiritual trajectory. This chapter will examine that shift by exploring the argument of the *Eukleria*, published in 1673, and contrasting it with her *Dissertatio*, published in 1641. The following chapter will analyze van Schurman's theology as explicated in her correspondence with Johann Jakob Schütz, which fills in some of the gaps in her *Eukleria*. The theme of self-denial's "impossibility" will also be explored. With the widespread reception of the *Eukleria*, new questions arose, and van Schurman went to lengths to further articulate her position through these letters.

This turn in van Schurman's thought, finalized in the 1660s, was coupled with her decision to join the Labadist movement, a decision that led to the overthrow of her fame throughout Europe. In 1669, van Schurman made the controversial decision to leave the life of intellectual pursuits in order to devote herself to a life of piety within the Labadist community. Jean de Labadie (1610–74), formerly a Jesuit, had converted to Calvinism (a rare move given the strident polemic of the era), only to sever affiliations again to form his own movement.[5] Van Schurman's renunciation of her elite past created upheaval among those who had been her most loyal supporters. It also marked an upheaval in her own thinking about what theology and the reading of scripture were ultimately to attain. This contrast with her past, as she herself presents it in the *Eukleria*, and as her earlier writings confirm, is almost as stark as her conclusion about the centrality of self-denial. Understanding this radical change will enable us to analyze better van Schurman's rhetoric of self-denial.

FROM "STAR OF UTRECHT" TO DEFAMED "SPIDER EATER"

Anna Maria van Schurman was widely regarded as the "brightest star" of seventeenth-century Europe, having demonstrated intellectual gifts unequalled among women and men alike. While she was recognized for her intricate artwork, sensitive musicality, and philosophical acumen, it was her linguistic genius that gained her highest praise, and even access to the university as the only female student (albeit hidden behind a screen in the corner of the lecture hall). Hailed as Utrecht's finest Latinist, she was invited to compose a poem in honor of the University of Utrecht's opening in 1636. Upon entrance to the university, she learned Semitic languages directly from the illustrious theologian Gisbertus Voetius. Van Schurman continued to impress elite intellectuals and traveled in the highest circles, exchanging letters and gifts with key philosophers, theologians, artists, and poets. Eulogies repeatedly described her as a *miraculum* or *monstrum naturae*, a "marvel of nature."[6]

Not only was van Schurman's towering intellect the object of enthusiastic praise, but her virtue and modesty were also of particular appeal, especially to theologians. The most prominent theologian from Leyden, André Rivet, for example, when remarking on her intellectual brilliance, characteristically supplemented his words of elaborate praise with salutations declaring his "admiration for your virtues and above all for your exceptional piety and modesty."[7] Had her intellect stood alone, without virtue and piety to match, van Schurman might indeed have seemed a "monstrous" sort of marvel to her male counterparts. Her humility, however, served to make her gifts more palatable and less intimidating to them. Their approval of her work, and in particular of her *Dissertatio, de Ingenio Muliebris ad Doctrinam, et meliores Litteras aptitudine* of 1641, gained her a wide readership, and her writings quickly circulated throughout Holland as well as Europe. This unusual integration of genius and humility was the object of intense admiration, and van Schurman became the pride of Europe.

Nevertheless, after enjoying nearly five decades of international renown, in the late 1660s van Schurman was decried by many as having "gone mad." Her fame was now reduced to a "dimmed, invisible star,"[8] and this "astre éclipsé" was said to have resorted to "eating spiders" ("On dit qu'elle aimait beaucoup à manger des araignées")—the equivalent of saying in our day that she had "lost her marbles" or "gone batty."[9] As Eberti explained in 1706, "This crown of the female sex would undoubtedly have been seen by posterity as a shining example of all learned women had she not somewhat tarnished her own luster and her fame by her reprehensible doctrines."[10] Van Schurman herself admits in her *Eukleria*, "It is now evident to all from the public writings of a number of celebrated men, who used to be extraordinarily well-disposed towards me, that my new manner of life displeases them greatly."[11] What was this "new manner of life"? Which of her doctrines earned the title "reprehensible," and for what reasons did this star lose its gleam? Did these detractors object to specific aspects of van Schurman's theology, or was mere cohabitation under Labadie's roof sufficient to raise eyebrows?[12]

Although van Schurman's intellect had been highly praised by her contemporaries for several decades, she paints a picture of growing dissatisfaction with this life in the *Eukleria*. Her mother had passed away in 1637, and as early as 1638 van Schurman had assumed some of her mother's former responsibilities, particularly her works of charity. Nonetheless, she reports in retrospect that all of her learning had imparted not a jot of genuine love in her heart for the tasks, and people, at hand. One may surmise that at some point during these years of charitable works van Schurman began to be disillusioned with the theological systems that had buttressed her life.[13] Finally, in 1653, van Schurman had to leave altogether the life of focused intellectual pursuits in order to tend to her ailing aunts.[14]

As one reads the *Eukleria*, it appears that a series of disenchantments had set her up for her introduction to Jean de Labadie in 1666. Though the treatise details neither the time line nor the specific ways in which she gradually departed from her academic training, hints are scattered throughout. She explains that she had become increasingly aware of the spiritual impotence of her former ways of doing theology. In addition to the lack of change within her own heart, she began noticing the ineffectiveness of the theology that surrounded her. As a result, she fled from the company of those whom she calls "worldly theologians . . . not only because they contained not a whit of solid learning or genuine eloquence, but primarily because they did not savor or give off the scent of even a drop of that oil that the Spirit of Christ pours into the hearts of his own."[15] She continues: "I was strengthened in this opinion by experience, and no one could easily persuade me [otherwise], since it was most truly false, namely, that the words of life that are dead in the mouth of a dead preacher (as someone said more elegantly than accurately) bring life to dead listeners. For the preacher can indeed say the words but not grasp and give voice to the meaning and life or Spirit of Scriptures; the listeners, moreover, have not the ears to hear spiritual things in a spiritual manner or to grasp them inwardly."[16]

In 1662, her brother Johan wrote to her of the Calvinist minister Jean de Labadie, reporting that his heart had been "set aflame" by his encounter with this "clear and living image of Christ." With these words, van Schurman turned in a new direction. She yearned for a theology that effected an inward change of heart. Upon meeting Jean de Labadie four years later, she concurred with her brother that this man was different from the other "representatives" of Christ she had known. Her intellectual trajectory had already taken a turn because of the demands of serving others, and now her spiritual journey was also to be redirected. In August of 1669, van Schurman became one of the core members of the Labadist community. This was the year that Labadie broke away (or was expelled) from the official Calvinist Church of Walloon in order to establish his own sectarian community in Amsterdam.[17] Van Schurman gladly became one of the first to join this new movement.

We know from van Schurman's exchanges with the theological authorities of her day that her decision to join the Labadist movement set off great controversy. Jean de Labadie had been expelled from both the Reformed Church of Montauban and the Walloon Reformed Church in Middelburg for his sectarian, chiliastic, and "mystical" tendencies. Hence, her association with the "fanatical Labadie" cast a "dark shadow" upon her life. Not only did the unconventional (co-ed) living arrangements of the Labadist community appall the authorities, but they had difficulty understanding Labadie's preaching, as well as his passionate approach to religious issues.[18] Perhaps his Jesuit background also evoked suspicion. Why would van Schurman leave her past behind to join *this* man's community? Those who had been her strongest supporters now questioned her, and praise was silenced.

From van Schurman's perspective, joining the Labadists was the culmination of a process. She had been dissatisfied by what she perceived to be the ineffectuality and aridity of airtight Calvinist scholasticism. As a result, she began to remove herself from the confines of narrow doctrine and scholastic theological argumentation.[19] That which she had mastered with previous delight—the art of "making distinctions"—no longer appealed to her. Theological polemic, rampant in the seventeenth century as Protestantism sought to define and distinguish itself, proved a hindrance to the newfound goal of her theological enterprise. Though the core of her thought would remain Calvinist, van Schurman expanded her categories, embracing the thought and spirituality of both nascent Pietism and Catholic mysticism.[20]

With van Schurman's desertion of the institutional church for the community of the isolated and controversial Jean de Labadie, mainstream theologians seemed to have had no choice but to disown her. Her decision to leave her prior way of life led some to believe that "common sense deserted her at last" as she "fell prey to such weakness" of mind and will.[21] Former admirers marveled that such a brilliant mind would "waste" itself on simplistic religion.[22] From first to last, however, van Schurman defended her decision to join the Labadist movement as "the better choice" (*Eukleria*).

VAN SCHURMAN'S THEOLOGICAL SHIFT: FROM *SCIENTIA* TO *INTIMA NOTITIA*

To understand van Schurman's change of heart, we turn to the pages of the *Eukleria*, where her self-portrait emerges. Her masterpiece, noted for its erudition as well as its eloquent Latin prose, is not only a spiritual autobiography but also a defense of the Labadist movement, a theological treatise, and a chronicling of Labadist history. Most importantly for our purposes, she describes the break with her past and offers a clear rationale for why this shift of allegiances was necessary.

How did van Schurman understand her "choice"? In what ways had she chosen "the better part"? The title itself (*EYKΛHPIA*, or *Eukleria*) can be translated in various ways, as "the better choice," or "good fortune." More specifically, van Schurman refers to Luke 10:41–42, signaling Mary's "choice" to sit at the Master's feet as the "better thing." Inscribed on the cover page of her treatise, one finds: "Luc. 10:41, 42: *Unum Necessarium. Maria meliorem partem elegit*" ("One thing is necessary: Mary has chosen the better part"). She also provides for her reader the Latin equivalent of the title on that same page: "*Eukleria: Seu Melioris Partis Electio.*" Hence, one can render her usage of *Eukleria* as "choosing the better part."

Throughout the *Eukleria*, van Schurman attributes the break with her past to her newfound pursuit of the "one thing" that was "necessary" (Luke 10:41–42). This scriptural passage becomes central to van Schurman's thinking and dominates the whole of her argument. What was this "one thing," however? The reader is invited to discern from the whole of her writing, as well as from the scriptural context itself, that this "one thing" involves an intimate knowledge of God (*intima notitia Dei*), or, an experience of "being taught by the Master directly."[23]

My task here is to elucidate the contours of this "one thing" as van Schurman expands on the notion of direct and intimate, or inmost, knowledge of God. Her thought will come into sharper focus as she contrasts inmost knowledge with that which it is *not:* merely formal or external knowledge (*scientia*). Van Schurman's understanding of this "one thing" becomes the primary lens through which she reconstructs the story of her "change." She defends her choice to join the Labadists as a decision to sit with Mary at the Master's feet in order to learn directly, rather than indirectly, from him. Indirect knowledge involves a host of complicated theological and linguistic means. She, however, has "chosen the better part," the "one thing" necessary.

As van Schurman explains her change, she refers to her *Dissertatio de Ingenio Muliebris ad Doctrinam, et meliores Litteras aptitudine*, published in 1641 (thirty-two years earlier). This treatise was a vigorous defense of the education of women and had contributed to her rise as the "star of Utrecht." Yet now she could only "blush" to think of its contents. Indeed, one senses regret and remorse over her former way of life. She explains:

> Recently I was truly astonished at the lack of moderation in my studies from which I formerly suffered: when, on the occasion of looking through my dissertation on the studies of a Christian Woman, which I wrote to Andreas Rivet, I could not but blush. . . . At that time I believed that I should learn everything that is knowable and indeed, as I argued there in the words of the philosopher, in order to escape from ignorance. But how far all my thoughts were from the admonition of our Saviour, "only one thing is necessary," is clear to everyone from the words alone.[24]

Van Schurman goes on to describe her former writings as "redolent of such superficiality of mind, or an empty and worldly spirit."[25] Upon closer examination of her *Dissertatio*, however, it becomes almost impossible to detect anything objectionable or potentially embarrassing to a religiously sensitive conscience. Indeed, it had won the praise of eminent theologians, including André Rivet and Gisbertus Voetius, precisely because she had declared in the *Dissertatio* that it is "fitting for women to study sciences instrumental to theology, since these lead to greater love of God."[26] In this treatise, she regarded theology as the supreme "science." Furthermore, the goal of study was to promote the glory of God, salvation, virtue, and magnanimity of spirit. What could be more noble or lofty? Wherein lay its "superficiality" or "empty, worldly spirit"? Van Schurman's previous call for the education of women had been precisely theological, not secular, in nature. Her "conversion" was not from a secular to a religious worldview; rather, she experienced a dramatic shift within her theological worldview. She now regarded her former ways of doing theology as sorely insufficient and devoid of true or lasting meaning.

Previously, neither the study of languages nor the "arranging into charts" of subtle theological "distinctions" could lead van Schurman to a "true" and "intimate" knowledge of God, the "one thing necessary."[27] In fact, one could never arrive at the "goal" of theology by entering headlong into discussions of theological subtlety. She explains: "It is evident from this that I did indeed subordinate everything to theology as preeminent but that this subordination extended almost *ad infinitum* before one would reach the *goal* of pure theology, since I considered so many and such different aids necessary for understanding Scripture that this study would easily overstep the bounds of this mortal life. In truth, had not the grace of God ordained otherwise, death would have overtaken me while still in these preparations."[28]

The "goal of pure theology," then, could not be reached by the most sophisticated intellectual and theological means. In fact, an "excessive desire to learn," as she puts it, would hinder the "simple and pure knowledge of the crucified Christ."[29] According to van Schurman, theology's proper aim was "union with the Highest Good," namely, God; this union was characterized by deep enjoyment of God, the soul's truest happiness. The "one thing" necessary for attaining that goal was an "inmost knowledge" (*intima notitia*) of God, as opposed to complicated theological reflection *about* God. This allowed for a deeply felt *experiential* knowledge of God that would penetrate within, while the latter left the individual detached or distant from God, even after complex considerations about the nature of God, the world, and self.

In van Schurman's view, erudite theological reflections functioned primarily in the realm of externals; God would remain outside the individual, and the individual outside God. Arid doctrine, marked by artificial systems and syntheses, prevailed within this mode, and the things of God would fail to penetrate the soul at a deeper level. Theological propositions might be placed in their proper order, but they would not be placed within the soul. "Inmost" knowledge of God, however, was marked by true change of heart and life. It implied *direct* communication with God and *intimacy* with the object of one's knowledge. One could attain union with God, in which God was not only "comprehended" but radically enjoyed as the soul's highest good and truest happiness.[30] Furthermore, this intimate (*intima*) connection with God alone had the power to effect a transformation of inward disposition and consequently to deepen one's love of God and neighbor. But how could one arrive at this "inmost knowledge"? Van Schurman notes her own failure to achieve *intima notitia* when she relays her failure to love her aunts, as well as others she was called to serve, upon her mother's death. Even after all of her theological investigations, she had found herself spiritually bankrupt.

To understand van Schurman's view of the deficiency of her former ways of learning, this distinction between "superficial," or external, forms of knowledge and "inmost" knowledge must be further clarified. Behind the perceived inadequacy of both theological and linguistic sophistication lay a fundamental opposition in van Schurman's mind between two kinds of "knowing." In the *Eukleria*, she contrasts *scientia* (a "*knowledge* so dry and superficial regarding divine matters") with *notitia* ("true, innermost, and salutary *knowledge* of God and his glory").[31] While *scientia* connotes knowledge, skill, and expertise of a more formal and academic sort, *notitia* (from *nosco*) is consistently qualified by van Schurman as true, health-giving, and *intima* (intimate or innermost). *Scientia* might leave the knower detached and outside the object of investigation, but *notitia* had the power to effect something—to create internal change. Doctrine could no longer remain outside the individual but would have to be incorporated into the very heart of one's life. She explains further that the object of *scientia* has nothing within it that "attracts our spirits to the contemplation and *innermost knowledge*" of God (quod animos nostros ad ejus contemplationem intimamque cognitionem alliciat) "unless its every essence be contemplated in a holy fashion." How, then, should God, the "end" of "true knowledge," be contemplated?

According to van Schurman, an inflow of grace was required to contemplate God "in a holy fashion." Grace would not be given apart from the reading of scripture, however. As one meditated upon the sacred page, divine love would be imparted—a love that would, in turn, become the key to unlocking scripture's inmost meaning. As van Schurman puts it, one had to be "instructed, not with philosophical modes of reasoning, or with human reason, but with the light of grace and scripture" as one is "truly imbued with divine love."[32] This kind of heartfelt instruction would overcome the superficiality and aridity of *scientia*. In fact, even the "slightest sense of God's love would provide a much more reliable and deeper understanding of the scriptures than the most extensive knowledge of biblical languages."[33] "Inmost knowledge" of God therefore ran parallel to an inmost understanding of scripture; theological insights would arise from the sacred page as the Holy Spirit shed light upon its hidden, or inner, meaning.

Van Schurman's former methods of theological inquiry were thrown into question, including her most finely honed skill, careful linguistic study.[34] The very subject into which van Schurman had dedicated her efforts would now avail little with regard to the knowledge of God she sought. As she puts it: "Let us look, for instance, at the study of languages, which scholars call the vehicles of sciences, and to which I have devoted so many hours. . . . I used to pride myself that I had to learn these by exhaustive labor, especially Syrian, Arabic, and [Ethiopic] because they have more roots from which derivations can be found in the Holy Scriptures. I thought that these languages would shed light upon the language of the Holy Scriptures and that I would find its most hidden meaning."[35] As van Schurman continues, she claims that the most detailed linguistic study contributes little, if anything, toward the discovery of scripture's "most hidden meaning." A merely intellectual "understanding" of the scriptures, or of the sacred languages, is incapable of bringing the believer into a direct and immediate understanding of God's truth. This kind

of knowledge cannot penetrate inward, nor is it an "intimate" ac-
quaintance with God. Rather, God must be directly present, and
God's love "sensed," or "experienced."[36] Van Schurman yearned for
the immediate instruction of "the Master," longing to sit in his presence with Mary. The *Eukleria* explains:

> But to be quite honest, is exhaustive language study not the same
> thing as to light torches before the sun, or to make an elephant
> out of a fly? Was this not, to put it lightly, playing around with a
> very serious matter? There are probably few words left which
> remain a puzzle to learned translators or to those trained in the
> Hebrew language. What is most needed is a spiritual framework,
> and none of these endeavors contributed anything to that. The
> Holy Scriptures are read either in the light of the Holy Spirit or
> not at all. If they are not, minute grammatical explanations will
> not help you find its innermost and spiritual sense. But if you are
> taught by the Master, then the true, total and general sense of it
> will not depend on one little word or on one special root to clar-
> ify how everything fits together, since God and His Spirit are the
> only undeceiving [infallible] Explainers of the Holy Scriptures.[37]

Thus, in place of complex linguistic analysis, van Schurman now
sought direct and inner illumination by the "Master," given through
the agency of the Holy Spirit.[38] Her previous search for scripture's
most hidden meaning had required many tools of inquiry, finely
crafted. Now they were replaced by "one thing"—"sitting" with
Mary at the feet of the "Master" and learning directly from him in
loving adoration.

Van Schurman presents a strict dichotomy, and one needs to be
mindful of the way she carries this to an extreme. "None of these endeavors," for *her*, "contributed anything to" a "spiritual framework."
She later qualifies that linguistic analyses *can* be helpful, though they
became problematic for her. She thus concedes that careful study
need not be a hindrance. The danger lay in the improper significance
and pride that she attached to these tools. Despite her caveats, van
Schurman still makes a problematic jump and applies this danger not

only to herself but to everyone. One wonders how careful study might be a helpful tool within her schema, rather than an impediment, but she does not address this question.[39] She simply suggests that erudition in and of itself is not the problem so much as the excessive attachment to learnedness.[40]

Instead of relying upon erudition, van Schurman's theological approach in the *Eukleria* seeks a different way of knowing God. She argues that *intima notitia Dei* is possible only when one is "truly imbued with divine love" and, as it were, rapt in loving attention of the Master. God's Spirit then illumines scripture's "most hidden meaning." The Spirit's illumination never occurs in a vacuum but only as guided by the "sacred page." These components are thus essential for the inmost knowledge of God: (1) an inner "sense" of the love of God (2) while reading the scriptures. God's love needs to be directly, personally experienced.

Had van Schurman stopped at this point, she would have sounded no different from the burgeoning Pietists of her day. She makes a striking turn, however. While love for God is the necessary handmaid of a "truer and deeper understanding of the sacred page," an unqualified love, in the end, will be deemed insufficient. *Caritas* is powerless in the absence of one vital element, namely, a *radical overthrow of the self*. One can never arrive at the "one thing needful" (*intima notitia Dei*) without it. In other words, a love that is not accompanied by self-denial is rendered inadequate.

In explicating this condition, van Schurman makes a threefold distinction among different forms of comprehension: "And yet, as in other things, the substance and the conception often differ greatly; thus also, I am learning daily that there is a great difference between those truths comprehended by the intellect, as if pictured in the mind, and even received by a certain love in the heart, and between a total overthrow, conversion, and emendation of mind and heart."[41] Three types of knowing or "comprehension" emerge: (1) the knowing of the mind, that is, "truths comprehended by the intellect" (illas intellectu comprehensas veritates); (2) knowledge received even "by a certain love in the heart" (etiam amore quodam in corde receptas); and (3) the kind of knowledge that can come only from a life radically changed in both mind *and* heart, that is, "a total overthrow, conversion, and emendation of mind and heart" (totalem mentis et cordis eversionem, conversionem et emendationem). In other words, if love is not attended by a complete "overthrow" of the mind and heart, it too will be insufficient in granting the individual *notitia intima,* "inmost knowledge" of God. This overthrow involves the entirety of the individual and cannot occur simply in one faculty. Loving devotion and direct illumination from the Holy Spirit therefore must be complemented by a radical overthrow, even "destruction" (*eversio*), of the whole self.

In distinguishing different types of comprehension, van Schurman thus separates two kinds of love. "Pure" love stands apart from a love for God that is mixed in with other loves.[42] Only when the latter is accompanied by a radical "overthrow . . . of mind and heart" does it gain power; only then is it distilled into its essential purity. Van Schurman's past loves were ineffective, and her earlier advocacy of education failed because it stopped at a partial love. In this manner, love is reckoned partial when it is unpurified; it is made complete and "perfect" once it has been honed or distilled.

Throughout her treatise, van Schurman offers examples of correctives to a stagnant intellect and limited (i.e., mixed) love. She also elucidates the meaning of the term *eversio,* which can be translated variously as "overthrow," "subversion," or "destruction." What would this "total overthrow" or "destruction" of the mind and heart imply? As she proceeds, she sets forth self-denial as the final cure for a mind and heart that are turned in upon themselves and hence unable to receive the fullness of *intima notitia*. In her attempts to describe both the goal of theology—namely, union with God—and the path toward this inexpressible union, she provides a fuller description of this radical overthrow.

SELF-DENIAL: THE KEY TO UNION WITH GOD

Expounding upon the conversion of one's mind and heart, van Schurman sketches out in the *Eukleria* a sort of itinerary, "the true

path" toward the "blessed life" and "union with the supreme good."
She argues that Christianity "teaches correctly and in orderly fashion" this "true path" and that this teaching leads to the destruction
and rejection of the self.[43] While the path to union with God is *im-
pervestigabilem* (literally, "unable to be investigated"), it has been
"revealed" by the Mediator. "Finally, [Christian truth] shows that the
Messiah is that unique Mediator who has revealed this uninvestigat-
able path to restore the union between the creature with his Creator
and supreme Good . . . infusing a new desire on the part of humanity
for his reconciliation and union with his supreme good; and moreover, the salvific knowledge of his supreme good, and love, and the
desire for seeking that, rather than the strength for elevating the self,
pursuing and possessing the self."[44] In describing this path, van
Schurman contrasts the desire for union with God with the pursuit
and elevation of the self. The pursuit of God *over* the self provides
the key to a successful journey.

Serving as a spiritual guide for her reader, van Schurman presents
specific means by which the believer may be united with God, his or
her supreme good. Clear prerequisites are outlined. For example:
"Altogether other and more lofty means has the Christian religion for
arriving at true union with the supreme good: when the Christian,
rejecting himself and all other created things, and through this abandoning imperfect, partial, dependent, and finite good, adheres to the
perfect, independent, infinite, and whole, content in that alone, and
desires nothing except [the supreme good] . . . through the sole desire
of pleasing [God] himself. And he seeks all his own good outside
himself and rejoices to rest in God alone."[45] A certain progression can
be traced, even in the brief passage above. The path to union with
God requires that the self be entirely abandoned in order for the
individual to cleave more fully to the supreme good. First, the individual is called to "reject" (*abdico*) the self and all other created
things. The individual must give up personal rights and desires and
subject them to something greater. Through this abdication of the
self, one abandons or relinquishes (*relinquo*) "imperfect, partial,
dependent, and finite goods." Once the imperfect and the finite are

abandoned, however, one is freed to "adhere" to that which is perfect and infinite. In other words, the finite self proves to be a barrier to full immersion in the infinite; it is a burden. Leaving behind the world of partial goods enables the individual to enjoy the realm of infinite, perfect good. Freedom and contentment are therefore impossible without one's having first renounced finite desires. When the self and its creaturely attachments are relinquished, or destroyed, the individual is able to achieve union with God.[46]

As seen in the frequent appearance of all-encompassing terms such as *total, alone,* and *nothing,* it is evident that singleness of heart is of critical importance to van Schurman. No other attachments are to have the slightest leverage in the heart. According to this understanding, undivided affection, desire, and attention are prerequisites for attaining the supreme good. This is the precise purpose of self-denial. One is to deny oneself in order to attach oneself to that which is supremely good and that which truly satisfies. The soul is thereby freed from the distractions and cares that keep the individual away from her one "good," and she becomes free to enjoy all else *in* that highest good.

Van Schurman presents in the *Eukleria* a radical either/or situation in which one desire alone is allowed to flourish. As seen in her subsequent letters to Schütz, no rival is welcome into the "throne-room of the King." Two opposing parties cannot share one's attention: either the self rules, or God does. She appeals to the words of Christ that "no one can serve two masters." A multiplicity of desires creates confusion, distraction, and paradoxically leads to incompleteness. Similarly, a divided love is considered to be a partial, imperfect love, as seen earlier. Singleness of heart—filled with loving desire directed toward its highest Good—ensures fulfillment and wholeness.

Together with the renunciation of self and all created things, however, one must also "cling to" (*adhaeret*) that which is "perfect, independent, infinite, and whole," contenting oneself in that alone. One "adheres" tightly to God, with a cleaving that is "full of desire" (*desiderat*). Then, seeking all his good outside himself, the individual rejoices to rest in God alone. In "resting" (*acquiescere*), one can be said to "become quiet," or even, in this particular construction, to "die."[47]

Significantly, the term *acquiescere* also suggests an element of pleasure and delight. One might therefore say that there is a certain pleasure in dying to the self. The individual finally comes to quiet, rest, and peace, finding delight in the singular object of his desire. According to this schema, self-denial leads to a profound peace and enjoyment. The self is abandoned and "destroyed" in order to create space, ultimately, for a greater joy. An alternate form of pleasure seeking is thus spiritually validated;[48] and paradoxically, self-denial is the precise means through which the greatest pleasure is achieved.

In a letter to Johann Jakob Schütz in December 1674, van Schurman further explains:

> Just as we are able to conquer all things, through him who loved us, and therefore especially our very selves, who were by nature the enemies of God, therefore that practice does not weary or weaken us, but strengthens [us] in a wonderful manner, in the way of life. Even more precisely, we believe that no Christian can enjoy perfect and constant inward peace, except after he has wrested his very self and all his possessions, temporal and eternal, by his own care and attention, through the denial of self and the transfer of all things into the hand and will of God.[49]

Though self-denial may seem like a difficult teaching to the novice Christian, van Schurman emphasizes that it is the key to great gain. It unlocks an inner strength and ushers in perfect peace. Once finite attachments are removed, the individual is free to enjoy his or her supreme good. The self is abandoned so that it may fasten itself anew to a greater object. Notably, self-denial here does not necessitate an ascetic lifestyle; rather, it entails radical trust and the surrender, or "transfer," of all things into the care of God. And trust is possible, because God is supremely good.

A central passage in the *Eukleria* demonstrates further that the path to union with God involves both a relinquishing *and* an embracing. We have already seen that "cleaving" to the Good necessarily accompanies a full abandonment of the self. Here again van Schurman argues that self-denial must be complemented by dedicating oneself to *another*. In other words, one does not deny oneself *for the sake of that denial* alone; this would result simply in a vacuum. Rather, one denies the self *for the sake of* filling oneself with something else, namely, dedicating the self, believing Christ's words, embracing Christ's truths, pursuing his will, and adhering to and following his steps.

> Briefly, the Christian truth alone reveals that the path to the happy life is in part the *abnegation* of the self and all created things; especially of the perverse love of self, and every created thing, outside or apart from the love of the Creator: in part, in *giving and dedicating* the self and his possessions to that redemption of his, and his Lord Jesus Christ, to *believing* all his axioms, and *embracing* all his truths and mysteries; and (in giving self to) *pursuing* faithfully, and absolutely, every will of his; and in truth, most of all, in *adhering* to and *following* the steps of that person. For from it, namely Christian truth, flows and is derived in us every light of knowing that supreme good, love of remaining in it, strength for pursuing it, and a faculty for uniting that eternity to himself.[50]

Once the individual has denied the self, she is freed to attach herself to the Creator and pursue her highest good. Self-renunciation enables the individual to come to "know that supreme good" (ad cognoscendum illud Summum Bonum),[51] to receive a love that is vibrant enough to "remain in" that good, and to find the strength to pursue it.

Although van Schurman does not explicitly make the connections at this point in her *Eukleria*, she has argued that this unwieldy self is associated with *scientia*, which she regards as a lower form of knowledge. Relying upon *scientia* alone proves to be an obstacle to *intima notitia*, and singleness of purpose is needed to remove its impediments. Former ways of knowing must be relinquished for the individual to come to a new place of delight and deepened knowledge. While *scientia* is not an inherent evil in her framework, it is insufficient on its own. It fails to provide the individual with wholeness of vision and attention because it does not require the renunciation of the self. *Intima notitia,* on the other hand, demands a radical overturn of the self. This "overthrow" (*eversio*) is the corrective to *scientia*'s limitations.

THE IMPORTANCE OF NOTHINGNESS: "IMMERSED IN THE MEASURELESS OCEAN OF DIVINITY"

Van Schurman's language in the *Eukleria* is extreme, troubling to some readers (such as Schütz, as we shall see). But her argument takes yet another turn. Van Schurman writes that one more step is necessary if God is to consume the seeker's desire. In addition to denying self and adhering to God, the individual must be reduced to nothingness. Her logic proceeds as follows: for Christ to be all, the individual, with his partial and incomplete desires, must become nothing. Only then will the "infinite ocean of divinity" fill and envelop the self.[52] In other words, one cannot join the realm of the infinite if one is still a finite entity, bringing distracting baggage and self-will to divine union. As indicated earlier, the finite becomes an obstruction to being lost in the infinite; it is a weight. Van Schurman explains that union with God, which she describes in various places as the happy "immersion" into the "infinite ocean of divinity," is inextricably linked with an awareness of one's own nothingness. She says: "Altogether other is the mind of the Christian man and the limit of his felicity, who considers his very self and all his own as nothing, or as if, gazing upon a tiny drop of the ocean, only then judges himself blessed, when immersed in the measureless ocean of divinity, enveloped, penetrated, and filled, by that goodness and happiness."[53]

Van Schurman employs the language of *becoming* nothing,[54] but she does not go so far as to say that the self is annihilated. The context of her words is essential. As she explains in the *Eukleria,* "I wish to be nothing, to own nothing or to do nothing *other than* that which he always shows through his workings to be his will."[55] In the above passage, similarly, the individual is to "consider" his very self as nothing—not to become nothing in actuality. The key here is one of perspective. When one regards the self as something, then God becomes less than everything to the individual. Once God becomes all, and the self is regarded as nothing, the individual finds himself "enveloped, penetrated, and filled" by that infinite "goodness and happiness." Again, van Schurman thinks in spatial terms, arguing implicitly that competing loyalties cannot occupy the same "space" in the heart, or in one's purview.

Throughout her writing, van Schurman attempts to qualify her emphasis on the soul's "nothingness" before God in order to preserve the integrity of the individual. Potential dangers remain in her language, however, especially when her theology is misconstrued or misapplied. There are limits to retrieving her thought today, and we shall return to this question in the concluding chapter of this work.

In the end, union with God, for van Schurman, involves an immersion into something that is infinite—a measureless ocean of divinity—and an awareness of one's own "nothingness" in light of God's magnitude. The way beyond finitude is to embrace one's nothingness. This recognition—that is, the "overthrow" (*eversio*) of self— is the necessary condition for immersion. One must either renounce oneself *entirely* or be left in the world of partial goods. One cannot have it both ways. This repudiation of the self coheres with a vision of God as infinite and measureless: because God is all-encompassing, the soul can enter that vastness only when it has lost sight of itself and become nothing. God becomes all-consuming, leaving room for nothing else.[56] As the soul is lost in God's fullness, it can finally be surrounded and filled by divinity.

3

The Impossibility and the Delights of Self-Denial in van Schurman's Theology

THE IMPOSSIBILITY OF SELF-DENIAL: VAN SCHURMAN'S FAILURE

If self-denial is the key to *intima notitia* and union with God, how does one "become nothing" and learn to deny oneself? Or, put another way, why do so many *fail* in the school of self-denial? While stressing its importance, Anna Maria van Schurman concludes that self-denial is an impossible task even for the most determined. The individual is so attached to the "I" that a greater force is needed to perform the extrication of the unwieldy self.

Interestingly, van Schurman's own experience parallels her theology. Convinced that self-denial was the secret to a more vibrant enjoyment of the *summum bonum,* she strove earnestly to achieve this state. In the conclusion of the *Eukleria,* however, the reader finds that while van Schurman was acutely aware of the need to deny herself, she was incapable of doing so. Deep within, she detected vestiges of creaturely loves (of both *earthly* and *spiritual* gifts) and bemoaned her inability to extricate herself from her imperfections and impure loves. Her dilemma is clear in the following passage, found in the closing pages of her treatise: "I was in high expectation of a renewal of grace, such as seemed to be promised to us from heaven. On the occasion of examining our paths, I was analyzing traces of spiritual avarice, an excessive love for the gifts and good things of God, and a certain impatience with my own imperfection, and especially the deficiencies in my own self-denial and my overall love of creation. I was greatly oppressed by the burden of this, because I seemed rather to be going backwards than advancing in strength and resolution in the ways of the Lord."[1] What is one to make of van Schurman's self-professed failure at self-denial? Other theologians of her day would have taken a kinder approach to her insistence on this practice.

In her later correspondence with Johann Jakob Schütz, van Schurman returns to the question of the difficulty of self-denial and why so many "fail" in it.[2] She also argues that self-denial is an *essential* and preliminary ingredient of Christianity, rather than being what Schütz called the "crown of perfection" or the final mark of maturity. In this unpublished correspondence from 1674 to 1678, van Schurman clarifies the argument of the *Eukleria*.[3] Her treatise, widely circulated upon publication in 1673, elicited new questions, and this series of letters offers important insights into van Schurman's theology.

An Essential Practice or the "Crown of Perfection"?

Shortly after the publication of the *Eukleria*, Schütz questioned the validity of van Schurman's teaching that self-denial ought to be encouraged "as a general rule," namely, among those young in the faith.[4] He countered her claim that self-denial is the most "fundamental" calling of the Christian by suggesting that it might rather be a mark of maturity. In fact, Schütz regarded the "denial of all things" as the most exalted expression of faith, the crown of one's love for God. He mused that those young in the faith ought to be "enticed and strengthened" by the promises of God, rather than taught from the start to deny all things rigorously. Hence, "failing" at self-denial was not an urgent issue for him. Indeed, he urged instead that "consideration should be given to the diverse status of persons" and that "the weaker ones should be stirred up by the promises of the New Covenant and roused by the hope of future glory . . . [since] . . . the Lord wishes to arouse our love." He thereby contended that self-denial, rather than being most fundamental to Christianity, marks "the highest step of the faith and love of God."[5]

In her response to Schütz, written in December of 1674, van Schurman argues that the "denial of all things" that are not Christ, including the self, is rather a "most universal truth," put forward by Christ to his disciples.[6] She answers Schütz's query with these words: "You concede that [self-denial] is indeed most just, rather, even most sweet: but you think that only a few people reach that place on account of human weakness. And for that reason, you think that they must be more enticed and strengthened by the promises."[7] Van Schurman, though she "concede[s] entirely that persons and their most diverse states should be distinguished: and not in any way are the most precious promises of the Gospel to be neglected," nonetheless argues that self-denial is not for the few but for all:

> But he who follows Christ does not walk in darkness or leave idle and incomplete the instruments of divine glory and salvation of the elect. And so I return to that first truth, which I have indicated, that *for the disciples of Christ all things must be denied* that are not God himself, *until they will have learned to love purely all things in God*: and placing before my eyes the example of Christ, I say that this fundamental principle or command of the highest evangelical Teacher *must be shown forth to everyone, and this at once, from its very beginning, if anyone will learn even very little concerning the excellence of our Divine Savior.*[8]

Not only is self-denial for all, it ought also to be regarded as the "first and lowest [step] of true Christianity, as the highest Teacher perfectly proclaims [it] to be (Luke 14:26),"[9] she insists. Why? "The reason is clear, since God most justly requires the whole heart for himself. . . . Impediments most especially opposed to the pure love of God, he ought for this reason to renounce before all things." She writes that nothing, including family or one's "own soul," is to "occupy [Christ's] place," nor is the heart to cling to anything or anyone but the supreme good alone. Self-denial, then, is a critical means of ensuring that Christ alone is Lord in the believer's life. "Nothing thus [is] to be excluded from this."[10]

But what is at stake in God's having "the whole heart for himself" from the very start? What is the problem with creaturely loves, self-love, and the failure to deny the self? She explains that the neglect of this teaching would be "a huge danger, lest before their self-love, whether spiritual or carnal, has been mortified through the Spirit of Christ, they snatch up those heavenly delights of promises and comfort to nourish and foster that impure love in a heart still living for itself and thus transform them into the poison and stench of death through truly natural foolishness and arrogance. They believe that they have already been reawakened and [are] inhabitants of heaven, although they have not yet learned properly to die to the world and to themselves and to that extent deceive themselves miserably."[11] In other words, the "poison" of an impure love can so easily creep into the life of a Christian that if it is not resisted it will cheat her of heavenly promises and comforts. In fact, this impure love is an indication that the individual has not yet been reawakened, or regenerated and converted. Moreover, van Schurman explains that an *impure love* is precisely that which is stained by the *love of self* and that this impure love of self prevents the individual from fully entering the "narrow gate." She continues: "For if anyone would wish to follow [Christ], it is necessary that he know what separates him from the very threshold of the narrow gate: surely, the love and possession of oneself."[12]

According to van Schurman, most Christians tragically believe that they have already learned to deny themselves and their "old man" (as Calvin also put it). They live in deception, preferring self and creature over God. In an earlier letter of 1674 to Schütz, she writes: "Many people nowadays, when they consider heavenly matters, think that their old man already has been subdued, despoiled, and buried in the ground: nevertheless, it even now lives in them, reigns, and powerfully stretches forth its wicked force, given the opportunity. The majority of those whom they call godly think that in these most calamitous times they are living for God, although meanwhile it is well known and it is not hidden from themselves that a large part of their lives is expended upon their very selves and is poured out most wretchedly for the love of the creature."[13]

She goes on to say that many consequently lose their way, precisely because they have not learned the true meaning of self-denial. As she explains: "I was not able to grasp how even the smallest little spark of a pure love of God, kindled by the spirit of God in the hearts of his people, so easily and so variously and crassly can be buried by worldly ash, with the result that it does not make its way toward its celestial and divine origin, often within a very long interval of time, and does not finally conquer and overcome the world by means of a living faith, which is the inseparable companion of a true love."[14] Put another way, van Schurman argues that the absence of teaching on self-denial would lead to a failed, aborted journey even before the pilgrim set out on her designated path.

The Pernicious "I": Van Schurman's Theological Anthropology

For van Schurman, self-denial means a surrender to God of the will and of one's loves and possessions. She endorses, not specific practices of asceticism or other concrete activities, but rather an attitude of the heart. Self-denial entails a willingness to let go of personal ambition and desires, for example, and a focusing of love upon God. Her rationale for why self-love hinders an individual from entering the "narrow gate" is that such self-love separates the individual from her highest Good, namely, God.[15] It causes a person to exalt the self at the expense of God's reign in one's life. As she explains earlier in the same letter to Schütz, self-love was the origin of Adam's "accursed falling." She says: "So in us now, too, it is the bubbling spring of all evil; that most pernicious 'I,' which elevates itself up to the throne of God and divides and separates our whole selves from the true and highest Good, most wretchedly flows from it."[16] This "I" leaves insufficient room for both the self *and* God to occupy the "throne" of one's heart,[17] for "the Highest Lord does not permit or endure a companion of his reign in the hearts of his own."[18] No middle ground is possible:

> But how can it happen that these two things, so greatly opposed, come together for the same subject? Let us confess the obvious: we live *either* unto ourselves *or* unto God; *either* we lose our lives, crucified together with Christ, *or* we cling wretchedly, connected to the world. But however much the remains of sin survive in the sanctified themselves, may it not be that its strength prevails in them so greatly that it attaches their hearts to the goods of the earth or to their own goods, outside of God, and devotes and surrenders a better part of their lives to Satan.[19]

A person thus has to make an ultimate choice at every turn between self and God. Yet the pernicious "I" cannot help but resist God's "holy will." Van Schurman explains: "The Divine Prophecy taught us that the heart of man is most desperately deceitful [Jeremiah 17:5f.], and therefore its cure and healing is difficult . . . since that disorderly love of self pillages all things, favoring itself without distinction, and does not want to quench itself or to submit to the most just love of God."[20] In this way, the love of self creates enmity with God and, in fact, belongs to the realm of Satan. With this stark contrast in mind, van Schurman reminds the reader that since God is the source of greatest good, diminishing God's place in one's life harms the self's truest good. Similarly, diminishing the reign of the self enables the individual to remove impediments to one's greatest happiness. The unwieldy "I" must therefore be defeated and extinguished, precisely for the sake of this greater good.

Self-denial, for van Schurman, becomes the only means by which one might successfully resist self-love and vanquish the pernicious "I."[21] Or, to borrow from the words of Paul, self-love "sets itself up against the [intimate] knowledge of God" by asserting its will over

God's.[22] From the start, then, removing this barrier is the key to enjoying God. From this perspective, self-denial is the source of "joy which the world does not know."[23] While van Schurman allows room for growth and progress in the Christian life, she argues that the "all or nothing" model provides the key to decisive, or authentic, Christianity. For without the obliteration of this barrier of self, one's knowledge of God remains external, "superficial and dry" and fails to penetrate within and change the self. Van Schurman calls this kind of Christianity "counterfeit." She concedes that "sincere denial of one's own self and of all things is not a small thing."[24] Nonetheless, the failure to deny the self or to submit one's will to God is not a symptom of one's spiritual "youth" or "tenderness" (as Schütz was wont to see it); rather, "one must consider whether that weakness, which shuns so greatly the crucifixion of the old man, is not the strength of one's own life and corrupt nature."[25] Van Schurman therefore boldly declares: "I will again state expressly that the abnegation and mortification of all things that are not placed under God and his most holy will are necessary and must be eagerly desired by all."[26]

While this assessment of the pernicious "I" might seem harsh, it reflects the Dutch Reformed background that van Schurman inherited. Many in the Catholic mystical tradition also taught that the self must be vehemently denied before intimacy with God could be attained.[27] For some thinkers, the self was an obstruction to "union with God" simply by virtue of its creaturely status. I will return to this theme when I analyze Madame Guyon's theory of annihilation.[28] At this juncture, it will suffice to note that the stark opposition between creature and Creator that van Schurman presents was nothing unusual for her contemporaries. In fact, like Bernard of Clairvaux, she argues that even while self-love is the fundamental problem, one must, in the end, return to the love of self—yet with a purified love.[29]

Purifying One's Loves

Although van Schurman cautions her reader against the power of "worldly ash," that is, the love of earthly goods and of the self, she goes on to explain that it is not so much the *objects* of one's love that are problematic as the *manner* in which one loves.[30] When the love of other things becomes an extension of self-love, one's love becomes "impure": "Christian abnegation does not so much consist in the disregard, scorn, and hatred of things that generally are good, as in the renunciation of one's own self, that is, of self-love [expressed] in those things."[31] The problem then is an impure love (i.e., love of self) that fails to love God first and foremost, and only then creatures in God. In fact, even the love of heavenly things can become impure in this manner: "Further, since that impure love stains and makes impure whatever it loves, whether it is natural or spiritual, worldly or heavenly, no one can doubt but that it must be denied entirely and in all things so that the love of God, which is able to love all things purely, alone may occupy the throne in the heart and preserve it in fullness of strength."[32]

Again, the exclusive reign of Christ is critical for van Schurman. There is room for only one Lord upon "the throne in the heart." One cannot love both the self and God, even in the early stages of faith. On the other hand, when one loves God alone, one is able to *return* to the love of both self and creature—but now with a purified love. As van Schurman reminds Schütz, the "love of God" alone "is able to 'love all things purely.'"[33] And it is through the school of self-denial that disciples of Christ will learn "to love purely all things in God."[34] In this Bernardian vein, she continues, "For these are able to enjoy all God's favors with joy purely; or I should rather say, they can virtuously love themselves and all creatures in God, and on account of God, since to the pure all things are pure [Titus 1:15]."[35]

Yet van Schurman fails to differentiate two kinds of self-love.[36] Though her theology may arrive at a renewed love of self, her rhetoric does not distinguish healthy from unhealthy self-love. In all of her usages of the term *self-love,* she assumes "impure" self-love. She does not have another term for healthy self-love but simply concedes that one must in the end return to loving the self "in God." Recognizing this rhetorical limitation may enable the reader to locate better the concerns that drive her thought.

Even so, van Schurman's prescribed path is so demanding that it is no wonder that many people fall short of it—including herself, by her own admission. Was Schütz, then, correct in placing the practice of self-denial later in one's journey toward God?

THE MEANS TO AN AUTHENTIC SELF-DENIAL: THE PRIMACY OF GRACE

Despite the difficulty, indeed impossibility, of self-denial, van Schurman explains in her correspondence with Schütz that "true Christians . . . have not received the grace of Christ in vain." They become and achieve that which Christ intends. Retaining her Calvinist theological core, van Schurman attributes all success in the Christian life to God, who begins and completes the work. According to van Schurman, all of Christian history attests to this work of divine grace: "We certainly have other examples of Christian faith and love, not only in the letter of the Apostle to the Hebrews, but also in the Apostles themselves and in all true Christians who have followed after them and have not received the grace of Christ in vain. And indeed God, who begins his work in his elect, also completes it. And he does not, therefore, kindle the midnight oil, in order that it be extinguished, hidden under a bushel."[37]

In another letter, van Schurman elaborates on the manner in which God's grace "works" in "true Christians." Grace spurs on the individual, empowering her to deny herself and enter a fuller knowledge of the Divine: "This grace of denying all things is poured out into all the elect, in its own time through the Spirit of Christ, who inspires, impels, and leads them there."[38] God is the primary actor from beginning to end. The Spirit is responsible also for purifying one's loves, actively carrying the individual along, says van Schurman: "This Spirit . . . leads and transports his own from an impure love of self and of all things, whether of natural and terrestrial things, or of supernatural and heavenly, to a pure love which does not seek those things that are its own, such that finally God himself becomes all things, [and] they themselves truly become nothing."[39] This outpouring of grace is the absolute foundation of self-denial. It works progressively and gradually throughout the whole of the Christian's life: "Moreover, it is most certain that the grace of Jesus Christ, reigning in the faithful, is the universal foundation of the denial of all things that are not God; whose general unfolding and, as it were, continuous series stretches out through all steps and intervals of life."[40]

Even the weakness of Christians cannot resist the work of grace, according to van Schurman: "For such weakness of Christians has not rejected this yoke of Christ, which is truly light and gentle. In fact, it becomes pleasing through his Spirit, which I said produces in his own the strength of abnegation and in equal measure love, to such a degree that it must not at all be supposed the work of our strength, or apportioned to the same. Thence sprang that old paradox of the Apostle, 'When I am weak, then I am strong.'"[41] Self-denial, then, is not the work of the Christian's own resolve; rather, it springs forth from her weakness as God's Spirit "takes over": "It must not at all be supposed the work of our strength." In other words, grace is given precisely to those unable to deny self and the world. Van Schurman here dodges the question of whether grace is then irresistible, even for sanctification. Many *do* fail in the school of self-denial, and she does not offer a clear explanation for this here, though elsewhere she would seem to argue that those in whom self-denial is not evident are not among the elect. Self-denial is, in fact, *the* sign of election, in her theology.[42]

As seen in the closing pages of the *Eukleria*, van Schurman admits to her own struggle with self-denial. Yet, parallel again to her theology, her struggle does not end in defeat. Something other than the self delivers her from her predicament. She describes a breakthrough in her efforts at self-denial, made possible by the "embrace" of the "vastness of God's own infinite Majesty." In other words, she is *unable* to "refuse" (*abnego*) or "forget" herself until she has the experience of being enfolded in God's presence. Self-denial in effect happens to her. In the final analysis, self-denial becomes contingent upon the divine "embrace." This embrace enables her ultimately to "surrender [herself] entire, all [her] desires, all [her] good and evil circumstances" and to become "profoundly forgetful of [her]self" as a secondary consequence. This profound lack of concern with herself becomes a source of freedom, and this self-forgetfulness is not a goal toward which to strive but an inevitable by-product of being consumed in the presence of God. This clearly appears in the text where she confesses:

> But then, instead of my consternation, which deserved divine abandonment, divine Mercy gazed at me with such kindness that, after first calming my soul a little, it surrounded me with all the vastness of its own infinite Majesty, and impressed upon me the sense of its own divine presence and goodness to such an extent that I surrendered myself entire, and all my desires, all my good and evil circumstances, both present and still in the future, to him, with greater perfection, as though starting afresh, and with a purer faith and love than ever before. I became profoundly forgetful of myself and looked upon myself as though I were the possession of another, that is, of God and Christ the Heir of all, and then became preoccupied more by shaping myself to the divine will than by anything else.[43]

Self-forgetfulness here is tantamount to the abandonment and denial of the self; and self-denial connotes surrender to and trust in another. She employs the language of reshaping, not of obliteration of the self. Furthermore, the emphasis is not on *becoming* nothing but on regarding herself as nothing in light of an infinite presence. Thus van Schurman equates self-denial with surrender to God, and with self-forgetfulness.[44] In the end, self-denial is not strenuous but effortless, for it flows out of a fresh vision of God as infinite and supreme.

During this moment of divine encounter, the "gaze" of "divine Mercy" and the enfolding of God's presence are critical for van Schurman. Her unrest and impatience are first quieted by kindness; she is then surrounded "with so great a vastness of [Mercy's] own infinite Majesty." God's "presence and goodness" are impressed upon her with the result that she is finally able to surrender herself completely, with a "greater perfection" and "purer faith and love" than before. Only afterwards does she become "profoundly forgetful" of herself and disregard herself, now that she is captivated by something much larger than herself. She does not need to focus on the act of denying herself. Rather, a new impulse, a new affection, consumes her and consequently expunges her self-loves. In the words of Thomas Chalmers, a nineteenth-century Scottish preacher and mathematician, one witnesses here "the expulsive power of a new affection."[45] Surrounded and filled with the presence and "infinite Majesty" of God, she realizes that she belongs entirely to another. There is no more room for self, because God reigns supreme. More accurately put, the "false" self, with its unhealthy self-loves, is expelled, and a new self is ushered in.

Van Schurman's theology comes full circle with this pivotal passage. As seen in her correspondence with Schütz, she explains this experience by analyzing how self-denial is the work of the Holy Spirit and not one's own effort. If one carefully heeds the sequence described in this keynote passage, however, an inconsistency seems to emerge in van Schurman's thought. In the previous chapter, I examined the conditions she prescribed for an individual who sought "immersion" into the "infinite ocean of divinity." She indicated that one must become "nothing" if one is to experience the vastness of God's "infinity." Reversing the sequence here, the imperative to "become nothing" is made possible only by an overwhelming experience of the magnitude and majesty of God. The individual *first* experiences the greatness of God and is *then* made aware of her relative nothingness. In the end, self-denial becomes impossible without this fuller revelation of God. That which leads to a deeper knowledge of God (i.e., self-denial) is rendered ineffective on its own merit, but it is granted, in fuller measure, by an intimate encounter with the object of one's desire. The goal becomes the impetus that again leads to a deeper appreciation of (and longing for) the goal—namely, the direct experience and enjoyment of the presence of God.

Rather than looking at self-denial as the prerequisite to union with God, one can conclude that deeper levels of self-denial make possible deeper levels of *intima notitia* and that self-denial is born out of a realization of the grace and majesty of God. This pattern leads, finally, to union with God. The goal and the means become interchanged in circular fashion, each leading to a more profound knowledge of God. In other words, once an individual experiences the vastness of God, he perceives that he is, by comparison, nothing. Similarly, once he sees how small he is, thereby "denying"—or regarding—himself as a "tiny drop in the ocean," he is able more fully to appreciate and enter the vastness of God's infinity.[46] Instead of asking which action comes first, one might see them as simultaneous activities, each leading to the other at progressive levels. Indeed, van Schurman writes to Schütz that "the grace of Jesus Christ" unfolds in a "continuous series" and "stretches out through all steps and intervals of life."[47] While the *Eukleria* argues that union with God is the end of Christian theology, the very awareness of God's intimate presence continues to propel the individual toward that goal.

Significantly, van Schurman writes in the concluding pages of her *Eukleria* that the soul is to be reshaped to the "divine will," as a "tiny drop" in the "ocean of divinity." She does not focus on her prior language of "becoming nothing" as the key to union with God. It may be that the extreme nature of her language (i.e., the use of the term *nothing*) serves as rhetorical flourish; for in the end, the soul is not asked to become nothing; it is asked simply to see its magnitude in light of the infinite. A mathematical analogy from calculus may be apt: whether one compares quantities of zero, ten, or two million to infinity, all finite quantities become zero.[48] And this realization of divine Majesty is a gift of God, not an awareness that can be attained by one's intellect.

At this juncture, one question remains. If divine grace is primary in van Schurman's theology, if it is the "universal foundation of the denial of all things that are not God," what is the individual to do?[49] For though an individual may strive to deny herself, the activity of God in one's life is seen as the guarantor of that denial, and the guarantor of *intima notitia*. Nonetheless, for van Schurman (and Guyon as we shall see), self-denial is not reduced simply to self-forgetfulness in the overwhelming presence of the Divine. The larger context of their thought reveals that while self-denial entails self-forgetfulness it also requires moments of decisive volition. Van Schurman argues in the *Eukleria* that it is still the task of the human, even if as secondary agent, to choose to relinquish herself and to attach herself to the infinite good. One is both to abandon oneself *and* to embrace one's highest good. Furthermore, had van Schurman not been in the position of seeking the grace of God in the first place, she arguably would not have experienced the presence and action of God in the manner that she recounts. The priority of grace in no way excuses the individual from acting or seeking, as she clarifies in subsequent correspondence, and can even be framed in terms of actively doing battle.[50] In Reformed fashion, however, God is for her the beginning and the end of all one's endeavors.

THE FRUITS OF SELF-DENIAL

Union with God

Although the *Eukleria* describes for the reader the "means" by which the goal of theology might be attained, it does not describe the content of this goal in clear detail. What constitutes "union with God"? And when is it achieved, or experienced?

In one of her letters to Schütz, van Schurman expands on this theme. She refers to "union with God" as the divine marriage between Christ and the church that is yet to come: "It is as you say, Dear Brother. The cross of Christ is pleasing and beloved to the faithful; death is pleasing, and eternal life is especially pleasing; when the sweetest Bridegroom of their soul, with all those, perfectly sanctified, belonging to him, enacts his most glorious, most just, and unending triumph and at the same time celebrates into all eternity his most divine nuptials with his most beautiful and beloved Church."[51] Later in the letter, she regards her time on earth as preparation for that future communion: "But as pertains to my position, it has not yet pleased that great guide and finisher of our faith to bring me into the most blessed possession of the same; since doubtless it more suits that one to train me in his School—indeed a heavenly school, but on earth—and to prepare me for that most narrow and holy communion with himself."[52]

In further passages of the same letter, however, van Schurman concedes that union with God *is* attainable in part, here and now, even while its final consummation is yet to come. Not only will the church be united with Christ, but individual members of the church are capable of experiencing the "intoxicating" joy of "divine nuptials . . . both in the present and in the future life." As she says to Schütz:

> Therefore, we conclude that you are in that state, with the spirit leaning forward and rejoicing as one to whom our highest King and also eternal Son of God seems to reveal, not so much as to a faithful servant, but as to a friend, the things which he has heard from his Father. And indeed so wisely and so spiritually do you speak concerning the union of the soul with her Bridegroom, both in the present and in the future life, that it is entirely evident that he not rarely brings you into his wine cellar and there intoxicates you with his delight.[53]

Christians may enjoy incursions of eschatological delights in this life; at the same time, van Schurman exhorts them to advance in grace and to follow diligently the will of God. One is yet in a preparatory stage: "In the meantime, through adversities and prosperities, through pleasant and bitter things, through battles and victories, his all-sufficient grace makes us advance with our heads held high, as long as we observe the most free and best will of our God—the observation and performance of which is our heaven on earth—and conform our will to it."[54]

Although this exchange with Schütz offers a better understanding of where van Schurman places the experience of "union with God," it is not clear what union with God precisely signifies for her.

The *Eukleria* presents it as the height of one's happiness, as God is the "supreme good" of the soul. Furthermore, van Schurman characterizes union as "immersion," "delight," and "penetration," as the soul finds herself "lost" in the "ocean of divinity." Van Schurman's writings also provide some indication of individual as well as corporate union with God; her emphasis on the "mystic body of Christ" as the bride of Christ is particularly notable as she stresses the importance of "fellowship" and "union" with the faithful.[55] While van Schurman does not provide clearer content than this, one may note that union with God at times *appears* to be synonymous with *intima notitia*, even as it is the *end* toward which one's knowledge of God aims.

Significantly, van Schurman does pose a further question with respect to union with God. Even while union with God is the "goal of Christian theology," it does not serve its own end when experienced upon this earth. She posits that there is a further purpose for experiencing this union. Immediately after writing to Schütz about his experiences of "intoxication" in the Bridegroom's "wine cellar," she continues:

> But to what end, I ask? Only that you may be delighted with the taste of celestial wine and overflow in joy? I think not: but so that, forgetful of yourself and the world, and strengthened by celestial ambrosia, you may fight bravely and, above all, conquer love of yourself, which, as in the first man it was the origin of his accursed falling, so in us now, too, it is the bubbling spring of all evil; that most pernicious "I," which elevates itself up to the throne of God and divides and separates all of ourselves from the true and highest Good, most wretchedly flows from it.[56]

Once again, the circular nature of van Schurman's theology emerges. An experience of union with God does not serve its own end, however pleasurable it may be. Rather, it provides the impetus to more vigorously deny oneself and the sinfulness that readily attaches itself to the "I." Celestial delights also result in forgetfulness of self and the world—a forgetfulness that strengthens one's self-denial. Self-denial, in turn, enables the individual to know God more deeply and to experience the fuller vastness of God. This pattern continues, stretching out "through all steps and intervals of life" until the marriage is consummated in celestial bliss.[57] Toward that goal, the individual is called to battle against the pernicious "I" and to follow more wholeheartedly in the steps of Christ. The false self must be vigilantly denied until the very end, even as the enjoyment of God marks every interval of the Christian journey.[58]

"An Unspeakable Joy"

Self-denial, for van Schurman, was not simply a theoretical construct. Her own life involved difficult decisions and the denial of loves she had once cherished. In the *Eukleria*, she portrays her "choice" as one between the theological world of partial goods and knowledge and a world that provides an intimate, all-consuming knowledge of God. Her choice was costly, however: her fame, intellectual pride, and social prestige were extinguished, together with her former loves and desires. In her own words, she willingly gave up her "good name," as well as her previous values: "I do not deny that I had all my life placed much weight on bourgeois proprieties, customary manners, and a good name, as if true virtues: but in this case I paid no attention to them. I considered them transient in comparison with heavenly matters or as a heavenly gift and entrusted good which I could give back to God, just as everything which is mine belongs to God and has been given to me by God. Thus I decided to offer all this with generous spirit as a sacrifice to God, the giver of all."[59]

In spite of the cost, she regarded this "sacrifice" as nothing—"for the sake of knowing" in a most intimate manner "Christ Jesus [her] Lord." She would gladly give up "dry, superficial knowledge" (*scientia*) for that which she considered "true, intimate, and salutary" (*intima notitia*). On the final page of her *Eukleria*, she identifies her "sacrifice" with the apostle Paul's and describes it as follows: "As far as the fame of my name is concerned, I have already previously indicated that in countless ways I value above it not only the glory but also the shame of Christ, along with his faithful servant Moses and his chosen vessel St. Paul, who 'considered all things loss on account of the towering importance of the knowledge of Christ Jesus his Lord' and indeed gave up all things, and considered them 'as dung, in order to gain Christ'" (Phil. 3:7–11).[60]

While derided for her decisions, van Schurman indefatigably holds that she has made the "better choice." Certainly, van Schurman's new life involved concrete sacrifices. In abandoning her former ways of knowing (*scientia*), she forfeited its accompanying fame. Speaking of her past life, van Schurman writes that she had "considered it [her] duty to preserve carefully the little honor of [her] fame as a common good of the republic of letters and, as much as modesty would permit, to increase it, so that among the other great lights [she] too, as a star of the sixth magnitude, might contribute some brightness to that sphere of vast knowledge or Encyclopedia."[61] However, her reputation was now tarnished, as she laid down that which she called her "excessive desire to learn." She regarded these prior pursuits as "dung," a loss that she would gladly relinquish for the sake of knowing Christ ("propter eminentiam notitia Christi").

In fact, van Schurman writes that an "unspeakable joy" arose in the place of loves she had previously nurtured. She says of her fellow members within the Labadist community: "We have seen clearly in all of them a complete denial of the world and scorn of all earthly things as well, on the other hand, as a true love of heavenly things and of Christ, a mortification of the old man and a vivification of the new, so much so that there has occurred in our house community a general resurrection; *this has brought forth among us all an unspeakable joy which the world does not know.*"[62]

Van Schurman's Empowered Voice: Theological Spokesperson of an Emerging Movement

A striking irony emerges in van Schurman's later years. Although disowned by the intellectual elite for her turn toward Labadism, she becomes more truly "voiced" within her new community. Despite her newfound emphasis on self-denial—or precisely because of it—she comes to own her voice. The topos of feminine humility, so prevalent in her earlier writings, vanishes.[63] The shift in rhetoric is astonishing. Van Schurman ceases to be apologetic in her writings, both in the *Eukleria* and in her letters, and she no longer bows to male authorities to validate her work.[64] Instead, she is open and forthright; the style, tone, and content of her writings reveal a new authority and confidence, not a weakened self. Even as she rails against excessive erudition, she shows no qualms about employing her own learnedness in the service of her newly found beliefs. The pages of the *Eukleria* unfold with remarkable precision and intellectual finesse.

Furthermore, van Schurman becomes a theological spokesperson for her superiors within the Labadist movement.[65] Indeed, she becomes an "authority," handing out advice to important leaders throughout Europe and influencing the development of early German Pietism in Frankfurt and beyond.[66] As Pieta van Beek has recently shown, van Schurman also rose to informal leadership in the established Dutch Reformed Church of her day before joining the Labadist movement; key theologians and pastors sought her counsel as they respected her foresight, her vision for the church, and her concern for reform.[67]

Having grasped the necessity of self-denial for an intimate knowledge of God, van Schurman seems to have gained an unexpected, quiet strength. As she wrote to Schütz, "Therefore that practice does not weary or weaken us, but strengthens [us] in a wonderful manner, in the way of life."[68] And, as depicted in the *Eukleria*, she is convinced that she has come to a deeper, more personal knowledge of her "supreme good." The final pages of this treatise describe the powerful effects of being "immersed in the infinite ocean of divinity": she is no longer consumed with herself or her personal fears and strivings, whether spiritual or earthly. Consequently, she is no longer defined or limited by the standards of her time. Confined neither by the demands of Calvinist orthodoxy nor by the "proper place" of women in society, van Schurman gained new muscle. Perhaps she experienced that quiet, rest, and delight of which she spoke in her treatise—the enjoyment that comes from denying the self, only to embrace more fully her highest good.

If for van Schurman self-denial was the key to a more intimate knowledge of God, for Guyon it was the entry into the most intimate marital chambers of the divine spouse. The analysis of Guyon's reading of the *Song of Songs* in the next chapter will reveal a more intensified language and logic than that of van Schurman's *Eukleria*.

4

"Oh, Happy Dying": Self-Annihilation in Madame Jeanne Guyon's *Commentaire au Cantique des cantiques de Salomon*

The marriage takes place when the soul falls dead and senseless into the arms of the Bridegroom, who, seeing her more fit for it, receives her into union.

Jeanne Guyon, commentary on the Song of Songs 6:4

The *Song of Songs* has been an important resource for the Christian mystical tradition throughout its rich history. Well-loved authors, such as Bernard of Clairvaux and St. John of the Cross, have taken its most intimate images and transformed them into tender accounts of the union that takes place between Christ and his bride.[1] Indeed, the *Song*'s lyrical poetry earned it the right to be called *the* song of love— whether it be the love shared between a man and his bride, God and Israel, or Christ and his beloved.[2]

Toward the end of the seventeenth century, however, the Song became a song of death under the pen of Madame Jeanne Guyon, who foregrounded her vision of a "dead bride."[3] In her *Commentary on the Song of Songs*, she heaps up one violent image after another as she details the union of the "annihilated bride" with her "bloody bridegroom," who is to her a "bridegroom of death."[4] The unsettling language may border on the morbid and macabre and potentially opens Guyon to charges of spiritual necrophilia. Her interpretation certainly shocked the religious authorities of her day, who quickly banned her work.[5] But even while offending some readers, Guyon's writings gained an extraordinary audience in many quarters.[6]

As one attempts to understand the controversial power behind Guyon's commentary, a few questions immediately arise. Why was the image of a dead bride so appealing to Guyon? Why did she suggest that only an annihilated soul could be received into the chambers of the bridegroom? And if death is the prerequisite, what does that say about the nature of this union? Guyon argues that full enjoyment of God in this life can be attained only after an excruciating spiritual death. Her goal, from the outset, is blissful union with God. From a human perspective, one would suppose that a dead spouse is the last thing a lover would desire. But in Guyon's treatment of the analogy, a dead bride is the *first* thing that the *divine* lover desires. Hence, if union with the Divine is contingent upon the annihilation (*anéantissement*) of the soul, the exact nature of this annihilation needs to be examined. *What* precisely needs to *die,* and in what manner? Put another way, who, or what, is the "self" that offers itself upon the altar of death?

This chapter will trace the progression toward union with God in Guyon's *Commentary on the Song of Songs* and will present her thought in a somewhat systematic fashion. Admittedly, trying to trace her argument, which moves like a torrent upon the page, is no easy task.[7] She seems to contradict herself in key places; the details she provides are elusive, even confusing, at times. One can nonetheless chart a sort of itinerary from the soul's spiritual betrothal to its "essential union" with God—a union that is at first transitory and then permanent. This union finds its culmination (i.e., "consummation") in the marriage chambers, and this marks the union as final and lasting.

In the next chapter, I will investigate the means by which the soul is brought from one stage to the other in Guyon's discourse, exploring specifically the relationship between human and divine agency. I will also elucidate the effects of this marriage, namely, the deepened joy and apostolic fruitfulness of the annihilated spouse. Death does not serve its own purpose, according to Guyon's commentary; it is rather the passageway to an experience of new power, a fully resurrected life. Last, I explore the questions of desire and joy. On this point it is likely that Guyon was charged with the "heresy" of Quietism. A more nuanced reading of her doctrine will emerge, however, by the close of these two chapters.

THE TREACHEROUS PATH FROM SPIRITUAL BETROTHAL TO MARRIAGE

The Song of Songs opens with an expression of longing—a yearning for the "kisses of [the lover's] mouth."[8] According to Guyon, these kisses represent the intimacy that the "soul desires of her God." More specifically, the kiss is a "real, permanent, and lasting possession of her Divine Object," equivalent to the "spiritual marriage of the soul with her maker."[9] In the very first paragraphs of the *Commentary*, Guyon points to the ultimate desire of the soul, as well as the goal of her commentary: final union with Christ.[10] This union is marked by deep pleasure and mutual satisfaction. As Guyon frequently asserts in her writings, "The end for which we were created is to enjoy God even in this life."[11] The path toward this goal is far from pleasant, however; it is characterized by suffering, humiliation, and death. In her exposition, Guyon lays out what she believes to be the difficult journey toward marital union. In fact, the whole of Guyon's work can be understood as an explication of this very path for the would-be traveler—an instructional handbook of sorts.

From the start, Guyon distinguishes two kinds of union. She tells her reader that a vast difference exists between (1) the "union of the powers," that is, the union of the "faculties of the soul," which she relates to spiritual betrothal; and (2) the "essential union," or "spiritual marriage."[12] Though the road to the first type of union is far from simple, the transition from betrothal to marriage is much more arduous. Much will be required of the bride-to-be. As Guyon puts it, "But ah! what a distance is yet to be traveled, and what sufferings are yet to be undergone, before this eagerly desired union can be granted and consummated!"[13]

The spiritual betrothal is significantly different from both the marriage and the marriage's consummation. Guyon asserts that many "spiritual writers" in the past have failed to make this distinction— and that in their confusion they regarded as "marriage" that which she places in merely the *preparatory* stages before marriage.[14] In other words, she claims that there is much more to union with Christ, even in this life, than others have imagined.[15] She cautions the reader that her teaching may offend those of a sensitive or weak spiritual constitution, that is, those who are not willing to ascend higher, or rather, deeper into the pit of darkness and death.

The Spiritual Betrothal

Guyon distinguishes the "union of the powers" from the "essential union" in that the former is not yet a "real, permanent, and lasting possession of [the soul's] Divine Object."[16] Rather, the soul is said to make "contact" with her beloved through "divine embraces." Tender caresses touch the soul, and affection of the heart is mutually shared. These exchanges, however, are not tantamount to a "possession" or "full enjoyment" of the soul's love. Instead, she likens this initial union to the promise of a future marriage, that is, a betrothal. Intimate conversation and warm affection certainly mark this period; *full* enjoyment of the soul's desire, however, awaits a future time.[17]

Although Guyon marshals rich imagery in her description of the "union of the powers," the reader is left with few resources to understand what a tender "caress" of the Divine actually signifies. What part of the soul makes "contact" with the Divine, and in what manner does divinity "touch" the soul? According to her schema, the three traditional faculties of the soul experience union with the distinct members of the Trinity respectively—albeit a union achieved by "mediated operation[s]."[18] While Guyon nods toward tradition in these opening paragraphs, she does not offer much detail.

Guyon writes in these first pages that the "union of pure intellect" involves the faculty of the *understanding* and its union with the second person of the Trinity, namely, the Word. How this occurs is another question—one that Guyon is content not to explain. She simply turns to the next faculty; when the soul becomes "profoundly forgetful of the creature," including the self, through an "absorption of the soul into God," the *memory* is united with the Father. As she later elaborates, the memory is held in suspension, so to speak,[19] and is capable of focusing exclusively on the Creator without interference from created beings, including the self. Beyond this, however, one encounters little of this particular union in her *Commentary*. Finally, "When [the union] takes place in the *will* alone, by a loving pleasure . . . it is the union of love, attributed to the Holy Spirit."[20] This "union of love" is the "most perfect of all because it approaches more than any other the essential union, and it is principally by this way that the soul arrives there."[21] The Holy Spirit effects this union and draws the soul to the inner chambers of the divine lover.

Beyond these initial hints, Guyon offers little explanation. The reader is simply to understand that the three faculties are united with the different members of the Trinity each in their turn, when they are fully "absorbed" into them through some sort of "intermediate operation." Guyon gives minimal detail regarding this process of "absorption" or "surrender." Again, this union is more "superficial" than the essential union, not yet leading to "the real pleasure of the object."[22]

The Spiritual Marriage

In contrast to the union of the powers, the "essential union" Guyon regards as a union of "essence with essence" and a "communication of substance." The distinction between the three members of the Trinity disappears, as well as any intermediate means or act whereby the initial union might have been achieved. Instead, God "immediately" reduces the entire soul "into unity and [possesses] it in the unity itself."[23] Even as the soul fully "possesses" her divine lover in the spiritual marriage, she is also "possessed" by him. Guyon considers this mutual "possession" to be the "essential beatitude," the "veritable enjoyment of the object."[24] Though the soul does not see her beloved during this life, she may yet fully enjoy him, just as at the beatific vision. In fact, the only demarcation between essential union in this life and the next is the joy of seeing. While this constituted a significant distinction in the history of the Christian mystical tradition, Guyon argues that lack of sight need not diminish the bride's rejoicing. She explains: "For, we are happy from the moment we receive the Supreme Good, and can receive and enjoy him without seeing him. We enjoy him here in the night of faith, where we have the pleasure of enjoyment without the satisfaction of sight; there, we will have the clear vision of God in addition to the happiness of possessing him. But this present blindness hinders neither the true possession nor the genuine enjoyment of the Object, nor the consummation of the divine marriage."[25]

Although Guyon has introduced a few of the differences between the "union of the powers" and the "essential union," her description is far from clear, as with many of the terms that she employs. The only insight she adds at this juncture is that the "union of the powers" is a union "without being mixed." A "mixing" with the Divine, on the other hand, is characteristic of the essential union. As she puts it, the spiritual marriage is marked by "union and admixture," as when "salt is liquefied, dissolved, and vanished" into water. For this to happen, however, "the soul loses its own consistency in order to live uniquely in God." She adds, "This is what is known mystically as the loss of self and as a loving and perfect recollecting of the soul to God."[26] Again, Guyon's terminology remains opaque at this point. She will make valiant, if unsuccessful, efforts in later passages to clarify her language.

Guyon does include one helpful hint at the close of this section. She explains that by the "loving and perfect recollecting [*récoulement,* or "sinking"] of the soul to God" she does not mean "the real detachment of the intimate subsistence."[27] Rather, she says: "What I am referring to may be illustrated by a drop of water falling into a cup of wine. It loses its own appropriate form and character, and is apparently changed into wine; but its being and substance always remain entirely distinct, so that, if it were the will of God, an angel could at any time separate the identical drop. In the same way, the soul can always be separated from God, though with great diffi-culty."[28] As Guyon puts it, the soul is "apparently" divinized, as it experiences the essential union with God. It loses *only* its "own ap-propriate form and character." Forever distinct, the soul retains its own "being and its material." It is not yet clear what is implied by the "loss of self-appropriation" through which one's being is only ap-parently changed. And if essential union is the height of intimacy with the Divine—an "intermingling" between human and divine "substance"—how does the soul find itself in this position? By what means does the soul become "ready" to be "united, mixed, and trans-formed within its God"?[29]

As the commentary unfolds, Guyon provides significant clues that further describe the essential union, as well as the path to that union, the "melting" of the soul into "the ocean of divinity."[30] As one pieces together her disparate descriptions, one finds that the most im-portant precondition for this "melting" or "loss" of the self into the immensity of God's own being is the "destruction" or "annihilation" (*anéantissement*) of the soul. Only when it has "lost" itself in God in a violent, destructive manner will the soul be "melted" and "sub-merged into" that ocean. As noted above, the "marriage takes place when the soul falls dead and senseless [*morte et expirée*] into the arms of the Bridegroom, who . . . receives her into union."[31] Guyon has just said, however, that she does *not* mean "that essential despoiling of its intimate existence."[32] If this is the case, what would it mean for the soul to lose itself in God and to be annihilated?

FOUR LEVELS OF ANNIHILATION: TOWARD UNION WITH GOD

The Bridegroom here calls her by the name of Spouse, and invites her to hasten in permitting herself to be destroyed and annihilated, and receive the spiritual marriage. He calls her to her wedding and coronation.

—Jeanne Guyon, commentary on the Song of Songs 4:8
(Metcalf's translation)

To grasp the progression of Guyon's argument in her *Commentary*, I address the following key questions: What within the soul needs to be annihilated? And what is the nature of this annihilation? Furthermore, for what reasons is this painful sacrifice required for the soul to experience deepest intimacy with God? That a self-destructive process would be the means by which union is achieved strikes the reader as highly suspect.[33] As Guyon describes the pathway to spiritual marriage, and as the chapters of the Song unfold, she attempts to explain the logic behind her strong and problematic claims.

Annihilation, or *anéantissement* (from *anéantir*), is a term that Guyon repeatedly employs as she traces for her reader the mystical path to union with Christ.[34] While an English translation might render her French simply as "death," "destruction," or "annihilation," her descriptions include rich expressions that help to elucidate the semantic contours of *anéantissement*. A simple listing of Guyon's terminology reveals verbal constructions as vivid as *détruite* (destroyed), *abattre* (to demolish, pull down, slaughter, or overthrow), *terasser* (to knock down), and *arracher* (to dig up, uproot, tear out, or snatch). In addition to these images that evoke the violent action of divine love, Guyon makes lavish use of other phrases to describe the soul, both during and after its annihilation: the soul is said to be "stripped" by this process (*dénuée*) and "skinned" or "pillaged" (*dépouillée*). On a "softer" note, she speaks of the soul finding itself "lost" (*perdue*), "melted" (*fondue*), and "sunk" or "submerged" (*abîmée*) into the "ocean of divinity."[35]

Although Guyon's choice of language provides a preliminary picture of the kind of action annihilation involves, she has yet to describe the recipient of this action. *What* needs to be destroyed, demolished, and stripped? *What*, or *who*, is the "self" that is pillaged, lost, and ultimately submerged into God's own being? If one equates the self simply with the traditional faculties of the soul (i.e., the understanding, memory, and will), this would appear no different from the first union, or "union of the powers," that Guyon described. This stage was but a betrothal, not yet an "essential union." How, then, is the spiritual marriage set apart from the betrothal? In what manner does the marriage involve a "union of essence to essence," as opposed to the union of the soul's discrete "powers" with God?[36]

Since Guyon does not provide a clear definition of the "self," I will reconstruct its likely contours by examining precisely what needs to be annihilated within Guyon's framework. In other words, I will work my way backwards from the data that Guyon does provide.

The Beauty of the Annihilated Bride: "Her Lovely Eyes . . ."

As Guyon begins to explain the process by which the "self" is annihilated, she writes that the first thing that needs to "die" is the *perception* of one's self.[37] One ceases to "discern" or recognize anything but God. Annihilation of the self is, first and foremost, an annihilation of one's *self-awareness*. From the start, it is an *action* of the self that is being destroyed, regardless of how one defines the self's "essence."[38]

In making this point, Guyon uses the analogy of a traveler approaching his destination; she argues that the soul must be "gifted with a single eye," just as the sojourner who "approaches an inn that is in plain sight has no need to deliberate about it, but fixes his eye steadily upon it, and having entered it, no longer beholds it."[39] According to this analogy, the soul is to enter into its own center—the dwelling place where God will be found—and there lose its self-perception.[40] In Metcalf's English translation of Guyon's commentary, selections from her *Justifications* appear as footnotes and elucidate further her interpretation of the *Song*:[41]

> So the soul, when it has arrived at its center, may be said to behold itself no longer—though, in fact, it has a mode of perception appropriate to its state. When, however, it passes beyond itself, it no longer feels nor perceives itself. The further it advances in God, the less it discovers itself, until at last, wholly lost in the abyss of God, it no longer feels, knows, nor discerns anything but him. At this point, it is plain that all self-reflections are

hurtful and deadly, for they turn the soul into the path that leads from God, and that would bring it back to self.[42]

I will return shortly to the "passing" of the soul "beyond itself." For now, it will suffice to note that the soul must move beyond its fixation with self and "lose" itself in the "abyss of God," no longer aware of anything but God alone.[43] Significantly, it is not that the *self* has been lost but that the "feeling," "knowledge," and "discernment" of itself is lost. The *perception* of self has been destroyed, not the self per se.[44] What, then, does she mean by "self-perception"? In other passages, Guyon describes self-perception as one of several things; in addition to beholding oneself, or feeling, knowing, and discerning oneself, it might be as simple as noticing oneself. On the other hand, it can be more focused in attention, suggesting a *regard* for the self or an "attending" to the self.[45]

Furthermore, as the passage above indicates, self-perception is connected in Guyon's mind to "reflecting" upon the self. She cautions that "all self-reflections are hurtful and deadly" to the soul that desires union with God. As one advances further, one is to avoid introspection, though it might have been helpful at the outset.[46] With the analogy of the traveler in mind, Guyon again explains that one must move toward one's center, only to move away from it in the opposite direction:

> Then, our progress in God should be measured by our *separation from self*, in relation to our *views, feelings, memories, self-interest, and self-reflection*. While the soul is advancing toward its center, it is wholly absorbed in self-reflection; and the nearer it approaches, the more intense is its absorption, though in greater simplicity. When, however, it arrives there, it *ceases to see itself*, just as we see everything around us, but not what is in us. But, to the extent that it moves away from and beyond itself, it *sees less and less of itself*, in proportion, because its face is turned the other way and it cannot look back. Therefore, *those self-reflections*, which were useful in the beginning, *become exceedingly injurious at the end*.[47]

This shift in perception is of paramount importance for the soul that aims to progress toward union with Christ. While self-reflection may have helped to focus one's concentration in the beginning, one must go beyond it. The pivotal criterion here is the object and direction of one's gaze. Guyon posits that a soul whose "eye" is "fixed" upon the self is unable to become united with God, for it retains a measure of self-love rather than directing all of its love to God alone. Put in another way, the gaze of the eye reveals the object of one's love.[48] If the soul loves God and is captivated by God's beauty, it will focus its attention upon that object. On the other hand, it might become like Narcissus, loving itself and therefore its own reflection. In either case, one's eye naturally tends toward that which one loves.[49] Consequently, it is the gaze of the bride that God seeks.

These eyes, in turn, ravish the bridegroom: "You have ravished my heart, my sister, my bride; you have ravished my heart with one of your eyes" (Song 4:9). Guyon comments on this verse in the bridegroom's persona: "For your pure and upright love kept you so steadily regarding me, that it did not permit you to *consider yourself*, nor your own interest, but *solely to contemplate me* with love as your Sovereign Object."[50] The object of the soul's love, namely God, has so captured her attention that she is no longer mindful of herself. The soul looks upon the loveliness of her beloved, and self-awareness fades away. Self-interest, too, is replaced by a desire to lovingly contemplate her lover. The first step, then, toward the annihilation of the bride is the annihilation of her self-gaze.

This shift in attention is no easy matter. It involves a decision to "come forth and abandon self," though it means "[leaving] this enjoyment within." Departure from self is so "difficult" and "bitter" that Guyon likens it to a death: "By issuing forth from self, she perishes and dies." The soul dies to self-interest and to prior preoccupations with (or "contemplation" of) herself, however noble they seemed at the start.[51]

Perception, Gaze, and Self-Awareness (or Self-Forgetfulness)

The soul's perception of, or regard for, herself is simply the first thing that needs to be extinguished, according to Guyon. To advance in her journey, an additional turn is required. Even as the bride ceases to see herself, she must also lose her awareness of the very act of perceiving. In other words, she becomes oblivious of her gaze, or the redirection of her gaze, having become utterly enrapt in the other. Self-reflection is thus annihilated to a second degree. If in the initial stages the soul could no longer say, "I see myself," at this more advanced stage it no longer says, "I see that I see." The soul has become steadfast in her focus upon her beloved but is not cognizant of her faithfulness. She even questions God with regard to what he has commended as her "steady gaze." As Guyon puts it: "'But alas!' exclaims this afflicted soul, 'how is it that I have steadfastly regarded You when I do not even know where You are?' She does not know that her look has become so purified that, since it is always direct and unreflective, it escapes her notice and she does not perceive that she always sees. . . . This fixedness of the interior eye upon God must be unfailingly pre-served, though unconsciously; in this way, the spouse never forgets her Bridegroom."[52]

The bride's singleness of attention thus "escapes her notice." She sees but is not aware that she sees, for the object of her sight has completely overcome her. Her gaze is "direct and unreflective,"[53] and she has become utterly "unconscious" of her own gazing. No-tably, this is impossible without the loveliness of the groom capturing her focus. As Guyon explains, self-forgetfulness "has its sole origin and cause in her unremitting application of her heart to God." The soul cannot simply "will" herself into forgetting herself in this way; even the act of volition is in danger of eliciting self-notice, or worse, self-congratulations. Rather, a greater object draws her attention away from self: "Every affection of the bride is concentrated in God alone."[54] This concentrated gaze, in fact, marks the beginning of the "essential union," albeit a union that at this stage is transitory, not yet permanent. For her to reach the marriage chambers, where the union is consummated and made lasting, further obstacles must be faced.

The Lure of Self-Praise

The soul's journey from spiritual betrothal to the marriage thus far requires a redirection of her gaze, a focus of attention upon her lover rather than herself. This focus becomes so all-consuming that she even forgets her act of gazing. The process of annihilation has only just begun, however. Along with this shift in perspective, the bride needs to redirect key attributions. That which she had previously credited to herself—righteousness, strength, and wisdom—must now be ascribed to her bridegroom alone. Put in another way, self-righteousness must be annihilated, as with any assumption that strength and wisdom belong to her. Only then will the marriage come closer to its consummation, where the essential union will no longer be fleeting but permanent.[55]

According to Guyon, the problem of attributing divine qualities to the self is fatal. A false estimation of the self quickly turns into "self-praise" and "keeps the soul in darkness." Like spiritual mud, it prevents her from uniting in joyous intimacy with God and is the "cause of all her melancholy nights."[56] A "secret presumption" underlies this usurpation of attributes that belong only to God, and it disqualifies the bride from entering the inner chambers of her lover. In fact, a "valiant" band of soldiers stands at the gate, exclaiming in loud voice, "Who is like unto [God]?"[57] Brandishing their swords, they come to "fight with and destroy the self-righteousness of [humanity]."[58]

These soldiers are metaphors for the divine attributes that bring to naught the pride and presumption of humanity. After attacking the bride's "self-righteousness," their next target is human power. They lead the soul into an "experience of her own infinite weakness, into the strength of the Lord." Without an acute awareness of her frailty, the bride would never learn to access divine strength;[59] she would remain separate from God, continuing to struggle on her own. This recognition of weakness is achieved through a series of events, a "bundle" of humiliations and crosses that the bride must bear.[60] Unable to stand on her own, she will at last draw strength from her maker. Apart from this "array of crucifixions," she would remain entrenched in the mire of self-reliance, thereby limiting her greatest potential. While this seems a ruthless requirement, its yield is abundant, unleashing enormous power. Last, "God's providence attacks human foresight. And so it goes with all the attributes." Human wisdom is laid low, in light of divine wisdom. As Guyon explains, the divine attributes "are all armed, for it is necessary for the soul to be destroyed in these matters before being admitted to the bed of Solomon, becoming a bride, and reaching the finishing and consummation of her marriage."[61]

It is surprising how starkly Guyon opposes God and humanity, denigrating the humanity of the soul in the process. Why does she depict them as polar extremes, with God being the exclusive source of righteousness, strength, and wisdom, and the bride the precise opposite? Furthermore, the divine bridegroom appears to be a selfish praise-monger himself, imposing unfair demands upon the bride. For instance, the bride must recognize her "wretchedness" as a precondition for the marriage's consummation, deprecating herself and lauding God at every turn. From the point of view of human marriage, this would be a most cruel arrangement indeed. It is one thing to claim that God is the "Author and Center of every good."[62] But does humanity never share in these attributes?[63] And what does Guyon make of the *imago Dei*, the stamp of divinity upon the soul? She seems to suggest that there is nothing within humanity that reflects the very being of God.

Finally, it is curious why *any* hint of self-congratulation becomes a misplaced pride, obstructing the soul from reaching her greatest joy. What might be regarded as healthy pride turns into spiritual sludge, creating "melancholy" in the soul. Guyon merely asserts at this juncture *that* it is, rather than giving the reasons for *why* it is. Her emphasis is that pride is a form of self-love, clinging to the soul with stubborn tenacity.[64] And this love of self makes the soul ill-prepared for the consummation of marital union. An "extreme annihilation" alone has the power to free the soul from her attachment to self so that she may be joined to her lover. Guyon's reasoning will become clearer as the reader ventures further and pieces together disparate strands of her thought; we will have occasion to explore these questions in more detail in the following chapter.

The Final Sacrifice of the Bride: A Bed of Suffering

The beloved of Christ has journeyed through various stages to reach the marriage chambers of her lover. When she draws nearer, however, she is met by a "gentle reproach." According to our commentator, the bride has desired too "soon to repose upon a flowery couch, before having rested with [him] upon the painful bed of the cross." In the voice of the bridegroom, Guyon explains: "I am, you say, the flower of the field, a flower that you do not pick while resting on a bed, but in the field of combat, of work, and of suffering. I am the lily of the valley that only grows in annihilated souls, so that if you want me to draw you from the earth and take up life in you, you must be in the last stages of annihilation. And if you want to find me, you must enter into combat and suffering."[65]

The would-be-bride is first called to enter a minefield of pain and hardship. She is not promised simple victories, however. This "combat" will, in fact, lead to her spiritual death. Unusual requirements are heaped upon the soul who yearns for the consummation of her marriage to Christ. We have already seen that radical shifts in such a bride's mind-set and vision are necessary, together with the death of self-praise; her introspective tendencies need to be replaced with a singleness of attention upon, and praise for, her lover. While this may sound simple, these shifts take place in violent fashion, according to Guyon. The soul is so glued to itself, in a manner of speaking, that it needs to be extricated, even if painfully, from its self-preoccupations.[66]

Toward this end, Guyon writes that an "extreme annihilation" is required. The bride does not easily die to self-regard and self-commendation; she needs to make a decisive "sacrifice" of herself upon the "painful bed of the cross." And God educes this sacrifice, by carefully placing the soul in "the field of combat, labor, and suffering." Through these difficulties, the soul will be overthrown, and therefore "fit" to be received into the bridal chambers of the Bridegroom.[67]

The severity of the brutal images that Guyon employs is disconcerting. Why is the process of becoming the bride of Christ filled with violent overtones? It seems needlessly cruel that the soul should endure manifold hardships in order to "prove" her love. She is rebuffed "gently" when she attempts prematurely to enter the bridegroom's chambers. Yet the demands of the bridegroom are anything but soft. The conditions that he places upon her seem merciless and overbearing. As Guyon states, "He is not yet a bridegroom whom I may embrace in the nuptial bed, but a bundle [*un bouquet*] of crosses, pains, and mortifications; a bloody husband (Ex. 4:25) and crucified lover, who desires to test my faithfulness by making me a partaker of a good share of his sufferings. For this is the portion given to the soul at this period."[68]

As the commentary continues, Guyon attempts to explain why a crucifying process alone has the power to rid the soul of her preoccupations with self, harsh though it may seem. Although the bride may begin to attribute divine qualities to God, vestiges of self-righteousness cling to her in hidden places. Hardships serve to uncover her "secret presumption," areas of self-reliance that she has not yet recognized. A series of crosses is given to her, both without and within, by which her pride is revealed and annihilated. They culminate in what Guyon calls the "final sacrifice," or "final renunciation."

External crosses, according to Guyon, involve not only the bitterness of suffering—that is, suffering of any kind, due to outside sources—but in particular, the ignominy of the cross one bears.[69] Among the examples that Guyon offers, not only does the bride endure the misunderstanding of others, but she is often slandered. (Presumably our commentator's own experience enters into her interpretation of the *Song*.)[70] For instance, the soul's longing for the bridegroom seems excessive to others, and onlookers mock the lengths to which she goes to draw near to him.

Adding insult to injury, inner crosses confront the soul anew. As the bride endures the shame of her various crosses, she faces inward humiliation through the experience of her own weakness. The beloved of Christ finds herself resistant to difficulty, unwilling to endure patiently the disgrace of others. Her past faithfulness proves insufficient to carry her through further trials, and she finds herself unable to imitate her bridegroom, unable to share in his suffering. The bride's personal failures thus devastate her as much as does the ridicule of others.

According to Guyon, the "final renunciation" that the soul must undergo is the relinquishing of this self-righteousness, including reliance on previous successes. To her dismay, she discovers that her crosses are too much to bear, and she laments the process. Feeble in the face of love's crucifying demands, she is at the same time keenly aware that those "who will not consent to this crucifying process must be content to remain all their lifetime in self and imperfection."[71] The bride therefore despairs of herself.[72]

Ironically, "holy despair" becomes the key to the fulfillment of the soul's desire. Once she has despaired of her*self*, a window opens by which she may breathe anew. Personal dejection leads her to make the "final sacrifice": she throws herself upon the mercy of God. She learns finally to offer nothing of her own righteousness and strength to him. Stripped of her self-reliance, the bride undergoes this "final" annihilation. However, an unexpected source of power is now released. As Guyon explains, "The more we despair of self, the more we trust in God." And trusting in God creates "space" for the power of God to infuse the soul anew. The less "self" gets in the way, the more God's strength can operate.[73] "Self-hatred," in fact, leads to a greater love of God, and the bride's love is made "perfect."[74] She adds, later: "This appropriation of the things of God to themselves must completely pass away, and all righteousness must be confessed as belonging to him alone. By the uncertainty in which they are placed regarding their own salvations, through seeing their wretchedness, they are caused to look only to the righteousness of God. They recognize his all and their own nothingness, his omnipotence and their own weakness. And they are therefore established in an abandonment that is never afterwards shaken."[75]

Guyon's language of "extreme annihilation" is difficult to digest, especially in the absence of qualification or cautionary words (which I will address in upcoming chapters). Returning to Guyon's framework for now, the bride when annihilated at these various levels is finally ready for the consummation of her marriage—a consummation that makes her union permanent. By this strange twist of providence, the "stripping" of the "veil of her own righteousness" allows the soul to "flow sweetly into her Original."[76] The bride brings nothing of her own righteousness to this union, thereby receiving all of God's righteousness.[77] She has become nothing; God has become all. Every hindrance of the self has been removed, and this excruciating death ushers her into the "immensity of God," where boundless joy comforts and surrounds her.[78]

"THAT ADMIRABLE FUSION": MELTING INTO
THE OCEAN OF DIVINITY

Through "many a trial and many a toil," the bride reaches the longing of her heart: she and her beloved are united in a marriage that cannot be broken.[79] Her long endurance has been rewarded by a "glorious participation of the immensity of God."[80] The pain of her treacherous journey is replaced by the assurance that she belongs to her beloved without reserve, surrounded forever by God's vast yet intimate embrace.

As at the beginning of her journey, the bride's attention is fixed upon her lover. In describing the consummation, Guyon returns to the theme of perception that began our analysis of the term *annihilation*. As we have seen in the earlier stages of the essential union, the soul becomes so enthralled by the loveliness of her groom that she is no longer aware of herself, or of her faithful gaze. Here again, our commentator explains that the bride "must then even lose the perceptible vision of God and all distinct knowledge [*Il faut même alors qu'elle perde la vue aperçue de Dieu et toute connaissance distincte*], as little as it may be."[81]

Immediately after stating this, however, Guyon provides a hint into another aspect of her thought; the *reason* that perception of the self (and of one's gaze) does not occur in distinct form is that there is no longer "division nor distinction" between the soul and God: "Remember that we see what is distinct from us, but not what is within us. Sight and knowledge no longer exist where there is neither division nor distinction, but a perfect fusion [*un parfait mélange*].

The soul in this state cannot look at God without also seeing herself, and perceiving at the same time the working of his love."[82] God and self have become one, and where one is, the other is necessarily found. What precisely does this "fusion" entail, however? Is it a fusion of "essences," or simply of "faculties" or "powers," albeit now in an unmediated fashion?

Guyon's terminology itself indicates that there is a union of "essence with essence," not merely of the soul's powers with God. Key passages also posit that the bride and groom become so "fused," "merged," or "intermingled" into one that they are no longer distinguishable—perhaps not only to one's perception but in very essence. Does this "union of essences," then, signify a loss of the essential self in its entirety? It might appear so, from certain turns of phrase in Guyon's argument. For example:

> Here the soul must no longer and can no longer make the distinction between God and herself. God is she and she is God [*Dieu est elle et elle est Dieu*], since, by the consummation of the marriage, she is flowing back to God and finds herself lost in him [*elle est recoulée en Dieu et se trouve perdue en lui*], without being able to distinguish or find herself again [*sans pouvoir se distinguer ni se retrouver*]. The true consummation of marriage makes the mixture of the soul with her God so great and so intimate that she can no longer distinguish herself or see herself.[83]

Here Guyon speaks in terms of equivalence between the soul and God ("God is she and she is God"). The soul has been "mixed" together with God. Other phrases further nuance her meaning, however. She writes of the soul losing her "power to distinguish or find herself" and to "make such a distinction regarding God and herself." The *perception* of self as distinct, that is, the ability to "distinguish and see herself," remains an important factor in her thought here, not the absolute indistinction of essences per se. Admittedly, it might be the case that one does not perceive the distinction because the distinction of *essences* is lost. In other words, it seems from this passage that there is nothing left to distinguish, as one has become absorbed, lost, and mixed into the other. However, other passages indicate otherwise.

Earlier in the commentary, when Guyon first introduced the reader to the essential union (and in particular its consummation) she described the soul as a "drop of water falling into a cup of wine." She averred that while this drop "loses its own appropriate form and character, and is apparently changed into wine . . . its being and substance always remain entirely distinct."[84] She added, "If it were the will of God, an angel could at any time separate the identical drop. In the same way, the soul can always be separated from God, though with great difficulty."[85]

Furthermore, Guyon explains that the soul's *actions* (notably, not its essence) are, "so to speak," "divinized": "It is this fusion that divinizes, so to speak," the "*actions* of the [creature] who arrives at this lofty and sublime position, for these actions emanate from a source that is wholly divine, as a result of the unity that has been effected between God and the soul who has been melted and absorbed into him [*fondue et recoulée en lui*]. God becomes the origin of her actions and words, though they are spoken and manifested externally through her."[86] Here, our author implies that God and the soul are distinct, even as they have become "one." God may be the primary agent, but the soul remains the vessel through which God acts and speaks. Although the soul is "fused" with, or "melted into," God, the soul acts distinctly on God's behalf. God originates the bride's actions, but she is the conduit.

Toward the conclusion of her treatise, Guyon celebrates the consummation of the soul's union with God using various illustrations. As might be expected in a commentary on the *Song of Songs*, she appeals to the analogy of human marriage; and this sheds further light on the distinction between God and soul. She reminds her reader that in marriage "two persons are rendered one flesh." Within this union, however, one finds two distinct wills, as well as persons. For example, Guyon speaks of "shared" possessions—a "common" bond that can exist only between two distinct entities. (In other words, I cannot create a joint bank account with myself.) The soul, retaining its own identity and integrity, willingly hands over its possessions to the "shared" or "common" ownership and control of another:

> Admirable oneness! All things are common between the Bridegroom and the spouse. As she has nothing that belongs to herself, the possessions of the Bridegroom become common to her also. She no longer has any property or any interests but His. . . . All that I have, my Well Beloved, is Yours, she says, and all that is Yours is mine. I am so stripped and pillaged of all things, that I have preserved, given, and laid up for you all manner of pleasant fruits, all sorts of excellent actions and results, whatever they may be, without a single exception. I have given You all my works, both the old, which You have performed in me from the beginning, and the new, which You effect through me from moment to moment. There is nothing that I have not surrendered to You; my soul, with all its powers and operations, and my body, with its senses and everything that it can do. I have consecrated all these things to You, and as You have given them to me to keep, permitting me the use of them, I preserve them wholly for You. I do this so that, regarding both the property and the use of it, all things are yours alone.[87]

Guyon concedes that this analogy is "only a faint image of this unity by which, in the words of apostle Paul, God and the soul become one spirit (1 Cor. 6:17)."[88] Nonetheless, she makes generous use of this image without further qualification. Within the union of husband and wife, the two parties never lose their separate identities; and she says this very thing of the soul and God. Even *within* their "inexpressible union" in which the two become "fused" into one, they remain "forever distinct." Union need not imply confusion of essences for Guyon. She states this at the beginning of her commentary, as well as at its conclusion.

After taking her reader through the arduous journey from betrothal to marriage, Guyon reiterates the theme: "Everything that is said of this inexpressible union is understood with all the essential differences between the Creator and the created [*avec toutes les différences essentielles entre le créateur et la créature*], though with a perfect unity of love and of mystical flowing back into God alone."[89] To the frustration of her reader, an apparent contradiction arises immediately afterwards. She adds that the soul "no longer fears losing him, since she is not only united to him, but has been transformed into him [*mais change en lui*]."[90] Furthermore, while positing a distinction earlier in the commentary, she claimed in the same breath that there is "neither division nor distinction" within the "perfect fusion" between God and the soul.[91] Where does Guyon stand on this question?

Union and Distinction

From certain vantage points, the self loses its distinct identity; it "becomes," or is "transformed *into*," God. The reader is not clear on what it means for the soul to "lose herself" and "flow back into God," however. Guyon simply posits, without elucidation, that the soul "passes beyond self" and "*into* God," with the result that "God is she and she is God" (Dieu est elle et elle est Dieu).[92] Regardless of these claims, she goes on to insist that the two remain forever distinct.

Guyon's language is certainly opaque. Some have gone so far as to consider it erratic and confused—the ramblings of a madwoman.[93] Indeed, Guyon repeatedly qualifies one claim with its opposite. For example, she writes in a pivotal passage:

> But the consummation of the marriage does not come to pass until the soul is so melted, annihilated, and freed from self that she can unreservedly flow into God [*lorsque l'Ame est tellement fondue, anéantie et désappropriée qu'elle peut toute, sans reserve, s'écouler en son Dieu*]. Then that admirable fusion of created and Creator is accomplished, which brings them into unity, so to speak, though with the same infinite disproportion that exists

between a single drop of water and the ocean. The drop has become ocean; yet, it forever remains a little drop, though it has
become assimilated in character [*elle soit devenue mer, toutefois
elle est toujours une petite gouttelette, bien qu'elle soit propor-
tionnée en qualité*] with the waters of the ocean, and is therefore
fit to be mingled with it and to make but one ocean with it.[94]

Guyon has been careful to note that even in the midst of the
soul's "mingling" with the divine, an "infinite disproportion" remains
between the soul and God, as between a "single drop of water and the
ocean." Creature and Creator are brought into "admirable fusion"
through an "assimilation in *character*"; but while the drop *becomes*
ocean, it "forever remains a little drop." She thus holds tenaciously to
a distinction of essences, even while positing an indistinction of some
sort (at the very least, perceptual indistinction).

At the end of the day, "union" of essences for Guyon is indeed
the fusion of two separate essences into "one." This "oneness," however, need not negate the distinctions that will "forever remain" between a little drop and the infinitely disproportionate ocean of which
it has become a part. While this may seem a contradiction in terms,
Guyon contents herself with ambiguity. It may be that she sees both
distinction *and* indistinction of essences as ultimately reconcilable,
perhaps even a necessary paradox.

Transgressive Language

One can easily concede that Guyon's language is erratic and extreme,
much like the torrents of the soul that she describes in an earlier
work.[95] If one were to conclude, however, that difficulty in language
implies irreconcilable confusion in one's thinking, one might have to
say the same of those who drafted the Chalcedonian formula. Wrestling with the mystery of the hypostatic union of Christ, their best
explanation at the time was to posit "two natures, without confusion,
without change, without division, without separation; the distinction
of natures being in no way annulled by the union, but rather the

characteristics of each nature being preserved and coming together to form one person and subsistence."

Notably, much of Guyon's language, as well as the tension in her thought, mirrors this very formula. Some of the language sounds surprisingly similar, in fact. The soul becomes united to God, while maintaining its own nature "without confusion." Likewise, "the distinction of natures" is in "no way annulled by the union." The difference for Guyon is that the soul *is* "changed" *into* God, in her account of the Song.

Appealing to the mysteries of the faith is certainly no way to absolve Guyon of the inconsistencies and tension in her commentary. After all, the hypostatic union of Christ is a singular, unrepeatable event; no human can claim such status, here or later. Nonetheless, this parallel might evoke one's sympathy if one considers Guyon's difficulty with language. If enough similarities exist between the perfect union of Christ's two natures and the marriage of the soul to Christ, it might be unfair to impose the restraints of formal logic upon Guyon at every turn.[96] She may have even intentionally presented her readers with this paradox, so as to stretch their categories.

Several scholars, most notably Michel de Certeau, have made this claim regarding mystics of Guyon's era in general.[97] Julia Kristeva also finds in these "disruptive uses of language" that which she calls "revolutionary potential"; the mystic reinterprets conventions in such a way that previously overlooked ways of understanding are opened.[98] As Susan St. Ville explains, "In the process of unsettling the conventions of language, mystical writing reveals the limitations of these conventions. Although incomprehensible, mystical discourse can have a powerful effect on those who read and listen to it. It is received and accepted as a 'testimony' to a beyond of which nothing is known but which is nonetheless taken as real."[99] Indeed, Guyon claims throughout her writing that she too desires to bring new avenues of understanding and experience to her readers,[100] and she may be employing deliberately transgressive rhetorical techniques toward that end.

5

The Impossibility and the Delights of
Self-Annihilation in Guyon's Theology

Like Anna Maria van Schurman, Guyon, in attempting to reach a deeper union with God (through self-annihilation), initially fails. As seen in the previous chapter, Guyon explains in her *Commentary* that the critical point at which the bride is united to her lover is in this place of self-despair. When the soul experiences the impossibility of her situation, she releases her hopes and makes a "final renunciation" or "final sacrifice." Guyon also speaks of these times of trial in her own spiritual journey and notes that desperation drove her into a deeper experience of God's kindness, mercy, and intimate presence. While this is not a comforting picture for most, through it Guyon reminds her readers that failure has the capacity to usher in a different and more profound success.

WHENCE THE VIOLENCE? GUYON'S THEOLOGICAL ANTHROPOLOGY

In charting the soul's painful journey toward union with God in Guyon's *Commentary*, we have yet to examine the rationale behind

Guyon's theology. It is not clear why the soul must be so violently extinguished along the way or why the experience of failure is the key to union with God. In what way is humanity so opposed to God that its destruction is required for it to achieve consummation in marriage, and why is self-praise detrimental to the soul's journey?

The query posed in the previous chapter thus returns in full force: What within the soul needs to be destroyed, and for what reasons? As already indicated, certain impediments must be demolished so that the bride can move closer to the inner chambers of her lover. It is no easy process by which her gaze becomes fixed upon the bridegroom and self-praise is removed. Yet the precise nature of these hindrances is unclear, and it remains perplexing why the soul needs to despair of herself in a "final sacrifice" in order to receive the fullness of intimacy with her beloved.

Guyon follows two lines of argument in response to these implicit questions. First, she explains that the soul must be purged of an "evil quality" that stands entirely opposed to God and thereby hinders union with him. A mutual repulsion, in fact, bars the joining of human impurity with the purity that characterizes God's essence.[1] The love of self, furthermore, is rooted in this "spoiled and corrupted nature," that is, the "infection" of sin passed on by the first parents; self-love keeps the soul from loving and desiring God fully. To give the soul its greatest good, God seeks by an extreme annihilation to deliver it from this "wickedness and the great evil of its depraved nature." This process eradicates the soul's wickedness, as well as its self-love. The annihilation is comparable with the pulling of a tooth that is too deeply infected by a cavity to be retained.

In this manner, God aims to restore the soul to its original purity before the Fall. This purity knew no "self-serving inclinations," and this is the destination of the bride of Christ.[2] The cure requires painful surgery, however, since the self is so stubbornly attached to the disease. The whole of the soul's journey can be likened to a healing process; medical images abound throughout Guyon's writing, as in many of her theological sources.[3] At the same time, the healing process envisioned by Guyon is not as gradual, as one finds in the works of her predecessors. It is disruptive, destructive, and violent.

From these and similar passages, it is evident that Guyon sub-scribes to a fundamentally low theological anthropology. To her, there is something desperately wrong with the soul—a distortion that prohibits her admittance into the inner recesses of her bridegroom's affections. The bride is not yet "cleansed of self" or purged of the in-fection of sin. God therefore "draws the soul out of self" by "long, powerful, and repeated operations." Through the crucible of suffer-ing, the disease of sin is removed, and God "reendows her with the grace of innocence . . . causing her to be lost in him."[4]

Though this process sounds unnecessarily cruel, the phrase "lost in him" provides a clue to the second line of Guyon's reasoning. Re-gardless of the sin with which the soul has been infected, her joyous end is to be lost in the vastness of God. By virtue of her limited, cre-ated nature, however, she remains cramped. She is simply too "small" to experience the fullness of God. The soul's nature is "bounded and limited" and therefore "harsh" and "unyielding." This limitation—which Guyon is careful to note is *neither a fault nor an offense*—"stands in the way of her happiness."[5]

According to Guyon, this "hard and contracted nature" has to be "enlarged" so that it may participate in the vastness of God and be "lost" there. The soul "suffers incredible pain" during this process, however.[6] It is excruciating for her to be "drawn out" of her "limited" self and into the vastness of God. Hardships serve to soften the un-yielding nature of the soul; severe annihilations make her fully pli-able. She is then ready to enter the joy of marital union "without ob-stacle, hindrance, or restraint."[7] Since the limitedness of the self posed this restraint, it is precisely the self that needs to be removed. Again, the fallenness of the bride's nature is not the issue here; her creaturely status alone is sufficient cause for her narrowness.

From this point of view, the created self is itself a burden. By im-plication, one's goal should be to be released of this weight.[8] Once the self and its preoccupations are extinguished, the soul knows true free-dom.[9] She is finally "disengaged from her hard, cramped, and limited nature" and can return to her original source; she is now ready to be "received into the nuptial couch of the bridegroom."[10] To possess God "without obstacle, hindrance, or restraint" thus requires the annihilation of the self, at the various levels described in the previous chapter; but this hindrance originates from both the infection of sin that plagues the soul *and* its sheer createdness. In her *Commentary*, Guyon addresses these impediments and proposes solutions to them.

According to Guyon, an "entire renunciation" of the self, both created and fallen, ushers the soul into the consummation of her marriage. In this newfound freedom, she is ready to be "sunk into his divine unity" and "lost in his bosom."[11] As Guyon puts it, "You are so fully your Beloved's that nothing hinders you from being lost in him. Since you have been wholly melted by the heat of his love, you have been ready to be poured into him as into your final consummation."[12] The Bride exclaims in response, "Ah! . . . if I am always for my Bridegroom, he is also all for me! For I feel once again his goodness; he gives himself to me in a way as ineffable as it is new. He pays back my pain with the most tender caresses."[13]

Serious implications arise from Guyon's claims. If the soul's sheer creatureliness is the issue, does this imply that the original creation was deficient and that perfect unity between God and the soul could not have existed in the prefallen state? As discussed earlier, Guyon speaks of returning to one's original purity "before Eve fell under the power of the Seducer"—but of what did that original union consist? Guyon does not fill in these gaps in her thinking and implicitly brings into question the original integrity of creation.[14]

In the final analysis, it is not clear whether there is a fatal flaw in the soul—something that stands in stark opposition to her divine lover—that must be extirpated or whether the sheer "creatureliness" of the soul poses a sufficient hindrance to this union that it warrants a final overthrow. Guyon has indicated that the limitation of the soul's "contracted" nature is a simple fact of her creatureliness and not a flaw. In other passages, however, she unabashedly speaks of the "infection of sin" that plagues the soul. As it turns out, the recognition of this infection leads to great gain: it causes the soul to be "well-persuaded of the all of God and [her] own nothingness," thereby preparing her to become lost in the vastness of God's divinity. "She is to enter into God by an absolute self-abandonment. . . . She herself, along with every other person, is merely nothingness. . . . And in this way, [she] may attain to union."[15]

Ultimately, Guyon fails to distinguish the soul's infection from its creatureliness. One cannot be understood apart from the other, for the glue of sin clings tightly to the self; the only way to eradicate the former is to extinguish the latter.[16] It may be that Guyon was unable to distinguish these existentially in her own life and that her experience played into her theology. Whether or not this was so, Guyon teaches that annihilation is necessary for the disease of sin to be expunged. Though she speaks of the "limited" nature of the soul—one caused by Creation and not the Fall—what is critical for her is that human nature is profoundly, irrevocably marred.[17] As a result, one is left with a soul that needs to be annihilated in its entirety.[18] A partial death will not do.

THE MEANS TO SELF-ANNIHILATION

Although Guyon's commentary details the trajectory by which the soul progresses from spiritual betrothal to marriage, the mechanisms *behind* this process yet remain unclear. The reader who seeks to follow Guyon's path may thus find herself befuddled as to *how* she might actually arrive at her goal. Guyon may have gone to great lengths to describe, and even prescribe, the journey that frees the soul from both the burden of sin and the limitations of her creatureliness, but if she is attempting to be a "spiritual guide" (as she herself claims), has she offered practical help to her audience?

The Virtue of Passivity and the Primacy of Grace

The very idea of progressing, or moving from one point to another, is problematic within Guyon's framework. The active nature of the process is called into question—and often negated by Guyon's predominant use of the passive voice. The soul does not "move" itself from one state to another; rather, it is "moved," or "taken," from the initial betrothal to the final union.[19] If the posture of the bride is to be passive, what role, if any, does she play in attaining this union?

Another way of framing the issue is to ask how the bride comes to die in the first place. *By what means* will she experience "mystical slumber," annihilation, and thereby essential union with God? Must she simply await "being taken," or can she actively crucify herself, which amounts to nothing less than spiritual suicide? Guyon piles numerous requirements upon the bride before she is made "worthy" of entering the innermost chambers of the bridegroom. Elsewhere, however, Guyon asserts that there is nothing the bride herself can actually do to be admitted. She must rely solely on the movement of God's grace and must "receive the spiritual marriage" by "permitting herself to be destroyed and annihilated."[20] As indicated earlier, the dichotomy of "all of God" and "none of the self" is key to an understanding of annihilation. What, then, can the bride actually do?

The manner in which human and divine agencies intersect has long vexed theologians. Guyon also runs into this conundrum but seems at times to disregard it, ignoring the inconsistencies that she presents.[21] The bride is to act responsibly—and yet is utterly dependent on God's action. The goal of annihilation is that the bride becomes entirely passive and allows God to be and do "everything." A further question then arises: If the key to self-annihilation is "all God," to the exclusion of any human element, does that necessarily and decisively eradicate human agency as well?[22]

Throughout her commentary, Guyon argues that it is the work of God to bring the soul to annihilation. The soul awaits the marriage and is brought to it by the grace of God. "Special grace" is given to her from the start to "prepare her for the sufferings that are to follow."[23] However, one may wonder how the soul would endure such mortification. When her lover tells her of the crosses that she must bear, what enables her to embrace them? For Guyon, special consolations from God strengthen the bride for the difficult process of annihilation. The soul experiences intoxicating joy in the bridegroom's "wine cellars," and this grace has the effect of purifying her loves and fortifying the soul.

Pleasure and the Purification of Loves

The experience of pleasure in God's presence significantly reorders the loves of the bride, so that she is prepared to endure suffering for him. In her explication of Song 2:4, Guyon argues that the divine lover brings the soul into his wine cellars and there sets "love in order" within her:

> The beloved of the King, issuing from her delightful interviews with him, appears to her companions to be intoxicated and beside herself. She is so in truth; for having tasted of the finest *wine* of the Bridegroom, she could not help being seized with the extremest ardor. Being quite sensible of it herself, she begs her companions not to be amazed at seeing her in so extraordinary a condition; my intoxication, she says, is excusable, for my King has *brought me into His divine wine cellars,* and there *has set love in order within me.* . . . I have drunk so abundantly of his strong and pure wine, that he has set love in order within me.[24]

This abundant imbibing of the delights of the bridegroom, namely, his "strong and pure wine," nourishes the soul, making her "wiser and stronger" for future hardships.[25] The strong drink of his love, like an aphrodisiac, creates a change within the soul and reorders her love.

Guyon explains, first of all, that an experience of God's delights causes the soul "to forget herself wholly that she may only think upon her Well-beloved." This includes becoming "divested of every selfish interest in her own salvation, perfection, joy, or consolation, that she may only think of the interests of God." The love of which she has drunk makes this possible, although Guyon does not explain how it is, only that it is. She simply adds, "It can only be known and enjoyed of those who have experienced it; the others have not yet tasted of the Bridegroom's wine."

Guyon further explains that the bride "can love nothing in herself or in any creature except in and for God, and not in and for self, however important and necessary it may appear."[26] Her love has become "perfectly chaste. All creatures are nothing to her; she wills them only for her God, and none of them for herself." The bride's affections are focused exclusively upon her lover, and all other loves are subordinated to, or subsumed into, that primary love.[27]

In fact, so great is the delight of his love that she no longer thinks only of enjoying his embrace but is willing even to suffer hardships for him. Having now "tasted of the finest wine of the Bridegroom, she could not help being seized with the extremest ardor," an ardor that gives her fresh resolve to carry her crosses. As Guyon puts it: "Ah! what strength does this well ordered charity impart for the terrible states that are to follow!"[28] Of course, we have seen that even this fails in the end. The bride's own experience and ardor fall short of the challenges that she later faces. At the same time, they bring her to the "final sacrifice" through which she renounces her own strength and enters into lasting union with God.

In addition to gaining strength for future trials, the bride "no longer asks anything for herself, but only that he might be glorified." The "intoxication" that she has experienced in his presence makes this possible, although Guyon again provides no further explanation. Her love has simply been fortified, purified, by the overpowering experience of God's presence. Last, the soul "enters fully into the designs of the divine righteousness, consenting with all her heart to everything it decrees with respect to her and in her, whether for time or eternity." Toward the conclusion of her commentary, Guyon adds: "If the manifold waters of afflictions, contradictions, miseries, poverty and distresses have not been able to quench the love of this soul, it is not to be supposed that the floods of abandonment to the Divine Providence could do it, for it is they that preserve it."[29]

With this purified love, Guyon argues that the bride loves God more deeply even through the absence of his pleasurable presence and, indeed, even in the midst of excruciating pains. In fact, the cross brings the bridegroom nearer to the bride, whether or not she recognizes his presence: "He is never more present to her than in those seasons of bitterness, during which he dwells in the midst of her heart."[30] The presence of God, even when imperceptible, guards the soul to the end. And as Guyon explains in a later passage, he is her constant delight, even during difficulty: "She goes on holding up to admiration the perfection of her Bridegroom; his abundance and his wonderful qualities are the joy of the Spouse, in the midst of her misery."[31] The soul is enthralled with the beauty of her lover, and the knowledge of his worth helps her to stay the course.

An "Array of Crucifixions": Active Reception

Although divine grace offers the consolation of pleasurable gifts, it also comes at high cost. The soul undergoes an "array of crucifixions," both external and internal, which are wrought by God and not the self, according to Guyon.[32] It is God's active will to test the soul and to "make her fit" for the marriage.

Furthermore, these trials are sent because the soul would not have the strength or resolve to extinguish herself (i.e., her preoccupations with self at the four levels described in the previous chapter). Spiritual suicide is not even possible, according to Guyon, as the individual clings too tightly to the self. This "terrible array of crucifixions" is therefore necessary, and it is by them that the soul is made to yield to death. Guyon adds, "If any one of them were missing, the part not assaulted in this way would serve the soul as a refuge and a reprieve, and would maintain her in her life of self."[33] In this crucible of suffering, attachments to the self are brought to the surface and destroyed, along with self-love and pride. The individual's only role is to consent to the process.

The question to be explored, then, is the manner in which the bride offers consent. What is her role in entering the spiritual marriage? Guyon indicates that many souls forfeit the marriage by refusing their death. They cannot, or do not, yield to the crucible of God; instead, they remove themselves from it.[34] In so doing, they fail to "die" to themselves and enter into full union with God. The individual's action therefore makes a decisive difference.

Even though the soul is annihilated in accepting its various crosses, Guyon calls the final renunciation a "pure sacrifice."[35] The soul actively offers herself upon the altar, even as the bridegroom has initiated the process by inviting her to partake in his sufferings.[36] Upon that altar, she receives a "Bridegroom covered with blood and seeped in grief."[37] Divine initiative is therefore followed by a human response—a response that is both passive and active. The soul receives the marriage but also actively offers herself upon this altar of "sacrifice." While Guyon insists on complete passivity, an active assertion of the will is also implied; it is even demanded.

In addition to actively offering the self, the bride must actively take up her cross. Guyon may not state it explicitly, but the task of the soul is to *receive actively* that which is imparted to it. She must *choose* to undergo her crucifixion, though she does not initiate it by her own will.[38] While this cannot be likened to spiritual suicide or self-destruction, it is still an active decision of the soul to be destroyed. Human agency cannot be fully erased, no matter how vigorously Guyon avers so. The individual consciously makes room for God and embraces the crosses given by God.

THE FRUITS OF SELF-ANNIHILATION

Death: The Passageway to Life

While the image of Guyon's crucified bride is disconcerting, even startling, one need only read further to find that the bride is imbued with *new life*. Fresh vigor, energy, and fruitfulness characterize her life in a way that was previously impossible. Death never has the final word within Guyon's framework. Annihilation of the self is, rather, a passageway from a feeble way of being to a newly transformed one. In fact, the door to new life remains shut, apart from *this* particular rite of passage, and the bride is unable to thrive most fully until she has first learned to die. As Guyon puts it, "the all-powerful voice of God" has summoned her "from the tomb of death to the spiritual resurrection."[39] To elucidate this transformation, I will trace Guyon's description of the contrasts between the soul's old and new manner of life.

Perfect Rest and Joy

Having experienced the consummation of her marriage, the bride finds ecstasy and rest in the bosom of her beloved. This repose is enduring, for the soul has "passed into God by her happy deliverance from self. This is rest from which she shall never be disturbed." The bride now knows the security and permanence of her essential union with God. She has become perfectly passive in receiving God's graces, even as she labors externally. Just as perfect rest and activity characterize God's own being, the bride too is "exceedingly active" and yet at "perfect rest."[40]

In addition to perfect rest, the bride experiences a profound level of joy, deeper than previously known. When the soul finally "possesses" the object of her love in the essential union, she comes to experience what Guyon calls "true enjoyment." Marital union with the divine is the "essential beatitude," the "veritable enjoyment of the object." She reaches the height of pleasure within the spiritual marriage.

Guyon writes in her *Vie* (published in 1720) that her own experience of annihilation ushered her soul into a more complete enjoyment of her divine lover. She explains that the individual loses herself within the embrace of the divine and discovers a "joy that accompanies [her] everywhere, still finding him, who had united [her] to himself, in his own immensity and boundless vastness!"[41] Annihilation, though an excruciating process, ultimately leads the soul to the greatest possible enjoyment of God in this life.

The Apostolic Bride

Once the soul has become the bride of Christ, passing from spiritual betrothal to marriage, she experiences an intensified vibrancy of life. Each of her faculties is endowed with a "double fertility," and she becomes an active servant of Christ. That which was dormant in the initial "union of the powers" rises back to new life. For example, the faculties of understanding, memory, and will are marked by an enormous surge in energy and effectiveness.[42] In Guyon's explication of Song 6:5 ("Your teeth are as a flock of sheep which go up from the washing. Every one of them bears twins, and there is not one who is barren among them") she writes:

> The Bridegroom repeats to His bride what He has already formerly declared, to show her that she now has in full reality what she then had only in the seed. Her *teeth* are her *faculties*, which have now become *so innocent, pure, and cleansed that they are perfectly washed*. The *sheep*, which they resemble, are no longer shorn, as they were before. Rather, *facility in the use of her faculties, in an admirable manner, and without confusion, is restored.* . . . Her faculties are *not barren*, since they have been endowed with a *double fertility*. They are *doing more than they have ever accomplished, and are doing it better*.[43]

The use of her faculties is thus restored to the bride with remarkable ease and purity; her understanding, memory, and will are no longer dead but fully alive and doubly fruitful. Guyon attributes this "wonderful facility" to the perfect liberty that the bride experiences, now that she has been freed from self-interest.[44] Hers is a perfect love; and this enables her to enter into an apostolic vocation.[45]

The surrender of one's understanding, for instance, ushers in a union of "pure intellect" in which the individual's mind is "so clear and empty of thoughts that those that come appear only for a moment and for just so long a time as is necessary to produce the effect God wants to work by them."[46] The "effect" that God desires to produce in "essential union" is far greater than the soul might have achieved on her own. As Guyon explains in her commentary on Song 7:4, when the bride's understanding "is lost in God, it becomes a fishpool, a source of every blessing and a remedy for every ill. God employs her mind, which has been willingly given up for his sake, in a thousand great undertakings that are useful for the good of her neighbor."[47]

The precondition for the multiplied usefulness of the faculties, as seen above, is that they be "lost in God" and "willingly given up for his sake." The faculties are then charged with greater energy. Having been surrendered to the vastness of God's own power, they can both receive and release a power greater than their own. This is made possible only by the loss of their own operation, however. And with the essential union, the soul has become so "intermingled" with God's own being that God's power and her own cease to be distinguishable. The faculties then become "a source of every blessing," poured out as a healing balm for others. As Guyon claims in her *Autobiography*, her own mystical marriage (made possible only by mystical death) ensued in an astonishing fruitfulness in her own "labors for her Lord."[48]

Perfect Passivity: The Active-Passive State

The "double fertility" of the bride's faculties is accompanied by a transition from sheer passivity to ceaseless action, according to Guyon. As she "unfolds" the meaning of Song 7:12 ("Let us get up early to the vineyards; let us see if the vine flourish, whether the tender grape appear, and the pomegranates bud forth; there will I give you my breasts"), she explains that the bride of Christ is now "full of activity." Far from remaining dead, the soul, after dying, can undertake vibrant, vigorous service of her Bridegroom. She becomes a spokesperson for her lover, teaching others of his perfections and beauty. Her speech drips with eloquence and unusual wisdom.[49] Having learned to receive from her bridegroom, she then gives generously "for the benefit of others."[50] Works of charity also flow from this enlarged spirit, and the apostolic bride is moved with greater compassion toward others.

Guyon explains in her *Justifications* (later footnoted in her commentary) that the "only true passivity, in its perfection," is "an active-passive state." In this state, "[the soul's] actions are no longer self-originated, but are wholly due to the gentle and loving influences of the Holy Spirit within."[51] Passivity in and of itself is no longer a virtue of the bride of Christ. She must be sent forth, engaged in her divine lover's work. The bride of Christ thus "faithfully represents" her Bridegroom and "notices a thousand things to be done" for his glory. She "labors with all her strength," even as she rests in him. As Guyon puts it: "She invites her Bridegroom to go everywhere, for she is *now* full of activity [*mise en action*]. And, as God is always acting externally and is constantly at rest within [*toujours agissant au-dehors et toujours reposant au-dedans*], so this soul, confirmed within in perfect rest, is also exceedingly active externally. What she did defectively a while ago, she now does in perfection."

Although the spouse of Christ is able to work and rest simultaneously, Guyon is careful to note that the bride's actions need to originate from perfect stillness within, only after she has experienced spiritual death. Had she chosen to act prior to her annihilation, her actions would have been gravely deficient. The bride needs first to learn complete passivity, dying to "all self-originating influences." Once she becomes "fully malleable," she enters into this "active-passive" state. As Guyon explains: "It would have been a serious defect in the soul if, when she should have remained entirely passive, she had chosen to act, for in this way she would have hindered the operations of God; she would have been acting from her own activity, when God required her to be perfectly passive, that she might die to all self-originated influences. Now, through her continued passivity, she has become like soft wax, or a perfectly manageable instrument in the hands of God, with which he does as he will."[53]

The bride of Christ, while ceaselessly active in her apostolic vocation, experiences at the same time an internal rest that is unshakable. The "active-passive" state may be the "only true passivity, in its perfection," but our commentator continues to place a heavy accent on the soul's stillness.[54]

Apostolic Self-Forgetfulness

Lest one lose sight of Guyon's emphasis on self-forgetfulness, one must keep in mind that the fruitfulness of the bride's faculties is an incidental by-product of her union with Christ, not the intended goal. In the transition from spiritual betrothal to marriage described earlier, the first requirement of the soul's annihilation was that she cease from self-reflection. Consequently, when the bride surrenders herself to her lover, together with her faculties, she does not seek explicitly to become more useful in his service. She is not to anticipate any particular outcome and must hold all things loosely. "Holy indifference" characterizes her attitude from beginning to end. As a result, she remains forgetful of herself and the "fruits of her annihilation," even when she experiences an astonishing effectiveness in her labors.[55] In other words, she is not to rejoice in her fruitfulness or pay heed to it. Fixation on the fruits, in fact, would immediately disqualify her from maintaining that state of self-forgetfulness. Guyon even remarks that the bride might forfeit her union with God at that point, though she adds that it is difficult, indeed nearly impossible, to lose that union.[56]

The bride therefore needs to be especially wary of noticing the *results* of her annihilation. While she labors incessantly on behalf of others, she is not mindful of her success.[57] Furthermore, even the desire to help others originates from God, not herself. Her only care is that God be honored.[58] The loss of self-perception and self-reflection, which marked the very beginning of her journey toward marriage, continues to characterize the bride to the end.

THE PROBLEM WITH JOY

The bride of Christ experiences the height of joy in union with her lover, but this remains a complex subject for Guyon. To understand the problem of joy, it is important to look back upon the bride's journey and retrace a few steps. In the initial stages of the soul's journey, the soul will have "tasted" the delights of intimacy with her divine lover.[59] She understands that God is the "center of [her] bliss" and "runs after him."[60] These delights serve as the impetus for drawing the soul further into union with God, causing her to yearn for an "enjoyment of himself more noble and more intimate." The soul exclaims regarding her current joy, "Ah! if this be so, even at the outset, what delights will there not be in the *nuptial kiss,* the kiss of his mouth!"[61] As Guyon explains in her commentary of Song 1:3 ("Draw me, and we will run after thee . . ."): "This young lover prays the Bridegroom to *draw* her by the center of her soul, as if she were not satisfied with the sweetness of the balm poured forth among her powers; for she already comprehends, through the grace of the Bridegroom, who continually draws her with more and more force, that there is an enjoyment of Himself more noble and more intimate than that which she at present shares. This is what gives rise to her present request."[62]

Even while enjoying God is the deep-seated desire of the soul, Guyon warns the reader against this desire. The pleasure of divine delights may attract the soul earlier in her journey, but she is no longer to seek these pleasures the further she advances. The desire for enjoyment is in fact a marker of immaturity. In these initial stages, "perceptible grace . . . penetrates the soul" and is "the sweetness by which God advises the hearts that he wants to engage in his love." As Guyon puts it, this sweetness is poured forth "with so excellent an odor that the young soul finds itself wholly penetrated by its power and sweetness. This takes place without violence, and with so much pleasure that the soul, still young and feeble, suffers itself to be carried away by these innocent charms. This is the way God causes himself to be loved by young hearts, who are not as yet capable of loving except on account of the pleasure they experience in loving."[63]

As the soul progresses, however, she is called to rise above the desire for delights. She is tested to see if she will display "sufficient fidelity to be willing to dispense with all the gifts of God that [she] may reach God himself." Guyon exhorts her readers to "not stop at the graces or gifts of God, which are only as the rays that issue from his face, but which are not himself." Rather, they are to "mount up to his very throne and there seek him; *seek his face evermore* until you are so blessed as to find it."[64] The giver is to be preferred above all his gifts, even in the painful absence of gifts that were once the source of youthful delight. In fact, the divine lover often disappears before the state of marriage (a recurring theme within the Song of Songs) and hides his "sensible grace" in order to strengthen and test the heart of his beloved.[65] The soul must learn to seek God rather than the "spiritual consolations" of God.[66]

If this is the case, what is the proper role of the enjoyment of God as a motivating force for the bride of Christ? She is appropriately drawn by the desire for more of the pleasures of God. However, she is to love *God* over the *enjoyment* of God and to prove that love during seasons of darkness and trial. Through excruciating hardships, she is faced with the question of whether she desires God or simply the pleasures of God.[67] Is she willing to forgo the gifts of God, indeed her very life and salvation for the sake of God?[68] The bride is asked to undergo a "total death" in order to confirm her faithfulness: this is the ultimate test of her desire. She is, in fact, warned of the crosses she must endure before she is to be united to her lover. As Guyon writes:

> When the Bride, or rather the betrothed (for she is not yet a bride), has found her Bridegroom, she is so transported with joy, that she is eager to be instantly united to Him. But the union of perpetual enjoyment has not yet arrived. He is *mine*, she says, I cannot doubt that He gives Himself to me this moment, since I felt it, but He is to me, as it were, a bundle of myrrh. *He is not yet a Bridegroom whom I may embrace in the nuptial bed, but a bundle* [un bouquet] *of crosses, pains and mortifications; a bloody husband (see Exodus 4:25), and crucified lover, who desires to test my faithfulness, by making me partaker of a good share of His sufferings.*[69]

Even while the bride is being tested, however, she is not bereft of all consolation or promise. Her hope is that sorrow will lead to a far greater joy. She undergoes suffering for the sake of her bridegroom, but only for a time. Following the example of Christ, she endures the cross "for the sake of the joy that is set before [her]."[70] Guyon appeals also to the writings of Paul in her description of the soul's mystical death:[71] "Though the soul suffers greatly in the search after her

Beloved, its pain is but a shadow in comparison with the bliss arising from the possession of its adorable object. The same thing is asserted by Saint Paul, who tells us that the greatest sufferings of this life are not worthy to be compared with the glory that shall be revealed in us (Romans 8:18). Her Well-beloved will not have her waked, because it would hinder her death and retard her happiness."[72]

Indeed, the "glory that shall be revealed" far outweighs the suffering the soul may have endured to reach her goal. The "gain" is far more "wonderful" than any sense of loss, and her delights are abundant and rich. As Guyon puts it, "O precious gain, the loss of all created stays! God himself is received for our sole support, in exchange for them!"[73] In describing the joy of union with the divine bridegroom, Guyon exclaims:

> The moment the soul is wholly freed from self-appropriation, she is all ready to be received into the nuptial couch of the Bridegroom, where she is no sooner introduced, than, tasting the chaste and holy delights of the kiss of his mouth, which she desired at first, and which she now enjoys in that essential union which has been bestowed upon her, *she cannot refrain from expressing her joy in these words, I am my Beloved's, and my Beloved is mine! O wonderful gain! I can describe it no farther than that I am unreservedly given up to my Beloved, and that I possess him without obstacle, hindrance or restraint!*"[74]

Despite the joyous conclusion to the soul's journey, tension arises within Guyon's argument. While the soul is not to be motivated in the advanced stages by the pleasures of God, her greatest desire is for God—the source of all her happiness.[75] She yearns for him at every step of her journey. The problem is that desiring God is nothing less than desiring the height of happiness that he is to the soul that loves him; but the soul was to have relinquished any such desire for joy.[76] Furthermore, the soul is aware that her death ushers in a greater happiness. Guyon has gravely warned her reader, however, that the soul is to submit all of her desires to the will of God—even when it means the loss of all sensible pleasure.

A key distinction is helpful here: the *result* of the crucifying process of annihilation turns out to be the greatest joy imaginable for the bride—but this joy is not to be her explicit, intentional *goal*.[77] Nonetheless, the desire for joy remains an important aspect of her journey and a valid source of motivation, not only at the outset but further along in her journey as well. While she is to be wary of misplaced desire, she is yet encouraged to long for more of God—a God who cannot be separated from what God is, namely, the fountain of "joy unspeakable."[78]

Again, ambiguity remains in Guyon's thought. In the final analysis, can the soul be properly motivated by delight in the more mature stages of faith? We have seen that Guyon sanctions this only in the early stages of her journey; maturity requires that the bride relinquish this desire. Yet Guyon concedes that it is the desire for God, ultimately equal to the desire for happiness in God, that draws the soul to the end. She even encourages this pursuit of joy, presenting this desire as exemplary for others: "The Spouse of this Canticle is set forth as a model . . . to every other spouse of the Celestial Bridegroom, that they may be animated in the pursuit of a similar felicity."[79] In addition, the divine lover woos his beloved with the promise of joy at critical turns, even while warning her of pending sufferings: "*Come, My Spouse*, He says, for there is but a single step to take before thou wilt be so in reality. Until now, I have called thee *My fair one, My Well-beloved, My dove*, but never as yet *My Spouse*. Oh! how sweet is this name! but the reality will be far more pleasant and delightful!"[80] Marital union is promised as the "height of felicity"—and this promise is never once withdrawn, even when seemingly dead for a time.[81]

In spite of these concessions, Guyon argues indefatigably that the soul needs to surrender this desire and lay down the promise of joy. The bride must be willing to endure pain with no hope of resurrection on the other side. Together with Job, she is to cry out, "Though he slay me, yet will I praise him."[82] Only when hope is relinquished does God's initial promise come to fruition. This process is not to be short-circuited in Guyon's framework, for the testing of the bride's faith will not have been complete.

The enjoyment of God serves more than one function within Guyon's commentary. It is not only the promised end and the desire of the soul (albeit fully abandoned); it is also the source of strength for trials to come. The experience of intoxicating joys in the bridegroom's presence reorders the bride's loves, enabling her to endure the testing of her love.

In the end, the soul's longing for her lover, even through depths of hardship, is not without reward. Indeed, her loves have been reordered such that she loves *not for the sake of this reward*. The delights to come, however, far surpass the sufferings that are endured. The "most tender caresses" of the Bridegroom compensate for her pains and melt them away.[83] All that the soul now experiences is "unutterable happiness." As Guyon exclaims in her *Autobiography*,

> The joy [of union] that such a soul possesses in its God is so great, that it experiences the truth of those words of the royal prophet, "All they who are in thee, O Lord, are like persons ravished with joy" (Psalm 16:11). To such a soul the words of our Lord seem to be addressed, "Your joy no man taketh from you" (John 16:22). It is, as it were, plunged in a river of peace. . . . Oh, unutterable happiness! Who could have ever thought that a soul, which seemed to be in the utmost misery, should ever find a happiness equal to this? *Oh, happy poverty, happy loss, happy nothingness, which gives nothing less than God Himself in His own immensity,* no more circumscribed to the limited manner of the creature, but always drawing it out of that, to plunge it wholly into His own divine essence. . . . *Oh, happy dying of the grain of wheat,* which makes it produce a hundred-fold! (John 12:24).[84]

In surprising fashion, these joys in union with God become unhindered and free. Once the bride's testing has come to its conclusion and she is received into the marital chambers, joy is no longer to be feared as in the earlier stages. She "runs over with delights" but is no longer attached to them and can freely enjoy them. As Guyon explains:

The soul has come up gradually from the desert since she abandoned it; not only the desert of pure faith, but of self. She runs over with delights because she is full, and like a vessel filled to the brim with water from the spring, runs over on all sides for the supply of those about her. She is no longer self-supported, and hence she no longer fears the abundance of these delights. She does not fear being overthrown, for her well-beloved, who sheds them into her bosom, carries them himself with her, and suffers her to walk, leaning upon him.[85]

Continually abandoned to these delights, the bride no longer needs them. They are nonetheless hers in abundance, her unexpected reward.

THE PROBLEM OF DESIRE:
CHRISTOLOGICAL ANALOGIES

Annihilation is not only the surrender of joy, in Guyon's commentary, but also the death of desire. As we have seen, the bride's longing for divine pleasures needs to be fully abandoned. The desire for the delights of paradise, or her own happiness, is extinguished, as the bride places all of her happiness in God alone. In addition, Guyon states that the bride is not to have *any* desires of her own: "She is in such an absolute state of abandonment regarding everything, that she could not fasten a desire of any kind upon anything whatsoever."[86]

More properly stated, annihilation is the death of "self-originating desire," for Guyon notes that God reserves the right to plant desires within the bride, as the author of both her desires and her actions.[87] "God still excites in [the soul] from time to time such desires as seem best to him. But they are not like those of the former days, which had their basis in the selfish will. They are stirred up and excited by God himself, without any thought on the part of the soul."[88] According to "his own good pleasure," the bridegroom "both takes away and implants in the soul . . . the desires of which it is conscious."[89] Likewise, the bride's prayers, as with any perceptible thought or hope, await God's prompting and never find their source in herself.[90]

The beloved thus has no need to "voice" her wishes to her divine lover. She is not to have any will of her own (i.e., tainted by selfish motives), nor is she to think, desire, pray, or act on her own. All she asks is that God be the "author of every emotion" and that she will only what he wills. "Having lost all her will in the will of God, she can no longer will anything."[91] "All the perceptible desires of the soul are merged and swallowed up" in God.[92] The reason for this is clear, according to Guyon: "A desire that relates to self is the necessary result of a will *still contaminated from self*. However, as the whole design of God is to destroy the will of a person by making it one with his own, he must, at the same time, necessarily absorb and destroy every self-originating desire."[93]

The bride's volition is thereby erased entirely, leaving the divine to overpower all that was human within her. Indeed, according to Guyon's description of "essential union," the divine and human elements have become so intermingled that the human sphere is decisively uprooted and replaced by the divine. Following the tradition of other mystical authors, Guyon often uses the analogy of liquid to describe the soul's relation to God.[94] Just as water has "no perceptible qualities of its own," the soul loses its own "properties" in order to be fashioned into those of God. Having no qualities of its own, it becomes "fluid and yielding," pliable in the hands of God.[95]

Another problem arises, however. Through this process, *the soul loses the integrity of its own identity.* The fallen nature has been "crucified," but there is no place for the redemption of human nature, or a new self. As noted above, "A desire that relates to self is the necessary result of a will *still contaminated from self*." Even after the consummation of marriage has been effected, the wounds of sin mar the bride. Yet Guyon avers that perfection is possible. The bride is now likened to a "costly mirror," free from distortion. She perfectly represents Christ's beauty and now participates in the attributes of God.[96] However, the only way to become this mirror is through an annihilation of the entire self, infected as it has become through the sin of the first parents. And the bride has to remain, from beginning to end, dead to herself. In the end, she cannot trust even her redeemed self.

This position may appear no different from the tradition that Guyon inherited concerning self-denial. She goes one step further, however. In her schema, the only way to free the self from this "infection" is to destroy its activity altogether. In the above discussion of the soul's violent death it was difficult, if not impossible, for Guyon to distinguish the fallen self from the created self, and we are left with a similar dilemma here.[97] With this reading, it appears that a redeemed human nature does not replace the fallen self. Instead, Guyon aims for a supplanted self, one that is defined exclusively by divine action and initiative.

The strange result of this particular crucifying process is that the bride emerges from these pages as arguably more divine than Christ himself. Once the marriage has been consummated, human volition and desires appear nonexistent within the operations of this newly transformed soul. In other words, that which was most harmoniously blended in the soul's divine exemplar (i.e., the perfect union of the divine and human natures in Christ) finds no place in the life of his bride. There would have been no need to struggle with the Father in the Garden of Gethsemane. One would no longer hear the cry of the suffering servant "Not my will, but Yours be done," for the will of the human nature has been utterly obliterated.[98] The fallen will has been destroyed, and a sanctified will does not rise in its place. Rather, the human will is forever annihilated and replaced by the divine will alone. The distinction between "my will" *versus* "God's will" therefore finds no meaning.[99] Admittedly, one might concede that in Guyon's mind the best way to surrender "my will" and thereby remove opposition to God's will is to demolish the human will. As a result, however, the image of the God-man sweating to the point of shedding drops of blood finds no analogous place in Guyon's system. It is simply eradicated. With the death of the human will comes the death of genuine wrestling with God. Quiet acquiescence to the divine will is not the end-product of inner wrestling; it is merely the norm.

Guyon might respond, in turn, that the entire *process* that led up to the spiritual marriage is to be likened to the struggle within Gethsemane. Indeed, Guyon avers that the bride now enjoys the resurrected life, even as the earthly Christ died and was raised to new life. At the "right hand of the Father," Christ no longer wrestles in his human nature as he did at Gethsemane.[100] Guyon seems to be suggesting that this is the perfect harmony with God that the bride too experiences. With Christ, she has passed from Gethsemane to the cross, and finally to the Resurrection. As described earlier, Guyon argues that the consummation of marriage to Christ can be experienced on earth and in this manner she departs from other streams of the Christian mystical tradition. To argue, however, that wrestling necessarily ceases with marriage may compromise the perfection of Christ's own hypostatic union while on earth. According to Chalcedonian Christology, Christ was perfectly united to the Father, in a union far deeper and more "essential" than the bride's, even in his (preresurrected) incarnate existence. Yet Christ's (perfect) human nature "struggled" with the Father, both voicing *and* submitting its own desires. Christ's struggle does not disappear simply by virtue of the union of two natures within Christ. As the Chalcedonian formula attempts to elucidate, this union occurs "without division" and "separation" but also without "confusion" or "change." Significantly, "the distinction of natures" is "in no way annulled by the union, but rather the characteristics of each nature [are] preserved and [come] together to form one person and subsistence."

One may suspect that an implicit Apollinarian Christology lurks in the background for Guyon (the teaching that Jesus did not have a human mind or spirit). Not only does her resurrection theology fail to do justice to the redeemed, earthly humanity of the soul, but she may be ignoring the full humanity of Christ, by implication. Guyon has said that the "effect of the deepest annihilation" is that the soul no longer wills anything; it is now "clothed" in Christ.[101] But even Christ had a vibrant human will, distinct (though not separate) from the divine will. The hypostatic union joined two distinct, even if indivisible, natures.[102] In removing from the lips of the bride the cry at

Gethsemane, "Not my will, but yours be done," Guyon would seemingly exalt the divinity of Christ at the expense of his humanity—and likewise for the bride of Christ.

To be fair, it may simply be that Christ's resurrected life is the model for Guyon's bride after she has passed through annihilation. The risen Christ no longer wrestles with the Father's will. This is the freedom of the resurrected life of Christ, and also of Guyon's bride. At the same time, Guyon's framework suggests that there is something deficient about the act of wrestling, and this assumption problematizes Christ's own wrestling. If the hypostatic union is to hold its weight, how might Christ's struggle at Gethsemane be explained? One can infer that his struggle arose not because of some defect or sin but because of the frailty of human flesh that Christ shared with all of humanity. Christ, in his (perfect) human nature, did not *want* to suffer excruciating pain. Arguably, then, neither are humans expected to *desire* such crucifixions. A "thirst" for pain (arguably present at times in Guyon's portrayal) does not make the would-be-bride of Christ more "advanced" in her journey—if one is to take Christ's own struggle seriously. Guyon's vision does not allow for a legitimate struggle of the will that finds its origin not in sin but in the dignity of one's humanity.

Contrary to Guyon's view, when one looks at the trajectory of Christ's life on earth, one might argue that the point of struggle in the Garden was not his weakest moment but his most heroic. It is in the active laying down of a will that is vibrant, kicking, and fully alive that the death of self-will gains any meaning at all. And this kind of struggle is no longer possible for Guyon's bride.[103] She no longer fights to follow the will of God but rather experiences harmonious union with God, having been resurrected with Christ.

What kind of earthly life, then, is this? What manner of living characterizes this bride? And is it authentic? Furthermore, might the path of annihilation be an easy way out in the long run? From certain vantage points, Guyon's bride appears lifeless—she has lost her own will completely, to the point of having nothing more to "surrender" continually. One might conclude that Guyon's prescribed path is, in the end, easier than a life of active, passionate surrender, a life that knows ups and downs along the journey. There is no more need for the soul to confront and overcome the challenges that continue to test its desires. Indeed, Guyon has likened this bride to a "living sepulcher."[104] And though "the all-powerful voice of God" has summoned her "from the tomb of death to the spiritual resurrection," resulting in profound joy and multiplied fruitfulness, one might argue that the bride's human will has not been fully resurrected. It has simply been replaced by the bridegroom's will.[105]

In Guyon's *Commentary*, the soul's journey from the betrothal to marriage with Christ is filled with struggle. The soul agonizes to lay down its will as it surrenders itself to a decisive death. It makes the "final renunciation." The bride's new life, however, is depicted as struggle-free. There is no more ambiguity; her actions are now divinized and she has been made "perfect."[106] From one point of view, this is perfection stagnant and sterile. The bride, in her freedom from struggle, emerges as more self-controlled than the earthly Christ. On the other hand, Guyon regards the bride as perfectly united with the resurrected Christ, risen and free from any struggle on earth, and this may be the Christological analogy Guyon had in mind.

ANNIHILATION AS RADICAL HOSPITALITY

Any attempt to systematize Guyon's thought must, to some degree, disregard her precautionary words. The mystical life defies human reason, she writes, and it ought not be straitjacketed by intellectual attempts to grasp it. She might therefore accuse the theologian of engaging in "textual harassment" of her works.[107]

Admittedly, the scholar who writes about mystical theology does not necessarily pursue the life of a mystic and so may be exempt from Guyon's precaution. But Michel de Certeau is right that the academic enterprise need not be divorced from the object of its study, namely, God and the experience of God. Indeed, Certeau writes that mystical authors attempted to pull their readers into their own lived experience—and this may indeed include the scholar of mysticism.[108]

Mysticism has long claimed to be that which is beyond words, beyond rational "knowing."[109] However, there must be a way to join the pursuits of reason with the desire for God, while honoring the integrity of each.[110] The hypostatic union of Christ is again instructive for the theologian. In Christ, the divine and human (including human reason) come together as one. Yet neither nature is compromised. It should then be possible to unite human reason with the enterprise of seeking the divine. Why should human reason be disregarded, if that was not the case even in Christ's person? Rather than destroying the human element, the operative word might be to "redirect" that which is human, including the faculty of reason.

Guyon may have made the error of devaluing the human will; this human faculty is replaced completely by the will of God. Likewise, human reason seems to be supplanted by the divine and is denigrated in the process. These excesses in Guyon's thought, however, do not immediately disqualify her from speaking meaningfully into the life of the church. That her writings have inspired many in the Protestant world is some indication of the power of her thought.[111] Though she speaks in exaggerated terms, often transgressing the conventions of language, her overall message might yet be applicable to a church that has resigned itself to a convenient, self-centered faith. Perhaps the constant preoccupation with self, and with one's accomplishments and successes, is one of the impediments that the soul faces in experiencing deeper union with the divine. The self has become small, rather than enlarging into a generous, hospitable space for God. Guyon challenges her reader to focus on Another and to see all of one's strengths as flowing from the divine. She invites her audience to lose their fixation on self by becoming lost in the grandeur and beauty of God.

This, in the end, is what "annihilation" means for Guyon. It is the cessation of human striving, for the sake of radical receptivity to the graces, power, and wisdom of God. "Annihilation" is not so much the violent destruction of the human component; it is rather a complete surrender of the self, so that it comes under a new guidance and control. This may appear very much like death, and Guyon certainly calls it so: all things human need to be "slain" so that they can be resurrected. However, death and radical hospitality toward God amount to nearly the same thing in the final analysis of Guyon's writing. Once human faculties are decisively redirected, or "annihilated," Guyon teaches that multiplied facility flows from the divine source. The task of theology might indeed benefit from such a resurrection.

6

The Challenges and Promise of Retrieval

From their inception, the writings of Anna Maria van Schurman and Madame Jeanne Guyon have elicited dramatically different responses from their readers. Some have been understandably repelled by the extreme rhetoric of self-abnegation, whereas others have imbibed their writings deeply. The question remains for their students today: Should we set aside their teachings because of the unsettling elements, as did the theological authorities of their day, or can we retrieve something of value for contemporary theology?

Gaining wisdom from thinkers from another era does not require agreeing with their presuppositions or conclusions. But the challenges in retrieving van Schurman and Guyon's thought may seem insurmountable to some. This chapter will explore the limits of appropriation but will also consider the ways in which their theological vision offers fresh insight. Their integration of a theology of sacrifice with a theology of delight rehabilitates the often hidden beauty of self-denial and offers an important corrective to a culture marked by convenience and consumerism. And though they invite their readers to take seriously the cost of discipleship, they argue that the road of self-denial leads, paradoxically, to the deepest fulfillment in this life.

REFRAMING SELF-DENIAL AND SELF-ANNIHILATION

Anna Maria van Schurman and Madame Jeanne Guyon use extreme language when speaking of the "destruction" of the soul for the sake of union with God. But for them, denial, or death, of the self is the precondition to enjoying God most fully. Apart from this radical surrender of one's life to God, one is unable to enter deeply into communion with God; the individual becomes too preoccupied with self to welcome the intimate, abiding presence of the other. In the end, self-denial can more properly be understood as self-forgetfulness and self-giving, as we shall later see.

Despite their emphasis on self-denial as the key to a fruitful Christian life, both van Schurman and Guyon conclude that the individual does not *initiate* the denial of the self and that such attempts lead to failure. In fact, to speak of "self-denial" or "self-annihilation" can be misleading if the action of the derivative noun is taken incorrectly. God is the primary actor, and God's grace enables the joyful surrender of self.[1] Furthermore, one must be careful not to read modern notions of the "self" into their formulations.[2] Van Schurman and Guyon did not see the "self" as an autonomous entity, defined primarily by reason. Rather, they often employed reflexive verbs to speak of the Christian *denying* him*self,* or the beloved of Christ allowing her*self* to be *annihilated.* Because of the limitations of language, these reflexive verbs are best translated with the slippery term *self.* Hence, the expressions *self-denial* and *annihilation of the self* are the best English shorthand to encapsulate their teaching.

For van Schurman and Guyon, "self-denial" or "self-annihilation" is ultimately a surrender of one's vision, orientation, or mentality to the refashioning of one's Creator. This may include the denial of ambition, hopes, or reputation (as it did clearly in the case of van Schurman), as well as one's possessions and gifts, earthly or spiritual. Neither of them emphasizes ascetical practices; there is little, if any, reference to the deprivation of physical necessities.[3] The key to self-denial is thus a shift in perspective, as well as a surrender of one's desires.

The choice to deny the self, of course, belongs to the disciple, in that she lays down her will for the sake of Christ. At the same time, it is God that enables the individual to lose sight of herself and ultimately to lay down all that she attaches to herself. She does not determine to "annihilate" herself; it happens to her as the result of other events, other actions.

Van Schurman's and Guyon's use of the term *destruction* seems in the end to be a rhetorical device intended to shake their readers into a deeper surrender or release of their self-enclosed anxieties. As we see in the concluding pages of van Schurman's *Eukleria*, God's action with her was perceived as gentle and sweet, not "destructive,"[4] despite its leading to a radical reorientation of her preoccupations. She was no longer concerned for her security, reputation, or progress; these were now at rest in a newfound trust. She no longer had to burden herself with self-care when she found herself "lost" in a larger, divine embrace. In the words of Julian of Norwich, "All is well, all manner of things shall be well." Notably, this paradoxical melding of the terms *lost* and *found* hearkens back to the Gospel saying: "Those . . . who lose their life for my sake will find it" (Matt. 10:38–39).

The self, with all its attachments, is thus "offered up" so that it may be received anew. The key, however, is that this new reception is impossible unless there is first a release. Guyon means much the same as van Schurman, except that she alerts the reader to the fact that this surrender is often excruciatingly difficult for the individual. She is convinced that the Christian holds so tightly to her will, her desires, her "preoccupation" with self (whether vainglory or the attribution of uniquely divine qualities to the self) that a decisive "annihilation" needs to occur in order to rid the self of these attachments. This leads to the rather violent imagery that she employs.

Augustine, in his *Confessions*, described a similar bondage of the will—the *viscum* that held him so tightly bound to his lesser loves. Lesser attachments ultimately demeaned, even strangled him. He writes that it was God's "affliction" that set him free from his despair, bringing him back to his one, true Good.[5] Likewise, van Schurman and Guyon are all too familiar with this unwieldy self. For van

Schurman, it is the "bubbling spring of all evil," and for Guyon, it is in need of constant repair. They recognize the negative effect that self-preoccupation has on the individual, and it is this from which they want to be free. Toward this end, they call their readers to a complete upheaval of thought, volition, and affection.

One needs to keep in clear focus the goal of both van Schurman and Guyon's itineraries, even as they employ the language of sacrifice, destruction, and denial. What they seek is a *new* self: a God-made self, rather than a "self-made" self.[6] The best version of self that one can create is still, in their eyes, a poor substitute for the divinely empowered, resurrected self that they envision. Yet resurrection comes only on the other side of a dark and painful death. Put another way, new wine cannot be poured into "old" wineskins. And old wineskins are best not repaired by being stretched or stitched; they are tossed out and replaced by something completely new.

THE LIMITS OF RETRIEVAL

Although van Schurman and Guyon offer important challenges to their readers—challenges that they promise bring new life—one must confront aspects of their writings that remain problematic. Before turning to the promise of retrieving their thought, we address some of these difficulties. One serious weakness in their theological discourse lies in their failure to distinguish the *imago Dei* from the "fallen self." Calvin himself maintained the integrity of the *imago Dei*, which van Schurman's theology did not adequately adopt.[7] The soul is so thoroughly stained by sin that, for them, an entire overthrow of the self is needed. Hence, they write in totalizing, disconcerting terms. Surrendering one part (or several parts) of the self to "God's will" does not suffice: one must offer the entire self—all of one's faculties, actions, and attitudes. In addition, the lack of differentiation between the fallen and redeemed self can lead to confusion and devalue the integrity of creation, as discussed in the previous chapter.

In light of this totalizing rhetoric and the extreme conclusions that follow, can we reasonably appropriate their works for theological discourse today? One answer might focus on their influence on the culture around them. Van Schurman's impact on the rise of German Pietism has been explored, as well as the importance of her arguments in favor of women's education in the seventeenth century. A linguistic genius and brilliant thinker, she became an icon, hailed as the "tenth muse of Europe." This seems reason enough to re-examine her life and work. Likewise, Guyon's influence upon the Methodist movement, the Holiness movement, early Quakers and Moravians, and figures like Kierkegaard has been established, not to mention the ways in which Fénelon's thought and Pierre Poiret's publishing efforts were deeply indebted to her.[8] Arthur Schopenhauer also wrote in Guyon's defense: "To become acquainted with that great and beautiful soul, whose remembrance always fills me with reverence, and to do justice to the excellence of her disposition while making allowances for the superstition of her faculty of reason, must be gratifying to every person of the better sort, just as with common thinkers, in other words the majority, that book [*Autobiography*] will always stand in bad repute."[9] Today, Guyon's influence on the American churches can still be traced in the Holiness movement, as well as in prayer conferences that focus on her work. Her books continue to be reprinted by a wide variety of publishers in multiple languages.

Nonetheless, there are limits to the retrieval of any past relic, regardless of appeal or influence; and retrieving van Schurman's and Guyon's works seems particularly difficult. Further dangers emerge as one considers other aspects of van Schurman and Guyon's theologies.

Limitations in van Schurman's Thought

Although van Schurman's theology acknowledges the enjoyment of creaturely goods "in God," this enjoyment is so weakly emphasized as to go almost unnoticed. Her theology struggles to find a balance between one's love for God and for God's creation. For instance, she recounts in her *Eukleria* that she grieved the lack of love that had been in her heart when engaging in works of charity. This realization contributed to her theological conversion, as she began to seek a new way of internalizing what she studied. Within the Labadist community, however, it is unclear whether its members valued works of charity or other means of extending love to those beyond their circle. They rejoiced in the love they shared among themselves and extended "fellowship" to the "faithful" across Europe, but they separated themselves from the world.[10] Thus the way in which they translated love for God into love for neighbor may have left much to be desired. Certainly, one cannot make an argument from silence, but the community's lack of engagement with the world is telling.[11] It appears that the Labadists did not quite know how to live in relation to the world, relishing instead their sectarian stance. They awaited a new millennium, a new "Age of the Spirit."[12]

As indicated earlier, another way in which van Schurman's thought devalued creation concerns her late suspicion of learnedness. She was wary of an "excessive love of learning" or an excessive love of creation in general. In response, she recommended what she perceived to be antidotes to those extremes, thereby creating extremes of her own (i.e., an excessive fear of the "excessive love of learning").[13] Ironically, even as this fear led van Schurman to a wholesale disregard of academic theology, it did not stop her from employing it in service of her own arguments, most notably in the *Eukleria*.[14]

One may, of course, disagree with van Schurman on any number of points. *Scientia* serves a vital purpose and ought not be undervalued. Here, Leclercq's advice in *The Love of Learning and the Desire for God* might be instructive for a wider audience. Despite his clear preference for monastic theology, Leclercq concludes that monastics and scholastics need one another's gifts. According to Leclercq, those in the monasteries read scripture in a way that directly nourishes the soul and its affections for God. A certain type of study stirs the individual's yearning for and "adoration" of God. On the other hand, Leclercq warns those pursuing meditative reading to pay special heed to scholastics. One cannot thrive without the other. He was mindful that monastics needed the special skills of the scholastics to keep them intellectually sharp, and he exhorts them to remain open to theological insights "from the schools."[15]

Van Schurman may have gone too far in discounting the "theological schools" of her day (though, again, she uses their insights and training precisely to demonstrate her point). But if one brackets her excesses, one uncovers enduring truths in her work. Failure to do so deprives the church today of important perspectives and potential correctives. Her voice can serve as an antidote for our tendencies toward lifeless, sterile theology. Her discussion of *intima notitia* challenges theologians to ask anew whether they actually "know" the object of which they speak and write, in a manner that is "true, intimate, and health-giving." It may be that we have become too easily contented with ruminations about God while forgetting to enjoy the *summum bonum,* the Satisfier of all human desires.

Challenges in Guyon's Thought

Guyon's language is more difficult to accept than van Schurman's. She speaks of death and destruction more frequently and more intensely. One ought to be vigilant against applying her insights unreflectively, particularly in contexts of deep suffering, where Guyon's rhetoric of self-annihilation may perpetuate or exacerbate the pain. Appropriation of these difficult themes must be handled with sensitivity to the context in view. To that end, it is important to clarify what Guyon means by the "suffering" that tests the bride. For Guyon, "annihilation" may come in the form of outward persecutions or slander (the most difficult of afflictions, from her point of view) or in other forms of suffering and sacrifice.[16] Suffering *for the sake of* the Beloved, however, is the highest form of suffering in Guyon's mind; and the inability to be steadfast in such situations can lead to a painful revelation of where one's true loves lie. When the bride in Guyon's *Commentary* passes that particular rite of passage, through her failure and "final renunciation," she discovers a deeper joy. The beloved recognizes the immeasurable kindness of her Divine Lover and is embraced by his "tender caresses," in spite of—or in the midst of—her despair;[17] and her desires are enflamed anew.

Guyon distinguishes suffering for the sake of God from other types of suffering. There is gratuitous suffering, which we daily see in the world around us and in our own lives. Then there is the kind of suffering that we bring upon ourselves by our foolish mistakes and misguided choices. The kind of suffering that Guyon focuses on is righteous suffering, that is, suffering for the sake of God. Guyon would concede, however, that other forms of suffering also have the potential to bring the individual closer to the Bridegroom—if the individual can cleave to her divine Lover during times of trial, rather than escape his loving embrace.

Bruneau argues that Guyon was able to face the horrific circumstances of her life (in particular, the years of solitary confinement in the Bastille) thanks in large part to her theology. Her spiritual exercises (prayer and self-surrender) were the key to Guyon's mental strength, giving her endurance in the midst of great pain. They enabled her to accept her circumstances with courage and with confidence that God's presence would be sufficient to see her through. Bruneau even speculates that others in similar straits would not have survived emotionally or mentally.[18] (Indeed, we know that Father La Combe did not.)[19] Similarly, Dianne Guenin-Lelle and Ronney Mourad write that Guyon's "writings present a model of resistance based on a spiritual practice that inculcates an indifference to or even a valorization of suffering and an absolute devotion to the will of God. By these means she was able to maintain her integrity and sanity during long periods of imprisonment in a way that inspired her friends and confounded her persecutors."[20]

Despite the strength that Guyon may have found from her theology, others still wonder if her emphasis on self-annihilation is pathologically masochistic.[21] Guyon may hold out the promise of joyous union with Christ in this life, but is that joy a worthwhile goal if one must endure suffering and self-annihilation to attain it? Indeed, Guyon's language confounds even the most sympathetic reader. Her thinking cannot, and must not, be appropriated without attention to context. Perceiving the truth behind the rhetoric while acknowledging the problematic nature of the rhetoric itself is not an easy task.

A careful analysis of her theology shows Guyon's conclusions to be largely coherent with the mystical tradition that she inherited and in that manner unsurprising. At the same time, other aspects of her thought remain problematic. For instance, Guyon ascribes more to the bride of Christ than the tradition does to Christ himself. As discussed in the previous chapter, the bride's volition is no longer functional; her will is swallowed up in God's will. The resultant picture is that of a bride with a seemingly lifeless will, even while active in her apostolic vocation. (The bride of Christ is said to do "more" than ever, in exponential measure and with "better" effect.) The idea of "total passivity" leading to deification on this side of the eschaton is also questionable. It may be that the bride participates so fully in the resurrected life of Christ that her will is perfectly joined to his, thus never in conflict with God or in need of its own activity. Complexities remain, however, that invite further exploration beyond the scope of this volume.[22] Guyon's blanket response is that those who have not experienced what she describes are simply incapable of understanding her thought. Indeed, if her reader has not experienced "mystical death," it would be difficult to comment on the joys that are said to come on the other side.

THE PROMISE OF RETRIEVAL

Even with the challenges in appropriating van Schurman and Guyon's language, important insights in their thought make the task worthwhile. First, I will explore some of the ways in which van Schurman and Guyon crossed theological boundaries and how these bold forays might be instructive for others. They were so committed in their pursuit of an intimate knowledge of God that they refused to be constricted by the teachings promulgated by their respective institutions.

I will then consider their emphasis on the enjoyment of God, even if reached through the painful path of self-denial. Last, I will look to the courage necessary for this difficult pursuit of the greatest joy. The path to union with God involves risk and requires the utmost resolve and trust. Through it all, the bride's longing for God keeps her on the journey, treacherous though it may be.

Crossing Boundaries: A Broad Theological Ecumenism

Content at the margins of conventional religion, van Schurman and Guyon found the freedom to explore and express fresh ideas. They were unabashed about integrating insights from traditions other than their own. Had they remained rooted within the rigid systems in which they had lost faith, their creativity would likely have been hampered, and they might not have made such daring moves in their thinking.

In an era of religious wars and theological strife, seldom do key players "cross sides." Seventeenth-century Europe, in particular, experienced a dramatic hardening of theological lines. Religious polemics were fierce. The ability to argue one's position against another became a virtue, and Protestants were intent on creating their own theological systems. Following the methods of the Scholastics of the Catholic Church, Protestants were now in the business of defining themselves with new precision.[23] Theological controversies *within* the Protestant world also demanded detailed argumentation; new camps, along with their demarcations and distinctions, proliferated. Rivalries between Protestant and Catholic thinkers continued to grow, adding more fuel to the controversy.

Occasional figures, such as Labadie, made daring leaps and switched allegiances. Such characters were widely regarded as enigmas, however, and not to be emulated. In other instances, "transgressors" tried desperately to remain within their own "school" but were forced out by those who had once supported them. Neither van Schurman nor Guyon wanted to desert her theological home. Van Schurman was from first to last a faithful Calvinist, and Madame Guyon was devoted to the Catholic Church to the end of her life. Nevertheless, their ecclesial communities felt compelled to disown them.

Other than their shared fates, van Schurman and Guyon were worlds apart, at least theologically speaking. Roman Catholicism and "orthodox" Calvinism appeared to have little in common but mutual enmity. Persecution abounded, and converts were sought by both of the opposing parties' "missionary" endeavors. Not even Jansenism, an alleged "middle position," was immune, as Jesuit and Jansenist rivalry broke out in France.[24] Despite this polarized environment, Anna Maria van Schurman and Madame Jeanne Guyon defied religious lines, moving fluidly from one camp to another—if not in institutional affiliation, at least in significant strands of thought. Such defiance was not left unchecked and created intense difficulties for Guyon in particular. What then caused Jeanne Guyon and Anna Maria van Schurman to challenge institutional boundaries? Other than sociocultural circumstances, their theological creativity was a significant impetus behind their bold maneuvers. Opening themselves up to new (or more accurately, foreign) trends of thought, both women crafted for themselves a synthesis of mystical elements in Reformed and Catholic theology.[25]

Van Schurman's Theological Synthesis

Van Schurman stood in the midst of this seventeenth-century polemical tradition and bridged the different worlds that clashed around her. Having been trained in the rigors of Protestant scholasticism, van Schurman was more than well-acquainted with "theological distinctions."[26] The "arranging of concepts into subtle charts" had been a particular source of intellectual pleasure for her. Having been a serious theological student, she was also able to debate the finest theological Catholic minds, and she attests that she did precisely that, with delight.[27] Along the way, however, van Schurman's appetite for this mode of theology shifted. She relinquished prior methods—methods that were in fact relatively novel with the rise of Protestant scholasticism—and embraced other ways of doing theology. With this shift came a change in her perspective on truth and, more precisely, on the "true knowledge of God." Her underlying question found its source in her pursuit of an interiorized religion—a religion that involved more than rational argumentation. What was "knowledge of God" if it lacked the power to transform the knower? In what sense, if any, might this kind of (external) knowledge be reckoned "true"? Van Schurman's newfound goal was to reach a "true, health-giving, and inmost" knowledge of God, as opposed to one that remained distant and exterior.[28]

"True" theology, then, necessarily entailed inner transformation. Theology that did not make a claim upon the individual, that was not internalized within the person's core, was for van Schurman severely limited. It inhabited the realm of partial knowledge and failed to penetrate the deepest part of the individual. Whether or not van Schurman articulated it, she found resources in other traditions to help her fill this gap. Admittedly, she did not have to seek answers in other traditions. Calvin himself said much about a true, health-giving knowledge of God.[29] Nonetheless, the Calvinist culture that surrounded her did not encourage her to drink deeply from that well. Even the strands of Dutch Pietism that surrounded her focused more on moralism rather than on vibrancy of life and enjoyment of God.[30]

Seen from a wider angle, van Schurman was among the first to challenge the rise of Protestant scholasticism from within the Protestant camp. In her *Eukleria*, she essentially questions a movement as it arises. A forerunner to early Pietism in Germany, van Schurman's thought arguably shaped the genesis of German Pietism and the penning of Spener's *Pia desideria* in 1675 (which appeared two years after the *Eukleria*).[31] What is unique about van Schurman, however, is that she was able to point to the deficiencies of academic theology only after having immersed herself completely in it. Had she not experienced and embraced the rigors of her theological training, she would not have been able to deliver as sharp a critique as she did. Furthermore, unlike some of the later Pietists, van Schurman borrowed from the rich resources of the Catholic mystical tradition.[32] While her insights remained fundamentally Calvinist, van Schurman's thought converged with elements of Catholic mystical teaching.[33] This, in and of itself, may have contributed to the alarm that her work caused.[34]

From Labadie, van Schurman inherited ideas beyond her earlier academic formation.[35] Her mature theology manifests a unique blending of elements from the Catholic tradition with her Calvinist heritage, even if a Calvinism taken to its "mystical" edges.[36] This particular synthesis of various streams finds expression in van Schurman's *Eukleria*, which provides an itinerary by which the individual might reach the "true knowledge" of God. In this treatise, van Schurman offers her prescription for the soul that seeks to attain "true knowledge" of God and, in so doing, become united with the divine. The result of "true knowledge" is intimate union with the object of one's knowledge—an "immersion into the infinite ocean of divinity" that sounds remarkably similar to that of which the mystics have spoken.[37]

On the other hand, undertaking this path is impossible apart from serious prerequisites: the individual must first heed the injunction to "deny herself" entirely. Only when the soul has learned to "die" will it become a ready recipient of the full graces of God. In many regards, this is no different from what Calvin himself argued in his *Institutes*.[38] For example, van Schurman's writings were largely based on Calvin's understanding of mortification and vivification.[39] The "old man," as she said, needs to be destroyed so that a "new man" may rise in its place. And this occurs when one willingly lays down the old, "carnal" self. (Again, van Schurman speaks of her ultimate failure to achieve this apart from a special dispensation of grace.)

However, van Schurman pushed the envelope of "orthodox Calvinism" in significant ways. She took Calvin's language further when she spoke of an "immersion" of the soul into the "ocean of divinity"—an immersion that is both the source and the result of her self-denial. Her thought also went beyond Augustine's by placing the soul's union with God both in this life and in the next.[40] Furthermore, van Schurman ventured beyond both Calvin and Augustine in making the inseparable connection between self-denial and *intima notitia*. Her claim that one cannot truly *know* Christ until one has first learned to live (and "die") for Christ made some of her contemporaries, scholastic and Pietist alike, uncomfortable.[41] And she believed that one had not learned to live for Christ until one had "denied," or relinquished, the world and self for Christ. Discipleship for van Schurman meant that the Christian should immediately heed the words of Christ, as later interpreted by Bonhoffer: "When Christ calls a man, he bids him come and die."[42] Van Schurman would not have a diluted Christianity; any other form was in her mind "counterfeit" (*fucatus*). *Intima notitia Dei* was her goal, though a costly one. And this kind of knowledge was the only source of true pleasure, or enjoyment in God.

Guyon's Theological Synthesis

Like van Schurman, Madame Jeanne Guyon became a stranger in her own theological home. Just a few decades later than van Schurman, Guyon would be charged with teaching "new ideas" and banished to the Bastille. Like van Schurman, Guyon was not content to remain within the confines of established tradition.[43] Even while under house arrest during the later years of her life, Guyon welcomed many visitors, including Protestant disciples, to her home and continued to teach her way of prayer.

Though condemned by the Catholic Church, Guyon gained a loyal following, some of whom surrounded her at her deathbed in 1717. Fénelon, as bishop of Cambrai, continued to promote her teachings, even if in disguised form. The French Protestant Pierre Poiret preserved and published her works, and her thought was well received in the Netherlands, Germany, Switzerland, England, America, and China, particularly among Protestants.[44]

Contrary to van Schurman, Guyon was neither a trained academician nor a lover of books. She claims in her autobiography to have read nothing but the scriptures up to the time shortly before her initial trial in 1686.[45] In addition to her reading of scripture, to which she devoted much time and energy, Guyon learned from spiritual advisers like Father La Combe and imbibed what she received from regular attendance at mass.[46] Nonetheless, Guyon seemed almost to pride herself on having little formal education—aiming, perhaps, to make more credible her claim to be divinely illuminated.[47] She was convinced that the "knowledge of God" offered through traditional means was in the end lacking, and she arrived at similar conclusions to van Schurman. The controversial *Moyen court* ("A short and easy method of prayer") was Guyon's attempt to teach everyone, without distinction, a "truer" way of knowing God, through a certain type of prayer. In this treatise, she introduces the notion of self-annihilation as the key to intimate prayer. In her *Commentaire au Cantique des cantiques de Salomon*, she analyzes further what she means by *annihilation*.

While Guyon did not have the erudition that van Schurman had almost effortlessly attained, learned men and women would soon give themselves over to her teachings and integrate them into their own. One such scholar, Bishop Fénelon, would strive to make Guyon's ideas palatable to even the most well trained of intellects, such as Bossuet. Of course, Fénelon failed to win over Bossuet, and these two bishops engaged in sharp rivalry over the fate of Guyon to the bitter end.[48] Yet Guyon (arguably with Fénelon's help) produced the *Justifications* in 1684, six years after publishing her *Commentary on the Song of Songs*, to demonstrate that her work was, indeed, not so new in Christian mysticism.[49] In this three-volume defense, Guyon quotes widely from figures respected at that time, such as St. John Climacus, Bernard of Clairvaux, Thomas à Kempis (*Imitation of Christ*), John of the Cross, Francis de Sales, and John of St. Samson (*Contemplations*), among others. The writings of Teresa of Avila also affected her. Whether she was influenced by their thinking from the start or sought out their validations after controversy erupted is unclear. She claims that she arrived at her thought through the illumination of the Holy Spirit alone; yet she certainly imbibed contemporary theological trends, whether or not she recognized it at the time.

Guyon's teachings may have gone beyond the comfort level of Bossuet and other bishops of her day. Yet it is not an easy task to pinpoint just where she departs from the mystics whom she quotes in her *Justifications*. For instance, her writing sounds much like that of St. Francis de Sales when she speaks of the mingling of the human with the divine; and her image of entering and then passing through one's center hearkens back to Teresa of Avila (although without the structure of the "Castle").[50] Guyon, of course, has come down in history as a major proponent of the Quietist movement, along with the Spanish priest Miguel de Molinos, who published his *La guía espiritual* ("Spiritual guide") in 1675 in Rome. Quietism advocated perfect stillness and passivity in the Christian life and allegedly taught "holy indifference" to all things, including even the forfeiting of one's salvation, ideas that were condemned by Pope Innocent XI in 1687.[51] There is, however, no evidence of Guyon having read Molinos's work.[52] There is also little in Guyon's writing to suggest that she would gladly forfeit the presence of the One she loves. Admittedly, her understanding of extreme passivity sounds like the Quietist teaching of "holy indifference," even if she later qualified this phrase by teaching that the perfect form of passivity is "active passivity."[53] To be sure, Guyon does surrender joy, and even desire, but at the same time her ultimate goal is to be with the One who happens to be the source of all joy.[54]

In the end, Guyon's language is erratic and extreme and often difficult to digest. Her teachings on sacrifice, suffering, and submission, for example, provoke conflicting responses. And her low anthropology, surprisingly similar to that of the Reformed theologians of her day, is not appealing to most readers.[55] Yet her writings convey a persuasive power even when she elaborates on abandonment to God's providence or complete surrender to the gracious hands of God. Guyon's theology comes close to that of van Schurman's when she argues, both in her *Moyen court* (1685) and in her *Commentaire au Cantique des cantiques de Salomon* (1688), that an interior, intimate knowledge of God can be attained only when the individual has "died" to self. This kind of "true theology," according to Guyon, does not and must not confine God to the limits of human reason. Again, "true knowledge of God" necessitates that the "object" of study not remain an "objective" entity (thereby removed and aloof).

The object must rather become the subject, the initiator, and, to borrow both van Schurman and Guyon's term, the "All."[56]

A *Shared Vision of the* Summum Bonum

Despite the disparity in their theological trajectories, van Schurman and Guyon reach the same conclusion: the ability to reason, or to argue for one theological position over another, does not contribute to a greater knowledge of God. In fact, they argue that an excessive love of reason hinders it. In other words, finely tuned argumentation may give a theologian something more to say "about" God, but it does not mean that the theologian "knows" God.

Striking also is van Schurman and Guyon's shared emphasis on an inward knowledge of God in conjunction with two elements: joy and self-denial (or self-annihilation).[57] Knowledge without intimate enjoyment of the object of knowledge is, for them, no knowledge at all. Though the path of self-denial reaches union with God circuitously, they argue that in the end it leads to the deepest knowledge of God and the most profound delight. As Guyon puts it, in words similar to the Westminster Shorter Catechism: "La fin pour laquelle nous avons été créés est pour jouir de Dieu dès cette vie."[58] Both van Schurman and Guyon sought a greater enjoyment of God than the theological culture of their day had provided them. Their descriptions of the difficult path that leads to this "end" are also similar. It is surprising that these two women, writing from different ends of the theological spectrum, would agree on both the goal of theology and the means to its end.[59] That their thought converges at the locus of self-sacrifice is further revealing. Self-denial emerges as a core element of the Christian gospel, significant in both Reformed and Catholic thought of the seventeenth century. For both van Schurman and Guyon, however, self-denial is never an end in itself. Their goal is the attainment of a profound level of joy in the Supreme Good. Even though reached at a steep price, this joy ushers the individual into an intimate knowledge of God that surpasses all sense of "sacrifice." This resonates with Apostle Paul's proclamation that "whatever were gains to me I now consider loss for the sake of Christ. What is more, I consider everything a loss because of the surpassing worth of knowing Christ Jesus my Lord, for whose sake I have lost all things. I consider them garbage, that I may gain Christ and be found in him. . . . I want to know Christ and the power of his resurrection and the fellowship of sharing in his sufferings, by becoming like him in his death, and so, somehow, to attain to the resurrection from the dead."[60] Keeping his eye on the prize and impelled by a desire also for *intima notitia* (to borrow from van Schurman's terminology), Paul writes that power and resurrection can indeed be reached—after one has passed through death.

This emphasis on a total self-denial, or self-annihilation, remains troubling to many contemporary readers. One needs to keep in mind, however, that the object of van Schurman and Guyon's final pursuit is God, the source of all pleasure. They seek a deeper joy, though it comes at great cost. Even Kristeva, who searches for the pathological in Guyon's mysticism, acknowledges that the mystics, in general, pursued some "good."[61] Indeed, van Schurman and Guyon argue that self-sacrifice or self-surrender is the path to the deepest enjoyment of the greatest good. When preoccupations with the self are removed, whether in attitude, a sense of self-importance, or even self-protectiveness, space is created for the *summum bonum* to fill and satisfy the soul. This too was Augustine's struggle and his ultimate yearning.[62] And it may be a universal cry in every age.

Self-Denial as Self-Forgetfulness

To understand the priority of self-denial in van Schurman and Guyon's theologies, it is important to note that self-denial for them becomes equivalent to self-forgetfulness in light of God's overwhelming love. One does not seek to deny or forget oneself; it happens as one becomes lost in God's care. Likewise, one does not strive to protect or preserve the self, because one becomes secure in God's wisdom, provision, and strength, having experienced the shelter of God's wings. This self-forgetfulness leads to a deeper freedom, so that one is no longer anxious about oneself or about how one is perceived. Rooted in divine grace, one need not examine how effective one's labors have been. In fact, there is freedom to fail, and this failure results in a profound recognition of one's finitude, which further transforms self-reliance into a dependence upon God's infinite resources. This dependence, in turn, leads to a greater release of divine resources, because self-reliance no longer limits God's free activity in the individual's life.

When surrounded by this expansive vision of God's love, one also becomes freed from self-interest, for all one's deepest interests are held safely by God's goodness. In other words, God, as the highest good, seeks also the greatest good of the individual, which frees him or her to love others. Freed from anxious striving, the "pernicious I" no longer operates willfully but relaxes into a trusting posture. And self-love is redeemed as one learns to love self, among all other creatures, under the umbrella of God's care.

Self-Denial as Self-Giving

Van Schurman and Guyon argue that the surrender of self, in addition to creating greater freedom in the individual's life, creates space for the divine to dwell as one becomes radically hospitable to God's presence. From this perspective, self-denial might be called "self-giving," the offering of the self in love to another. Indeed, the reverse of self-denial is not healthy self-affirmation but rather a destructive form of self-interested egotism. This kind of egotism is closed off, unable to love or give freely. It may be argued, then, that a self-interested posture (i.e., the opposite of self-denial) is that which precisely *destroys* life and deeply loving relationships. For van Schurman and Guyon, "following after Jesus" indeed requires "picking up [one's] cross" and "denying [oneself]" for the sake of an Other.[63] Yet denying oneself *for God* never entails the ultimate repression of one's gifts. A joyful surrender of the self to God rather offers deep spiritual nourishment and strength, and it results, ultimately, in a greater intimacy with and enjoyment of the *summum bonum*.

What does this theology look like in practice? Might the reader of van Schurman's and Guyon's texts find something life-giving in their approach to the theological task and also in their coupling of self-denial with the joyful pursuit of God? The purpose of self-denial or self-annihilation for van Schurman and Guyon is to create more room for God's presence in one's life. Letting go of one's own agenda opens up space for God's Spirit to work, to lead, and to create the individual anew. This surrender is at times painful, as one clutches to the things that one cherishes. Releasing one's loves, however, only allows the Divine Lover to offer new graces in the place of lesser loves previously grasped.

In surrendering herself, the bride of Christ waits upon her bridegroom. As she waits for God's leading, strength, and wisdom, she is also an active worshipper who places her life upon the altar. Certainly, courage is necessary for such a surrender. The offering of oneself to God and God's purposes does not come easily. Apart from a deep trust in God's beauty, good designs, and trustworthiness (as seen in the case of the bride in Guyon's *Commentary*, as well as in van Schurman's own experience at the close of her *Eukleria*), the courage to release one's hopes and ambitions would elude the individual.

Van Schurman's understanding of *intima notitia* is instructive here. Just as she argued that self-denial is the doorway to a deeper knowledge of God, she also demonstrated that the surrender of oneself occurs only after one experiences the tenderness and compassion of God. An inmost knowledge of God as kind, generous, and gracious is thus necessary for the individual to place her trust in God. At the same time, when one makes the offering, or "sacrifice," of oneself, one comes to experience the beneficence of God again and again.

In fact, self-denial is made possible only because of *God's self-giving* toward the individual. The offering of the self to God is simply a response to God's tremendous sacrifice on behalf of humanity. In her *Commentary*, Guyon keeps her eye on this crucified lover, seeped in blood, because this self-pouring death was the highest expression of God's love for humanity. Van Schurman, likewise, focused on this theme. Her life motto, "My love has been crucified," had double meaning for her in that, as Christ's life had been poured out for her, so too lesser loves in her life would be crucified for Christ, her single love.[64]

In this place of surrender, van Schurman and Guyon claim that the soul comes to find the deepest enjoyment of God possible on this earth. A series of difficult "renunciations" precedes this delight, but with the apostle Paul they count these losses as nothing, for they are in pursuit of "the better thing" (*Eukleria*). Guyon writes of this immeasurable gain: "Oh, unutterable happiness! Who could have ever thought that a soul, which seemed to be in the utmost misery, should ever find a happiness equal to this? *Oh, happy poverty, happy loss, happy nothingness, which gives nothing less than God himself in his own immensity. . . . Oh, happy dying of the grain of wheat,* which makes it produce a hundred-fold! (John 12:24)."[65] Van Schurman and Guyon exclaim that they have found an inexpressible happiness, and they invite their readers to risk, to trust, and to offer themselves with abandon for the sake of this greater joy.

Appendices

APPENDIX A
*Letter 2 from Anna Maria van Schurman to Johann Jakob Schütz,
Altonae, 12/22 August 1674*

Manuscript G2.II.33, fols. 2r–3v, University of Basel Library Archives

Altonae, 12/22 Augusti, Anno 1674

Fideli Jesu Christi Summi Regis Servo, nobisque plurimum dilecto Fratri Domino Johanni Jacobo Schutz Salutem Plurimam Dicit Anna Maria a Schurman.

Ita revera est, ut dicis, Care Frater, Fidelibus grata et amata crux Christi est, grata est mors, et maxime grata est vita aeterna; ubi dulcissimus eorum animae Sponsus, cum omnibus suis, perfecte sanctificatis, gloriosissimum, justissimum, atque interminabilem agit triumphum, simulque nuptias suas divinissimas cum pulcherrima et dilectissima sua Ecclesia, tota aeternitate celebrat.

Ad meum autem statum quod attinet, nondum placuit illi Archiduci et Consummatori nostrae fidei, me in possessionem eiusdem beatissimam introducere; cum illi procul dubio magis conveniat, ut me in Schola sua, coelesti quidem, sed in terris, exerceat, ac praeparet ad arctissimam illam et sanctissimam cum ipso communionem.

Per adversa interim ac prospera, per dulcia et amara, per pugnas et victorias, nos omnisufficiens eius gratia erecto capite incedere facit: dum liberrimam optimamque Dei nostri voluntatem, cuius intuitus, et exsecutio coelum nostrum in terris est; in omnibus conspicimus eique nostram conformamus.

Quid autem aequius aut iustius [**p. 2**] est, quid summo Domino rerumque omnium Arbitro dignius, et gloriosius est, quam ut omnes curas in ipsum devolvamus, nos et nostra omnia ipsi fidamus, eiusque libertati ac supremo Dominio nos totos consecremus?

Anna Maria van Schurman sends best wishes to Sir Johann Jakob Schütz, faithful servant of our highest King, Jesus Christ, and our greatly beloved brother.

It is as you say, Dear Brother. The cross of Christ is pleasing and beloved to the faithful; death is pleasing, and eternal life is especially pleasing; when the sweetest Bridegroom of their soul, with all those, perfectly sanctified, belonging to him, enacts his most glorious, most just, and unending triumph and at the same time celebrates into all eternity his most divine nuptials with his most beautiful and beloved Church.

But as pertains to my position, it has not yet pleased that great guide and finisher of our faith to bring me into the most blessed possession of the same; since doubtless it suits that one better to train me in his School— indeed a heavenly school, but on earth—and to prepare me for that most close and holy communion with himself.

In the meantime, through adversities and prosperities, through pleasant and bitter things, through battles and victories, his all-sufficient grace makes us advance with our heads held high, as long as we observe in all things the most free and best will of our God—the observation and performance of which is our heaven on earth—and conform our will to it.

For what is more fair or just, [p. 2] what is more worthy of the highest Lord and overseer of all things and more glorious, than that we roll off all our cares to him, entrust ourselves and all we possess to him, and consecrate our whole selves to his freedom and supreme Lordship?

ita ut ipse de nobis, juxta eius sanctissimum beneplacitum statuat, sive in tempore, sive in ipsa aeternitate; ad summam illius gloriam, quam, ut omnium finium Finem, ipsi inserviendo consequimur.

Eo in statu te esse, prono ac gaudenti animo, conjicimus; utpote cui summus noster Rex atque aeternus Dei Filius, non tantum ut servo fideli, sed ut amico, quae a Patre suo audivit, revelare, videtur.

Etenim tam sapide, tamque spiritualiter de unione animae cum suo Sponso, et in praesenti, et in futura vita disseris, ut illum te non raro in cellam suam vinarium introducere, atque ibidem deliciis suis inebriare satis appareat.

Sed cui, quaeso, fini? Num tantummodo ut sapore vini coelestis delecteris, et gaudiis abundes? Non puto: sed ut tui ac mundi oblitus, coelestique Ambrosia corroboratus, fortiter pugnes, et inprimis expugnes amorem tuiipsius, qui, uti in primo homine eius detestandi lapsus origo fuit: ita in nobis etiamnum est omnium malorum scaturgio; unde perniciosissimum illud <u>Ego</u>, quod in thronum Dei usque se elevat et nos [p. 3] totos a vero ac summo Bono dividit ac separat, infelicissime profluit.

Haec quamvis tibi non ignota esse arbitrer, attendas tamen, mi Frater, ne inter agendum quicquam de tuo zelo ac fidelitate remittas, quin in proeliis Domini forti intrepidoque animo decertes, apertasque inimicitias cum mundo ac Satana exerceas.

Non parva res est suiipsius rerumque omnium sincera Abnegatio; abque qua tamen nullus est nisi fucatus Christianismus.

Multi hodie, cum coelestia intuentur, existimant veterem ipsorum hominem iam esse debellatum, spoliatum, et humi reconditum; cum tamen etiamnum in ipsis vivat, regnet et vires suas impias, data occasione potenter exerat.

so that he himself may decide according to his most holy will, whether [it is] in time or eternity. By serving him we reach toward the highest glory of that one, the End of all ends.

Therefore, we conclude that you are in that state, with spirit leaning forward and rejoicing as one to whom our highest King and also eternal Son of God seems to reveal, not only as to a faithful servant, but as to a friend, the things which he has heard from his Father.

And indeed so wisely and so spiritually do you speak concerning the union of the soul with her Bridegroom, both in the present and in the future life, that it is entirely evident that he not rarely brings you into his wine cellar and there intoxicates you with his delight.

But to what end, I ask? Only that you may be delighted with the taste of celestial wine and overflow in joy? I think not: but so that, forgetful of yourself and the world, and strengthened by celestial ambrosia, you may fight bravely and, above all, conquer love of yourself, which, as in the first man it was the origin of his accursed falling, so in us now, too, it is the bubbling spring of all evil; that most pernicious "I," which elevates itself up to the throne of God and [p. 3] divides and separates us all from the true and highest Good, most wretchedly flows from it.

Although I imagine that these things are not unknown to you, nonetheless listen carefully, my Brother, lest you relax any of your zeal and faithfulness in action, but rather that you fight in the battles of the Lord with strong and dauntless spirit, and practice open enmity with the world and with Satan.

Sincere denial of one's own self and of all things is not a small thing; without which nevertheless there is no Christianity except one that is counterfeit.

Many people nowadays, when they consider heavenly matters, think that their old man already has been subdued, despoiled, and buried in the ground: nevertheless it even now lives in them, reigns, and powerfully stretches forth its wicked force, given the opportunity.

Plerique eorum, quos Pios dicunt, hisce calamitosissimis temporibus se Deo vivere putant, cum interim constet, ipsosque non lateat, maiorem suae vitae partem sibiipsis insumi, atque in gratiam creaturae miserrime profundi: quomodo autem fieri potest, ut haec duo tantopere pugnantia eidem subjecto conveniant?

Fateamur, quod res ipsa loquitur, vel nobis vel Deo vivimus; vel cum Christo crucifixi comperimur, vel cum mundo conjuncti haeremus infelices.

Quamvis autem peccati reliquiae in ipsis sanctificatis supersint: absit ut eius vis tantum in iis praevaleat, ut ipsorum corda terrae, vel **[p. 4]** propriis, extra Deum, commodis affigat, potioremque vitae partem Satanae devoveat ac mancipet.

De te, dilecte Frater, non nisi bonum ferimus coram Deo iudicium. Applaudimus iis, quae ex intimo cordis prodeunt, maius aliquid pro te speramus, et de te expectamus. At ut in cursu, quem te incipere fecit Divina gratia, ne subsistas, aut te ipso quasi contentus, solummodo gaudeas obnixe rogamus, et per Caritatem Dei obtestamur.

Plura in dies procul dubio revelabit animae tuae Dominus, quo perfectius voluntatem eius excognoscas et ames, et fideliter adimpleas. Dilatarunt, fateor, paululum cor meum haec tua verba, quibus asseris te sincerioris Divini amoris igniculos plurmis in locis, citra conditionis et sexus differentiam etiam inter illustres seculi deprehendisse varios, utut cineribus mundi obrutos varie atque suppressos: cum illico pectus meum desiderio eos noscendi intus inflammari sentirem.

The majority of those whom they call godly think that in these most ca-lamitous times they are living for God, although meanwhile it is well known and it is not hidden from themselves that a large part of their lives is expended upon their very selves and is poured out most wretch-edly for the love of the creature: but how can it happen that these two things, so greatly opposed, come together in the same subject?

Let us confess the obvious: we live either unto ourselves or unto God; either we lose our lives, crucified together with Christ, or we cling wretchedly, connected to the world.

But however much the remains of sin survive in the sanctified them-selves, may it not be that its strength prevails in them so greatly that it attaches their hearts to the goods of the earth or to their own goods [p. 4] outside of God, and devotes and surrenders a better part of their lives to Satan.

Concerning yourself, dear Brother, I bring only a good judgment in the presence of God. We applaud those things that spring forth from your inmost heart, something greater we hope for on your behalf and antici-pate regarding you. But we ask resolutely and we implore through the Love of God that in the running, which Divine grace caused you to begin, you do not halt or only rejoice, as if satisfied with yourself.

The Lord will beyond doubt reveal more things day by day to your soul, in order that you may more perfectly recognize and love his will and faithfully carry it out. I confess that these words of yours have made my little heart swell—words by which you assert that you have dis-covered little fires of a more sincere love of God in very many places, without regard to distinction of situation and sex even among various illustrious people of the world, although in various ways buried and suppressed by the ashes of the world. By this I felt my heart inwardly inflamed with the desire of knowing them.

Verum mox ad Principia illa Christiana revertens, capere non potui, qui vel minima sinceri amoris Divini scintillula a Spiritu Dei in corde suorum accensa, tam facile, tamque varie ac crasse mundano cinere obrui possit, ut ad coelestum ac divinam suam originem, longissimo saepe temporis intervallo, non tendat, nec tandem per fidem vivam, quae verae caritatis individua comes est, ipsum mundum **[p. 5]** vincat, at superet.

Alia sane habemus fidei ac caritatis Christianae exempla, non solum in Epistola Apostoli ad Hebraeos: sed et in ipsis Apostolis omnibusque vere Christianis, qui illos subsecuti sunt, atque gratiam Christi in vanum non acceperunt.

Deus etenim, qui opus suum in suis electis inchoat, idem perficit. Nec ideo lucernam accendit, ut sub modio occultata consumatur.

Certe omnes isti, qui se Deum et Christum sincere amare sibi, et aliis persuadent, serio et exacte in fundum cordis sui inquirere debebant, annon ibidem coelum cum terra misceant, et annon ignis quidam fatuus sit, qui illos ducit?

si is nunquam concipit salutarem flammam, cuius luminis beneficio viam angustam, quae ducit ad vitam, a via lata multis parasangis separatam, feliciter inveniant.

Esurientes ac sitientes iustitam Christus se exsatiaturum promisit; sed non in somnio fallaciarum ambulantes, aut tantum ex amore suiipsius propriam suam salutem, ac gloriam desiderantes, cum illud desiderium, quod a creatura terminatur, sit injustissimum.

But soon returning to those Christian axioms, I was not able to grasp how even the smallest little spark of a pure love of God, kindled by the spirit of God in the hearts of his people, so easily and so variously and crassly can be buried by worldly ash, with the result that it does not make its way toward its celestial and divine origin, often within a very long interval of time, and does not through living faith, which is the inseparable companion of a true love, conquer and overcome the world itself. **[p. 5]**

We certainly have other examples of Christian faith and love, not only in the letter of the Apostle to the Hebrews, but also in the Apostles themselves and in all true Christians who have followed after them and have not received the grace of Christ in vain.

And indeed God, who begins his work in his elect, also completes it. And he does not, therefore, kindle the lamp in order that it be extinguished, hidden under a bushel.

Surely, all of those who persuade themselves and others that they sincerely love God Himself and Christ ought to search earnestly and precisely in the bottom of their hearts whether in that very place they are mingling heaven with earth, and whether it is some flickering flame that leads them?[1]

If it is so, it never contains a salutary flame, by means of whose light they may happily reach the narrow path that leads to life, separated from the wide path by many Persian leagues.

Christ promised that he would satisfy those who hunger and thirst for righteousness but not those walking in the fantasy of deceits, or desiring only from the love of their own selves their own special prosperity, and glory, since that desire, which is defined by the creature, is most unjust.

---

1. *Ignis fatuus* describes a thing or person that deceives by a false and fleeting appearance literally, "fool's fire": (probably) from flickering flames, ignited from the gases of decaying organic matter, seen at night in marshes.

Justitiam Dei istic universim intelligi non dubitamus, inprimis vero istam, quam Christus sibi, ac suis promeritus est. ut nempe hic, et aeternum in suis, et cum suis regnet, [p. 6] nominatim vero temporibus ultimis; quod gloriosi ipsiu regni in terris erit complementum.

Sed quomodo illi homines hanc justitiam amant et desiderant, qui, ut plerique hodie, illam vel non plene credunt, vel Christi regnum cum mundo, Satanae regno, conjungere, aut dividere student?

Totum hominem vult Christus, quem e mundo electum ad justissimum suum regnum evocat, cum passim et eos ipsos, qui ad Christi Regnum se aspirare profitentur, utroque pede in luto iniquissimi huius seculi haerere minime obscure videas.

Nos vero, licet Deum hisce temporibus Noae seculo simillimis suos habere in terris hinc inde dispersos, aut in coetibus etiam externis corruptissimis languentes ac gemibundos quosdam manere certissimi simus:

tamen ad Christi regnum in terris gloriosum propagandum novo quodam Spiritus Christi adventu opus esse credimus, minimeque sufficere putamus errores quosdam detegi aut nonnullas veritates, in Sacra Scriptura revelatas a quibusdam fidelibus Christi Servis orbi proponi.

Linguis igneis, vento quodam violento, qui excelsa mundi evertat, imo virtute Omnipotentis creatrice opus est, ut mortui ac somniantes excitentur, sibiipsis viventes destruantur, et novae creaturae producantur, ad vere Reformatas Ecclesias [p. 7] constituendas, de quarum felicitate ac bonitate gloriari ac laetari possit Christianismus.

We do not doubt that this righteousness of God is understood universally, especially indeed that righteousness which Christ has gained for himself and for his own, in order, to be sure, that here and eternally he may reign among his own and with his own, [p. 6] specifically in the last times, which will be the fulfillment of his glorious reign on earth.

But how do these people love and desire this righteousness who, as most today, either do not believe it fully, or strive either to join the kingdom of Christ with the world, the kingdom of Satan, or to divide [Christ's kingdom]?

Christ wants the whole person whom he calls forth from the world, chosen for his most just kingdom, although everywhere you see very clearly that even they themselves, who profess to aspire to the kingdom of Christ, are stuck fast with both feet in the mire of this most unjust world.

We, however, although we are very certain that in these times that are very similar to the era of Noah God has his own people scattered here and there, or even that certain ones remain languishing and groaning in most corrupt external assemblies:

nevertheless, in order to extend the glorious reign of Christ on earth, we believe that there is need of a certain new advent of the spirit of Christ, and we think that it suffices not at all that certain errors be exposed, or that a number of truths revealed in Sacred Scriptures be put forward to the world by certain faithful servants of Christ.

There is need of tongues of fire, a certain violent wind, to overthrow the lofty things of the world; more precisely, there is need of the creative power of the omnipotent, in order that the dead and dreaming be stirred up, those living for themselves be destroyed and new creatures brought forth, in order to establish truly reformed churches, [p. 7] concerning the happiness and goodness of which Christianity can glory and delight.

Deus noster admirabilis et adorabilis in viis suis omnibus, quae toto coelo nostris sunt excelsiores, suo tempore omnia faciet nova; et suos cultores, qui illum in Spiritu ac veritate adorant, sub Pastore sumo congregabit, et in Tabernaculo suo habitabit cum ipsis. Ipseque solus erit eorum Deus.

Cui sit in aeternum Gloria, et cuius gratiae omnimodae te commendamus.

Inprimis vero Dominus Yvon et Dulignon, quorum prior suas ad te literas cum hisce conjungere in animo habebat: sed hac vice illum detinuere aliae non differendae occupationes.

Our God, wonderful and worthy of adoration in all his ways, which are more exalted than ours in all heaven, will make all things new in his time; and he will bring together his worshippers, who worship him in Spirit and in truth, under the Chief Shepherd, and He will dwell in his Tabernacle with them. And He Himself alone will be their God.

To whom be Glory, for all eternity, and to whose grace of every sort we commend you,

especially indeed Messieurs Yvon and Dulignon, of whom the former had in mind to join his letter to you with this one, but other occupations not to be delayed have detained him.

APPENDIX B
*Letter 4 from Anna Maria van Schurman to Johann Jakob Schütz,
Altonae, 22 December 1674*

Manuscript G2.II.33, fols. 9r–12r, University of Basel Library Archives

[middle of p. 6]

Hic moves quaestionem discipulo Christi dignam, de Abnegatione suiipsius, quousque nempe in communi urgenda?

Ad quam respondebo primo, si verba Domini de hoc argumento simplici oculo intueamur, illa proponere veritatem universalissimam discipulis scilicet et asseclis Christi omnia esse abneganda, praeter ipsum.

Deinde hanc gratiam abnegandi omnia omnibus electis suo tempore per
Spiritum Christi infundi, qui illos eo incitat, impellit ac ducit.

Hic autem Spiritus, quem si quis non habet non est Christi, teste Apostolo, suos ab impuro amore sui **[p. 7]** omniumque rerum sive naturalium
ac terrestrium sive supernaturalium et colestium in purum amorem, qui
non quaerit, quae sua sunt, traducit ac transfert, ita ut tandem Deus is
omnia, ipsi vero nihil fiant.

Porro certissimum est gratiam I[esu] C[hristi] regnantem in fidelibus
esse fundum universalem abnegationis rerum omnium, quae non sunt
Deus; cuius explicatio gerneralis et veluti series continua sese extendit
per omnes gradus ac intervalla vitae.

[middle of p. 6]

Here you raise the question worthy of the disciple of Christ, regarding the denial of one's own self: How far, indeed, should it be spurred on as a general rule?

To which I will respond, first, if we consider the words of the Lord concerning this argument with a simple eye, that they clearly put forward a most universal truth to disciples: that the followers of Christ must deny all things, except Himself.

Next, that this grace of denying all things is poured out into all the elect, in its own time through the Spirit of Christ, who inspires, impels, and leads them there.

Now, this Spirit, whom if anyone does not have he is not of Christ, with the Apostle as witness, leads and transports his own from an impure love of [p. 7] self and of all things, whether of natural and terrestrial things, or of supernatural and heavenly, to a pure love that does not seek those things that are its own, such that finally God himself becomes all things, [and] they themselves truly become nothing.

Moreover, it is most certain that the grace of Jesus Christ, reigning in the faithful, is the universal foundation of the denial of all things that are not God; whose general unfolding and, as it were, continuous series stretches out through all steps and intervals of life.

Denique notandum Abnegationem Christianam non tam consistere in neglectu, contemptu atque odio rerum, quae plerumque bonae sunt, quam in abrenunciatione suiipsius, hoc est amoris proprii in illis.

Praeterea cum amor ille impurus quicquid diligit, sive naturale sit sive spirituale, mundanum sive coeleste, inquinet sibique impurum faciat, nemini dubium esse potest, quin omnio et in omnibus sincere sit abnegandus, quo caritas Dei, quae omnia pure diligere potest, thronum in corde sola occupet atque in plenitudine potestatis conservet.

Haec omnia illustrari ac probari possint variis S[acrae] Scripturae dictis st exemplis, sed mihi nunc brevitati studendum.

At quaeris quousque haec sint urgenda. Respondeo, urgenda sunt secundum rei [p. 8] veritatem. Pergis, annon sit ratio habenda diversi status personarum?

Et cum hic sublimis fidei atque amoris Divini gradus sit, annon potius infirmiores promissionibus Novi Foederis sint excitandi et spe futurae gloriae erigendi, quatenus et illa nos tangit, quandoquidem protestatione sui amoris amorem nostrum excitare voluerit Dominus?

Omnino concedimus distinguendas personas earumque diversissimum statum: nec ullo modo negligendas esse pretiosissimas Evangelii promissiones:

sed, qui Christum sequitur, non ambulat in tenebris nec ulla otiosa relinquit electorum salutis ac Divinae gloriae instrumenta ac media.

Redeo itaque ad primam illam, quam indicavi, veritatem, Christi discipulis omnia esse abneganda, quae Deus ipse non sunt, donec omnia in Deo pure amare didicerint:

In short, it must be noted that Christian Abnegation does not so much consist in the disregard, scorn, and hatred of things that generally are good, as in the renunciation of one's own self, that is, of self-love [expressed] in those things.

Further, since that impure love stains and makes impure whatever it loves, whether it is natural or spiritual, worldly or heavenly, no one can doubt but that it must be sincerely denied entirely and in all things, so that the love of God, which is able to love all things purely, alone may occupy the throne in the heart and preserve it in fullness of strength.

All these things could be illustrated and demonstrated by various sayings and examples of Sacred Scripture, but now I must pursue brevity.

But you ask how far these things are to be pushed? I answer that they are to be urged according to the truth of the matter. **[p. 8]** You go on, [asking] whether consideration should be given to the diverse status of persons?

And since this is the highest step of the faith and love of God, whether, rather, the weaker ones should be stirred up by the promises of the New Covenant, and roused by the hope of future glory; and to what extent also that touches us, seeing that by the declaration of his own life, the Lord wishes to arouse our love.

We concede entirely that persons and their most diverse states should be distinguished: and not in any way are the most precious promises of the Gospel to be neglected:

but he who follows Christ does not walk in darkness, nor by any laziness does he abandon the instruments and means of salvation of the elect and Divine glory.

And so I return to that first truth, which I have indicated, that for the disciples of Christ all things must be denied that are not God himself, until they will have learned to love purely all things in God:

mihique ob oculos ponens exemplum Christi dico omnibus proponendum esse hoc axioma sive mandatum summi Doctoris Evangelici idque ipso statim initio, siquis vel tantillum inaudiverit de excellentia Divini nostri Servatoris.

Nam siquis ipsum sequi velit, sciat necessum est, quid illum ab ipso limine angustae portae arceat; amor nimirum ac possessio suiipsius.

Cumque omnes posteri Adami in primo illo capite ac patre generis humani (qui suus esse voluit atque independens, perfectionem maiorem quaerens extra Deum) [p. 9] illius vestigiis insistentes seipsos in locum veri Dei constituant, antequam per Spiritum Dei regenerentur per gratiam, corruptae naturae contrariam, propriam illam sapientiam ac superbiam, qua nos aliquid esse extra Deum aut aliquid boni nobis deberi praesumimus, ut et proprium amorem, quo nos divisim a Deo diligimus, ante omnia abnegare tenemur; nisi nos ipsos Deo nostro, cum primo Adamo praeferre ac Servatoris etiam doctrinam, ductum ac viam salutis negligere pergamus.

Nec iste certe tam sublimis (quod innuere videris) perfectionis gradus est, quin et primus atque infimus veri Christianismi vere dici queat, cum Supremus Doctor absolute esse pronunciet, ut quis eius sit discipulus et assecla, qui odio non habet patrem, matrem, uxorem, liberos, fratres, sorores, imo et suam ipsius animam[1]: si nimirum eius locum occupent aut cor illis adhaereat.

Nihil itaque hinc excipiendum.

Et ratio manifesta est, cum Deus integrum sibi cor omni iure postulet.

---

1. Luk. 14,26.

and placing before my eyes the example of Christ, I assert that this fundamental principle or command of the highest evangelical Teacher must be shown forth to everyone, and this at once, from its very beginning, if anyone will learn even very little concerning the excellence of our Divine Savior.

On the other hand, if anyone would wish to follow his own self, it is necessary that he know what separates him from the very threshold of the narrow gate; surely, the love and possession of oneself.

And since all of the descendants of Adam, persevering in the steps of that one, in that first head and father of the human race (who wanted to be his own and independent, seeking greater perfection outside of God) [p. 9] set themselves up in the place of the true God before they be regenerated through the Spirit of God through a grace contrary to the corrupt nature, we are compelled to deny before all things that particular wisdom and arrogance by which we presume that we are something outside of God or that something good is owed to us, as well as that love of self by which we love ourselves apart from God. If not, we go on to prefer with the first Adam ourselves over our God, and neglect also the teaching of the Savior and the guidance and path of salvation.

And [self-denial] is surely not so high a step of perfection (insofar as you seem to think), but that it could truly be called both the first and lowest [step] of true Christianity, as the highest Teacher perfectly proclaims [it] to be (Luke 14:26), that whoever is his disciple and follower, who does not hold in hatred, his father, mother, wife, children, brothers, sisters, rather, also, his own soul, if surely they occupy his place, or if the heart should cling to them.

Nothing thus [is] to be excluded from this.

And the reason is clear, since God most justly requires the whole heart for himself.

Siquis autem v[erbi] g[ratia] patrem aut matrem excipiat, eo ipso osten-
dit ibi suum esse thesaurum ac fulcrum, cui cor affixum est atque inni-
titur: quibus, ut Dei puro amori maxime oppositis impedimentis, eo
nomine ante omnia renunciare debet. [p. 10]

Summus enim Dominus in corde suorum socium regni non admittit aut
tolerat.

Huius vero abnegationis totalis non solum in N[ovo] T[estamento], sed
et V[etere] illustria habemus exempla;

nominatim in Abrahamo[2] Patre credentium, qui vocationi Divinae res-
pondens patriae, cognationi simulque rationi propriae (nesciebat enim,
quo esset iturus) in ipso viarum Domini initio prompte ac fideliter
renunciavit;

atque in progressu filium[3] suum unicum, dilectum, optimum filiumque
promissionis Divinae minime cunctanter sacrificavit.

Et nos, qui eius filios nos profitemur, nec solum illius, sed et Patris
coelestis ac Filii eius unigenti exemplum habemus ante oculos; nobis
quicquam reservabimus, quod Deo nostro consecrare nolimus?

Illud quidem iustissimum, imo et dulcissimum esse concedis: sed paucos
eo pervenire putas ob humanam scilicet imbecillitatem. Eoque promissionibus potius eos censes allicendos ac corroborandos.

2. Gen. 12, 1ff.
3. Gen. 22.

But if anyone, for example, should exclude father or mother, that in itself shows that his treasure and support are there, to which his heart is attached and also on which it leans: by which things, impediments most especially opposed to the pure love of God, **[p. 10]** he ought for this reason to renounce before all things.

For the Highest Lord does not admit or endure a companion of his reign in the hearts of his own.

We have brilliant examples of this total denial, to be sure, not only in the New Testament, but also in the Old,

specifically in Abraham, the father of believers, who, responding to the Divine calling, in the very beginning of the ways of the Lord promptly and faithfully renounced his fatherland, family, and his own reasoning, for he did not know where he would go;

and without the least hesitation he sacrificed his only son, beloved, most noble, and son of the Divine promise.

And we, who profess ourselves his sons, have an example before our eyes not only of that [father] but also of the heavenly Father and his only begotten Son. Will we hold on to anything whatsoever for ourselves, which we would not want to consecrate to our God?

You concede that that is indeed most just, rather, even most sweet: but you think that only a few people reach that place on account of human weakness. And for that reason, you think that they must be more enticed and strengthened by the promises.

Quod tibi lubens concederem, nisi in applicatione particulari, in novitiis praesertim, ingens esset [p. 11] periculum, ne antequam eorum amor sui tum spiritualis tum carnalis per Spiritum Christi mortificatus sit, coelestes illas promissionum et consolationum dulcedines in corde sibi adhuc vivente ad impurum illum amorem nutriendum ac fovendum arripiant eoque in venenum odoremque mortis convertant, per naturalem nempe vanitatem ac superbiam, credentes se iam resuscitatos et incolas esse coeli, cum tamen nondum mundo ac sibi mori recte didicerint atque adeo misere se fallant.

Desperatissime fallax esse cor hominis nos docuit Divinum Oraculum, ideoque difficilis eius cura et curatio est: sed et minime dubium, quin plures pereant per spem imaginarium salutis quam per desperationem:

cum amor ille sui inordinatus omnia ipsi faventia sine discrimine ad se rapiat nec seipsum necare aut iustissimo Dei amori cedere velit.

Concludam igitur denuo abnegationem et mortificationem omnium, quae Deo eiusque sanctissimae voluntati non subiiciuntur, omnibus esse necessariam et adamandam.

Imbecilles autem quod attinet, videndum, an illa imbecillitas, quae tantopere fugit crucifixionem veteris hominis, non potius sit vis vitae propriae ac naturae corruptae quam vitae supernaturalis teneritudo anhelantis [p. 12] vires Spiritus Christi, quibus superare possint, quicquid in ipsis voluntati Divinae inveniunt contrarium.

Talis enim Christianorum imbecillitas non reiiceret hoc iugum Christi, quod revera leve ac lene est. Fit namque amabile per eius Spiritum, quem in suis abnegationis virtutem pariter atque amorem producere dixi; adeo ut opus nostrarum virium minime censendum nec iisdem metiendum sit.

This I would willingly concede to you, except in a particular application, especially in beginners, it would be a huge **[p. 11]** danger, lest before their self-love, whether spiritual or carnal, has been mortified through the Spirit of Christ, they snatch up those heavenly delights of promises and comfort, in order to nourish and foster that impure love in a heart still living for itself, and thus transform them into the poison and stench of death, through truly natural foolishness and arrogance. They believe that they have already been reawakened and [are] inhabitants of heaven, although they have not yet learned properly to die to the world and to themselves and to that extent deceive themselves miserably.

The Divine Prophecy taught us that the heart of man is most desperately deceitful, and therefore, its cure and healing is difficult: but there is little doubt that more people perish through the imaginary hope of salvation than through despair:

since that disorderly love of self pillages all things, favoring itself without distinction, and does not want to quench itself, or to submit to the most just love of God.

Therefore I will again state expressly that the abnegation and mortification of all things that are not placed under God and his most holy will are necessary and must be eagerly desired by all.

But as far as weak people are concerned, one must consider whether that weakness which shuns so greatly the crucifixion of the old man is not the strength of one's own life and corrupt nature, rather than the tenderness of the supernatural life, breathing **[p. 12]** the strength of the spirit of Christ, by which they may be able to overcome everything that they discover in themselves contrary to the Divine will.

For such weakness of Christians would not reject this yoke of Christ, which is truly light and gentle. In fact, it becomes pleasing through his Spirit, which I said produces in his own the strength of abnegation, and in equal measure love; to the end that it must not at all be supposed the work of our strength, or apportioned to the same.

Indeque natum illud paradoxum Apostoli,[4] "cum infirmus sum, tum potens sum."

Postremo dixeram in fidelibus esse fundum huius gratiae universalem, qui per totum vitae eorum cursum sese explicet, cum non ita plene a seipsis sint liberati in terra, ut non aliquando implicari aliquo eius laqueo aut circumveniri possint, etsi victores sui eiusdem nodum facile resecare valeant ac soleant.

Talibus vero, quorum corda per fidem purgata ac per Spiritum Dei renovata sunt, promissiones Evangelicae vere competunt, et, cum pro Regno ac gloria Regis sui praesertim ad sanguinem usque (ut loquitur Apostolus)[5] contra peccati reliquias decertant, tuto applicantur.

Hi enim pure omnibus Dei beneficiis cum exultatione frui, imo seipsos et omnes creaturas in Deo et propter Deum sancte amare possunt, [p. 13] cum puris pura sint omnia.[6]

Haec vero gratia abnegationis omnium, uti caeterarum initium et quasi basis nec non certissimum nostrae electionis, regenerationis et conversionis signum et indicium est: ita inter maxima Divini erga nos amoris beneficia merito numeratur nostraeque gratitudinis ac gaudii solidum perpetuumque argumentum et materiem praebet.

Et quemadmodum per eum, qui dilexit nos, omnia eoque inprimis nosipsos, qui natura Dei sumus inimici, vincere possumus: ita illud exercitium nos non fatigat aut infirmat, sed mirum in modum in via vitae corroborat.

---

4. 2 Kor. 12,10.
5. Hebr. 12:4.
6. Tit. 1:15.

Thence sprang that paradox of the Apostle, "When I am weak, then I am strong."

Lastly, I had asserted that the universal foundation of his grace is in the faithful, which unfolds itself through the whole course of their lives, since they are not so completely liberated from themselves on earth that they can never be entangled in or beset by any of its snares even if those who conquer themselves are strong and are accustomed to easily cut the knot.

[But] for those whose hearts have been purified through faith and renewed through the Spirit of God, the promises of the Gospel truly suffice and are safely applied, when the people fight against the remnants of sin for the kingdom and the glory of their King, especially (as the Apostle says) to the point of blood.

For these are able to enjoy all God's benefits with joy purely, or I should rather say, they can virtuously love themselves and all creatures in God and on account of God, [p. 13] since to the pure all things are pure.

This grace of the abnegation of all things, to be sure, as the beginning of all the rest and, as it were, the foundation, is indeed also a most certain sign and evidence of our election, regeneration, and conversion: thus, it is rightly counted among the greatest benefits of Divine love towards us and provides a firm and everlasting evidence and an occasion for our gratitude and joy.

Just as we are able to conquer all things through him who loved us, and therefore especially our very selves, who are by nature the enemies of God, therefore that practice does not weary or weaken us, but strengthens [us] in a wonderful manner, in the way of life.

Imo neminem Christianorum solida ac constanti tranquillitate interna frui posse credimus, nisi postquam seipsum ac sua omnia, temporalia atque aeterna, manibus ac curis suis eripuit per abnegationem sui ac translationem rerum omnium in manum ac voluntatem Dei.

Vide an mea brevitate prolixitatem tuam castigem? sed abrumpo.

Tibique et tuis omnibus fortitudinem iuxta ac pacem Christi indies cumulari exopto. Vale in eo, care Frater.

Altonae, 22, decemb. 1674 Stylo V[etere].

More precisely, we believe that no Christian can enjoy perfect and constant inward peace, except after he has wrested his very self and all his possessions, temporal and eternal, by his own care and attention, through the denial of self and the transfer of all things into the hand and will of God.

See whether I chastise your prolixity with my brevity? but I break off.

And I long, from day to day, to be gathered to you and all your own, according to the strength and peace of Christ. Be well in him, beloved Brother.

Altonae, December 22, 1674—Stylo V[etere].[7]

---

7. Different parts of Europe went from the Julian calendar to the Gregorian. However, the dates listed for the Netherlands (at http://webexhibits.org/calendars/year-countries. html) do not coincide with the year that Schurman made the transition. She was living in Friesland at the time, so that would indicate that she wouldn't go Gregorian until 1700. Perhaps her correspondent in Germany was on the Gregorian calendar by 1675, and she was still Julian, explaining why she gave two dates beginning in 1675. Essentially: different parts of Europe made the change at different times, and when she gives two dates the later one is Gregorian, the earlier Julian.

APPENDIX C
EYKΛHPIA, by Anna Maria van Schurman, Chapter 9,
Sections XIX–XXIV (pp. 198–207)

Full title: *Eukleria seu Melioris Partis Electio. Tractatus Brevem Vitae*
ejus Delineationem exhibens. Luc 10:41, 42. Unum necessarium. Maria
optimam partem elegit. Altona, 1673

[p. 198]

XIX. Babylon sc. sanari noluit ideoque sibi fuit relinquenda. Quid
autem aliud tandem exspectare debet, nisi plenam effusionem phialae
postremae irae Dei, eiusque plagarum ac iudiciorum ultimam periodum.
Haec quidem ex parte sentire coepit; sed nihil inde profecit. Dominum
Deum cogere velle videtur, ut se penitus destruat.

Dum eius infinita Bonitas quotidie nobis novam parat suae laudis ac
benedictionis materiem, & istam, inter alia innumera, quod nos eo
posuit loco, quo bellorum

[p. 199]

flagella non pertingunt: & quod maius beneficium divinum est, eam
nobis largitur gratiam, qua omnes etiam parati sumus ad osculandam
divinam voluntatem, si quidem ea nos cum reliquo terrarum orbe iisdem involveret. Nobis certe non minus amabilis est Deus, iustitiam,
quam misericordiam exercens, cum ab eodem simplicissimo principio
utraque proveniat, ac summum bonum, Dei nempe gloriam, semper
habeat pro fine.

Et revera Christiano nomine indignus esset, siquis minus sincere se in
sacrificiu obtulisset Deo & Christo, qui se Patri suo pro nobis in Sacri-
ficium prius consecravit, non mutabili proposito, sed ipso facto, quando
animam suam posuit pro multis Jes. 53.

[p. 198]

XIX. Babylon of course has refused to be cured and so has had to be left to herself. Yet what else is she ultimately to expect, except a full outpouring from the final flask of God's anger, and the final time of his punishments and judgments? She has indeed begun to be aware of this in part, but it has done her no good. She seems to wish to force the Lord God to destroy her utterly.

While his infinite Goodness affords us a new opportunity every day for his praise and blessing, and, among other countless examples, the fact that he has set us in a place

[p. 199]

where the lashes of war do not touch us, and the fact that an even greater act of kindness of his is divine, when he endows us with grace, thanks to which we are all indeed ready to kiss his divine will, if only it might join us to the rest of the world with the same blessings. Certainly God is no less lovable in exercising justice rather than mercy, since each originates from the same wholly simple principle and always has as its objective the highest good, that is the glory of God.

And indeed one would be unworthy of the name of Christian if one offered oneself as a sacrifice to God and Christ without complete sincerity, since Christ first consecrated himself as a sacrifice to his Father on our behalf, not with a resolve that was capable of change, but by the deed itself, since he laid down his life for many (Is. 53).

Itaq; in eo nostram ponimus beatitudinem, quod Deus nobis suo Spiritu eam mentem dederit, ut nostra omnia, vitam ac mortem, quin imo salutem simul ac semel & serio tradiderimus eius sanctissimae ae liberrimae dispensationi & consilio, cui inservire toto vitae nostrae curriculo, usque ad eius constitutum terminum, toto corde desideramus: ad exemplum Dei Servi Davidis, de quo legimus Act. 13: 36. *postquam etate sua* (nempe ipsi a Deo determinata) *inservivit Dei consilio, obdormivit.* Adeoque omni nostra cura de anima & corpore nostro (quae sane non nostra, sed Dei & Christi sunt) in Deum devoluta, nihil praeter obedientiae gloriam, aut verius Dei omnium Domini gloriam nobis in oculis & animo habendam esse putamus.

XX. Hanc vero, omnibus vinculis terrenis soluti, non solum corde & opere; sed & lingua ac cantu perpetuo celebramus in hac domo ora-

[p. 200]

tionum. Cuius argumentum nobis saepe suppeditant Psalmi eiusdem Prophetae, *amoeni Psalmista Israelitarum*, ut de eo loquitur Spiritus Dei 2. Sam 23. praesertim ii quos Evangelice composuit: sed & illi qui ab eiusdem insigni imitatore D. de la Badie titulo *Psalmorum Evangelicorum*, in lucem editi sunt: uti etiam sacri Cantus de Perfectionibus divinis, inscripti *Sancta Decades*, Gallice *Les Saintes Decades*.

And so we attribute our happy condition to the fact that the Lord, through his Spirit, has granted us a mind of such a kind that we surrender to him all we possess, our life and death, and indeed our very salvation, once and for all and irrevocably, to his most holy and free dispensation and counsel, which we wish to serve throughout the whole course of our lives, right up to its appointed end, with all our hearts, following the example of David, the Servant of God, about whom we read in Acts 13:36, "After he had served God all his days" (these of course were determined by God) "he fell asleep." So true is it that, after entrusting all care of our souls and bodies to God (for these are not ours, but belong to God and Christ), we consider that we should hold nothing before our eyes and minds apart from the glory of obedience, or, more truly, the glory of God who is Lord of all.

XX. This, however, after being freed from all earthly bonds, we celebrate not only with heart and deed but also with tongue and continual singing in this house of prayers.

[p. 200]

The Psalms of the same Prophet, "the loveliest of the Psalmists of the Israelites," as the spirit of God describes him in 2 Sam. 23, often supply us with a proof of this, especially those that he composed to spread the good news of God, but also those that have been published by that illustrious imitator of his, D. de la Badie, with the title of "Evangelical Psalms," and also those sacred songs about the Divine Perfections, called the "Sanctae Decades" (the Holy Decades), in French "Les Saintes Decades."

Praeterea Canticum regium Magni Regis JESU, *Le Chant Royal du Grand Roi* JESUS. Unum porro praestantissimum, quod omnia Dei Filii Admiranda proponit, atq; Ecclesiae nostrae celebranda ac depraedicanda exhibet, cum hac inscriptione CHRISTUS *de novo revelatus,* Gallice *Christ revelé de nouveau ou d'une nouvele maniere.* Ut taceam tot alia devotissima Cantica, quae omni occasione dictitat Amor JESU, & desiderium insatiabile Nomen eius glorificandi, quibus illum vel ut infantem in praesepi ac cunis vagientem, vel ut in aetate perfecta omnibus filiis hominum pulchriorem, vel in morte patientem, pro Ecclesia satisfacientem, eamque secum sanctificantem; vel per Resuscitationem triumphantem, nobis ad vivum repraesentat: quibus vel singuli seorsum, vel omnes congregati, elevamur ad amandum ac laudandum magnum, amabilem, atque adorabilem Dominum nostrum JESUM.

XXI. Nunc autem facile, puto, meis amicis ac notis ex modo dictis constabit, statum mihi quoad vitam spiritualem obtigisse exoptatissimum, sive nostros Doctores ac Duces, sive nostram Ecclesiam ac Familiam, sive me ipsam

[p. 201]

intuear. Certe si *in multitudine Consiliariorum salus est,* ut dixit regum sapientissimus in sanctis suis Proverbiis: sancta ac salutaria consilia nobis non desunt eorum, qui in omnibus Deum consulunt, & quibus, per optimam experientiam, viae Domini innotuerunt: ita ut in eo adimpletum quotidie sentiamus divinam hanc prophetiam sive promissionem: Daturus sum vobis Pastores ex sententia animi mei, qui pascent vos scientia & intelligentia.

Nam revera nos pascunt verbo, & pascunt exemplo: Verbo, quod ex eorum pectore & corde, tanquam e fonte perenni, depromunt. Et exemplo, ad exemplum vitae Christi efformato, quo simplici, puro, nativo ac constanti in viis Domini incedendi modo, nobis indesinenter praeeunt, sic ut eorum naturam in gratiam, imo & gratiam ipsis in naturam conversam dixeris; eoque vivam nobis imprimant Evangelici Pastoratus Ideam.

There is also the Royal Song of the Great King Jesus, "Le Chant Royal du Grand Roi Jesus." There is in addition one absolutely outstanding one, that sets forth all the wondrous qualities of the Son of God, and made available to be celebrated and preached about by our church, called "Christ revealed afresh," in French "Christ revelé de nouveau ou d'une nouvelle manière," to say nothing of so many other most devout Songs, which were on every occasion dictated by the Love of Jesus and an insatiable desire to glorify his name, in which he vividly portrays him either as a child in the manger, crying in his cradle, or fully grown and more comely than the sons of men, or suffering in death, giving satisfaction for his church, and sanctifying her with himself, or triumphing through returning to life. Through these, when we are either alone or gathered together, we are raised up to love and praise our great, lovable and the adorable Lord Jesus.

XXI. Now, furthermore, it will be easily agreed by my friends and acquaintances, to whom I customarily refer, that I have been granted a most desirable condition insofar as my spiritual life is concerned, whether I consider our Teachers and Leaders, or our Church and Family, or myself.

[p. 201]

Certainly "salvation lies in having a large number of counselors," as that wisest of kings said in his sacred Proverbs. We do not lack the holy and saving counsels of those who consult God in all things, to whom the ways of the Lord have become known by the very best proof. And so it is that we feel that this divine prophecy or promise is fulfilled every day in this: "I shall give you Shepherds of whom I fully approve, who will feed you with knowledge and understanding."

For in truth they feed us with the word, they feed us with their example; with the word, which they bring forth from their breast and heart, as if from an unfailing spring, and with their example, shaped to the example of Christ's life, with which they unceasingly go before us with their unalloyed, pure, inborn and resolute manner of walking in the ways of the Lord, so that one would say that their nature has been turned into grace, and indeed that through them grace has been turned into nature, and thereby they impress upon us the living idea of Evangelical Shepherding.

Quod si ad nostram Ecclesiam animo convertimur, siquidem veri Christiani, hoc est, sibi & mundo mortui, aut reapse quotidie morientes, Deo verò soli viventes, ac Christi genuini imitatores veram & optimam constituunt Ecclesiam: illam, iamdudum alibi frustra à me quaesitam, hoc tempore tandem cum magna consolatione hic certe conspicio, eiusque communione gaudeo.

XXII. Si vero me ipsam privatim respicio, quamvis ut sanctorum minimam, tamen ut verum ac vivum huius verae ac vivae Ecclesiae membrum, eiusdem Spiritus ac gratiae particeps, nihil mihi amplius deesse arbitror: sed omni parte, etiam ante obitum, mihi videor beata.

[p. 202]

Si enim *beatus est, qui habet omnia qua vult,& nihil vult male,* ut Ethnicus Christiane locutus est; vel omnium meorum amicorum calculo me probabo beatam, siquidem nihil nisi quae Deus noster vult, qui nisi optima velle non potest, per eius gratiam volo; & quia nihil praeter aeternum & optimum eius decretum accidit, aut ille ipse agit, ideo quoque nihil aliud quam quod fit, & ipse facit, volo.

Nunquam enim Deum, omnium Ordinatorem, primum Motorem & Gubernatorem fine suo, qui summa & sola eius Gloria est, solumque bonum necessarium, posse excidere extra controversiam pono. unde efficitur ut nec ego unquam meo, qui cum fine divino coincidit, excidere queam.

Et cum antea variis circumagerer desideriis, tum multa sciendi, tum agendi, ita ut nusquam mihi standum esse putarem: nunc nihil amplius scire cupio, nisi quod mihi Deus per suum verbum ac Spiritum, divinamque Providentiam vult revelare; nihil esse, aut possidere, aut facere exopto, nisi quod eadem perpetuo ipso facto se velle declarat: aut etiam nihil non pati velim (quod difficillimum videtur) quod Deus meus me vult pati. cum *omnia possimus* cum Apostolo, *per Christum, qui nos corroborat.* Phil. 4.

But if we turn in heart to our Church, then indeed true Christians, that is, those who are dead to ourselves and the world, or, in truth, dying each day, but living for God alone and genuine imitators of Christ, establish the true and best Church. I have sought her for a long time elsewhere in vain, but now at last with great consolation I see her here, and I rejoice in being in communion with her.

XXII. But if I regard myself in private, although I consider myself the least of the saints, I see myself nevertheless as a true and living member of this true and living Church, a sharer in the same Spirit and grace, and consider that I lack nothing, but I consider myself blessed in every respect even before my death.

[p. 202]

For if "he is blessed, who has all that he wants, and has no evil desires," as the Gentile Christian said, then I shall prove myself blessed by the caculations of all my friends, since I want nothing except what our God wants, who can desire nothing except what is best, and I want it through his grace; and since nothing happens unless by his eternal and excellent decree, or else he himself is the doer, on those grounds also I want nothing other than what happens and what he does.

For I assert that it is beyond debate that God, the Ordainer of all things, the prime Mover and Governor, can never abandon his End, which is his highest and greatest Glory, and the only necessary good. And so it is that I too can never abandon my End, which coincides with the divine End.

And whereas I was previously tormented by various desires, both to know and to do many things, so that I thought I should never have rest anywhere, I now desire to know nothing more than what God wishes to reveal to me by his word and Spirit and divine Providence; I desire neither to be, to possess, nor to do anything except what this same Providence declares it wants by its own unceasing action. Indeed I should not be unwilling (this seems the most difficult thing) to suffer anything that God wishes me to suffer, since, along with the Apostle, "we can do everything through Christ, who strengthens us" (Phil. 4).

XXIII. Plurimum autem in illa praxi & siducia nuper confirmata sum, cum divina benignitas nostram postremo renovavit Ecclesiam, ut supra recensui, ubi me communi illo verbo, quod *neminem praterierit*, inclusi, non enim aliorum membrorum gratia, minus quam nostra gaudemus: sed ad meam beatitudinem cla-

[p. 203]

rius, & speciatim depraedicandam hoc addam, quod cum ego una cum reliquis Ecclesiae nostrae membris, quae non paribus passibus, ut quaedam insigniora, *instar lucis splendentis & pergentis usque ad plenum diem* Prov. 4.

fuerant progrefla, in magna essem exspectatione renovantis gratiae, qualis nobis coelitus videbatur promitti; atque occasione examinis viarum nostrarum, reliquias avaritiae spiritualis, nimii amoris donorum ac bonorum Dei, meaeque imperfectionis quandam impatientiam, adeoque defectum abnegationis mei ipsius, atque universi amoris creaturae deprehenderem,

eiusque onere nimium deprimerer, quod retrogredi potius quam progredi in robore & constantia in viis Domini mihi viderer: loco meae consternationis, quae divinam merebatur derelictionem, tam benigne me respexit divina Clementia, ut primum tranquillato paulum animo meo, tanta amplitudine infinitae suae Maiestatis me circumcinxerit, suaeque divinae praesentiae ac bonitatis sensum impresserit, ut me totam, meaque desideria omnia, tamque mea praesentia quam exspectanda bona malaq; quasi de novo magis absolute, & fide ac amore puriore quam unquam antea in eum transtulerim.

XXIII. In this practice and faith I was furthermore very greatly strengthened recently, when divine kindness finally restored our Church, as I
have described above, an occasion when I included myself in that shared
quotation that "he shall pass by nobody," for we do not rejoice less in
the grace of other members of the church than in our own. But in order
to render my own blessedness clearer

[p. 203]

and more specific I shall add this: along with the other members of our
Church, who had advanced with unequal paces, since some were more
distinguished, "like a light which shines and remains visible even into
full daylight," Prov. 4,

I was in high expectation of a renewal of grace, such as seemed to be
promised to us from heaven. On the occasion of examining our paths I
was analyzing traces of spiritual avarice, an excessive love for the gifts
and good things of God, and a certain impatience with my own imperfection, and especially the deficiencies in my own self-denial and my
overall love of creation.

I was greatly oppressed by the burden of this, because I seemed rather
to be going backwards than advancing in strength and resolution in the
ways of the Lord, but then, instead of my consternation, which de-
served divine abandonment, divine Mercy looked back at me with such
kindness, that, after first calming my soul a little, it embraced me with
all the vastness of its own infinite Majesty, and impressed upon me the
sense of its own divine presence and goodness to such an extent that I
surrendered myself entire, and all my desires, all my good and evil circumstances, both present and still in the future, to him, with greater perfection, as though starting afresh, and with a purer faith and love than
ever before.

Meq; ipsa penitus neglecta, tanquam possessionem alterius, nempe Dei & Christi Haeredis omnium, intuens, de nulla re amplius, quam ut eius me conformem divinae voluntati, exinde fuerim sollicita. Plene nimirum ac plane me sentio convictam, per amabilem hanc veritatem, quod ille solus dignus sit, cui se omne genu flectat, eiusque sola fiat & ametur voluntas in nobis & de nobis;

[p. 204]

utque omnis creatura eo gaudeat, quod sit, & quod Deus gloriosissimus sit. qui, quemadmodum solus est ens necessarium, ita meretur ut solus sit beatus; quemadmodum etiam solus est bonus, testante eius Filio, qui solus novit Patrem, & ii soli, quibus ipse Patrem & seipsum vult revelare; ut qui solus eum recte & adaequate novit.

Itaque nihil aliud esse, quam quod Deus me esse vult, desidero; & ut eo modo quo ipse vult, glorificetur. Uno verbo, haec status mei renovatio mihi alter quidam vitae meae spiritualis partus est: cuius effectus melius sentire, quam effari valeo; & quales mihi forte plures exspectandi sunt ab eadem gratia renovante ac corroborante, donec in postremum coelestis perfectionis & gloriae sumar partum.

XXIV. Si vero externa, quae me, vel hanc Dei familiam spectant, hic quoque in censum venire debent, me certe primo, quoad locum meae habitationis, in alta pace & quiete video, qualem nunc Ultraiecti inter arma & armatos nemini etiam fidelium obtingere posse existimem. Si studia & occupatiunculas, mihi ibidem usitatas, considerem, quae mihi potissimum varietate placebant; certe abnegatio nimii sciendi desiderii, multiplicatarum scientiarum comprehensione, quae nos a simplici & pura cognitione Christi crucifixi ut plurimum abducere solet, nunc mihi longe carior est, & esse omnibus debebat.

I became profoundly forgetful of myself and looked upon myself as though I were the possession of another, that is of God and Christ the Heir of all, and then became preoccupied more by shaping myself to the divine will than by anything else. Assuredly I feel completely and clearly convinced by this lovable truth, that he alone is deserving that every knee should bend, and that his will alone in us and concerning us should be done and loved,

[p. 204]

and that every creature should rejoice that he lives, and is God most glorious. He is the only necessary being, and also he alone is good, as his Son testifies, who alone knows the Father along with only those to whom he wishes to reveal the Father and himself, since he alone knows him adequately and properly; and therefore he deserves to be the only blessed one.

And therefore I desire to be nothing other than what God wants me to be, and that God should be glorified in the manner in which he wishes. In a word, this renewing of my condition is for me a second birth of my spiritual life, as it were. I can feel its effects better than I can speak of them. What further effects must I by chance now await from the same renewing and strengthening grace, until I am taken up into a final birth of heavenly perfection and glory!

XXIV. But if I am to take account here of external circumstances also that concern me and this family of God, I see most certainly that as far as my place of habitation is concerned I enjoy deep peace and quiet, such as I think nobody even of the faithful may now be enjoying at Utrecht amid weapons and armed men. If I were to consider my studies and little occupations, which were customary for me in that same place, which certainly delighted me particularly by their variety, then certainly (in their place) there is now the denial of my excessive desire to learn from an understanding of the manifold branches of knowledge, which usually takes us far away from a simple and pure knowledge of the crucified Christ. He is now far dearer to me, and should have been to everyone.

Meas vero artes & varia epuscula manuaria, quae mihi alicuius videban-
tur esse pretii, nunc aranearum telis subtilitate vinci erubesco; & apes
nostras me sua sedulitate & sapientia in eo superare video, dum inge-

[p. 205]

niosis ac quadratis suis cancellis, suas aedes instruunt, quos non alieno
colore superficie tenus pingunt, sed ibi mel reale recondunt, sibique &
domino suo de optimo cibo provident.

Ita ut nunc quod bonum est, iuxta monitum Apostoli, manu mea operer,
unde aliquid fructus ad commune Ecclesiae bonum proveniat. Quodsi
porro consortia intuear eoru, quibuscudies transigo, nusquam mihi in
nostra familia alii occurrunt, nisi vivae imagines Christi, aut certe tales,
qui mundum spernunt, & se Christianae vitae studio devoverunt, &,
quod incredibilis iucunditatis est, loco unius aut alterius famulae mer-
cenariae, me saepe dignissimarum Sororum amabilissima corona cir-
cumcingit:

quarum singulas pro aliis vitam suam ponere, & quotidie consumere
paratas videas: tantum abest, ut earum manus amicissimae mihi non
opem ferant in omnibus, quae alterius auxilium desiderant. Curae do-
mesticae sicui Sororum demandatae sunt, quibus ego aetatis beneficio
sublevor, tractantur sine cura aut ulla molestia Caritate Christiana do-
cente & animante omnia.

Ordine vero iam pulcherrimo constituto, convenienter rebus & perso-
nis, omnia iuxta proportionem optimam magna hilaritate, facilitate ac
tranquillitate efficiuntur, ex amore mutuo, ut dixi, & vere Christiano.

Si olim Cicero non immerito magnum esse bonum iudicavit Amicitiam,
imo Solem e mundo tollere asseveravit, qui ex hac vita tolleret amicitiam, quam sane mira cum dexteritate descripsit, quod sit *omnium divi-
narum ac humanarum rerum cum benevolentia summa consensio*: Ego

As for my skills and various little handicrafts, which used to seem of value to me, I now blush to be surpassed in skill by the spiders' webs. I see that our bees surpass me in their unremitting toil and wisdom, while they

[p. 205]

equip their homes with their own cleverly wrought square framework, which as far as the surface is concerned they paint with a similar color, while concealing the real honey inside, and provide for themselves and their master with excellent food.

And so now, as is good, in accordance with the command of the Apostle I would perform with my hands tasks from which some benefit may be gained for the common good of the Church. But if in addition I look at the company of those, with whom I spend my days, nothing presents itself before my eyes within our family except true images of Christ, or at least such as despise the world and have devoted themselves to the study of the Christian life and, instead of one or two hired servant girls, a most lovable circle of most worthy Sisters surrounds me, which causes unbelievable joy.

You might see them prepared individually to lay down their lives for others and use them up every day. It is so far from being the case that their very dear hands fail to give me strength in all things that need the help of another. If any domestic responsibilities are entrusted to any of the Sisters, they are performed without anxiety or any unpleasantness, with Christian Charity teaching and animating everything.

But now a most attractive order has been established, suiting our circumstances and personalities, and all tasks are carried out in accordance with the best kind of sharing, with great merriment, ease, and calm, as a consequence of our mutual and truly Christian love, as I said.

Indeed once Cicero not undeservedly judged Friendship to be a great good and asserted that a man who would remove friendship from this life might as well remove the sun from the world. He described it with amazing aptness, because, he says, there occurs "the utmost agreement regarding human and divine affairs accompanied with kindness." I too

[p. 206]

quoque eo nomine omnium iudicio censenda ero beata: cum in nostra domo sive Ecclesia, amicitia Christiana, quae sola vera est amicitia, instar Solis omnes illuminet & animet.

Cumque inter amicos omnia communia esse, cum ipso statuendum sit, ipsa qui- dem primo commune nostrum omnium bonum est: deinde & omnia nobis interna, perinde ac externa bona, sunt communia; ita ut nemo quicquam sibi quid proprium esse dicat, ut in primaeva Ecclesia Hierosolymitana Act. 4:32. aut ullus egenus sit inter nos. ibid. v. 34.

Quod mirandum non est, cum inter nos *nihil se plus quam alterum diligat amicus*: quod idem auctor Ethnicus in amicitia requirit. Attamen veram ac divinam amicitiam non novit Philo-sophia Ethnicorum; sed sola Christiana Religio, eiusque viva praxis: cum Christi Spiritus, essentialis quippe Caritas, solus eam doceat & operetur inter fideles.

eo modo, ut non tam se invicem respiciant & ament, quam CHRISTUM qui in ipsis vivit & regit, amant & glorificant. Quam praxin fidelium commemorat Apostolus, quando de sua conversione loquitur ad Gal. 1. 24. *Glorificabant Deum in me*, ut habet textus originalis.

Mundus itaque, ac falso nominati Christiani hanc felicitatem non cognoscunt, qua toties Christi multiplicantur imagines, & in uno suo Proto-typo sive Exemplari uniuntur, unde omnes inseparabiliter, ut radii a suo Sole, pendent & sustentantur, quoties eorum numerus augetur:

quo lucro sane non minus inter nos oritur gaudium, quam Salvator in coelo existere, propter conversionem vel unius peccatoris, affirmat:

[p. 206]

shall have to be considered happy on that score in the judgment of all, since in our house, or Church, Christian friendship, which is the only true friendship, illuminates and animates everybody like the Sun.

And since it must be established through our being friends that all things among friends are shared, our friendship itself is from the first a shared good belonging to us all. And then, all our interior goods are shared just like all our external goods, so that nobody says that anything is her own property, just like the primitive Church in Jerusalem, Acts 4:32, nor is anyone among us in want, Acts 5:34.

This is not surprising, since "among us no friend loves anything more than his neighbor": the Gentile writer seeks the same quality in friendship. Yet the philosophy of the Gentiles is not since the Spirit of Christ, which is of course the essential Charity, alone teaches it and brings it about among the faithful.

In this way it is not so much a case of them regarding and loving each other as of loving and glorifying Christ who lives and reigns in them. The Apostle recalls this practice of the faithful when he speaks of his conversion in Gal. 24. "They will glorify God in me," as the original text has it.

And so the world, and those falsely called Christians who do not recognize this happiness, by which the images of Christ are multiplied so many times, and then brought together in one Prototype or Exemplar of him, on which all, like rays from the sun, inseparably depend and by which all are nourished whenever their number is increased.

At this gain, of course, no less a joy arises among us, than that which our Savior declares exists in heaven on account of the conversion of even one sinner,

[p. 207]

quod regnum Satanae subdito suo spoliatur, & Christi Regnum, quasi in eius praeludio, accrescit.

Ad famae autem meae claritatem quod attinet, iam antea indicavi, quod non solum illi gloriam, sed & ignominiam Christi, infinitis modis praeferam, cum fideli eius Servo Mose, & electo eius vase S. Paulo, qui *omnia damnum esse duxit propter eminentiam notitia Christi Jesu Domini sui*: imo omnium iacturam fecerat, & *pro stercoribus* habuit, *ut* CHRISTUM *lucrifaceret.*

Eundem ergo imitatorem Christi imitari serio desiderans, *ea qua a tergo sunt obliviscens, & ad ea qua a fronte sunt contendens, scopum versus feror, ad praemium superna vocationis Dei in Christo.* Atque una cum eius Ecclesia *nos omnes ut municipes coeli gerimus, unde etiam exspectamus Dominum Jesum: in eoque perstamus.* ut Apostolus Philippensibus loquitur. Ideoque postquam statum meum praesentem beatum esse, mihique partem ac sortem optimam obtigisse probavi, quam Εὐκληρίας nomine in hoc Scripto insignivi, cum Christi Ecclesia, ad Sponsi sui verba Apoc. 22. 20. *Etiam venio cito, Amen:* eius Sponsae verbis, *Veni igitur Domine* JESU! concludo.

SOLI DEO HONOR & GLORIA!

[p. 207]

since the kingdom of Satan is robbed of a subject, and the kingdom of Christ grows, as at its beginning.

However, as far as the fame of my name is concerned, I have already previously indicated that in countless ways I value above it not only the glory but also the shame of Christ, along with his faithful servant Moses and his chosen vessel St. Paul, who "considered all things loss on account of the towering importance of the knowledge of Christ Jesus his Lord" and indeed gave up all things, and considered them "as dung, in order to gain Christ."

Therefore, desiring with seriousness of mind to imitate the same imitator of Christ, "forgetful of what lies behind and hastening towards what lies ahead, I am borne towards the mark, to the reward of the heavenly calling of God in Christ." And along with his church "we all conduct ourselves like citizens of heaven, from where we also await the Lord Jesus and stand fast in him," as the Apostle says to the Philippians. And so, having proved my present condition to be blessed, and shown that I have gained an excellent portion and fate, to which in this work I have given the name Εὐκληρία, I conclude with the Church of Christ, in reply to the words of the bridegroom, Rev. 22:20, "Come quickly," with the words of its bride, "Come therefore Lord Jesus!"

To God alone be Honor and Glory!

Notes

1. Coakley's *Powers and Submissions*, for example, sparked many conversations. See also Mercedes, *Power For*, and Chau, "'What Could Possibly Be Given?'"

2. Anna Maria van Schurman, *Eukleria* [1673], chap. 9.IV, 187.

CHAPTER 1

1. The enjoyment of God is a hallmark of Augustinian theology, as expressed, for example, in the *Confessions*: "The person who enters into you 'enters into the joy of the Lord' (Matt. 25:21) . . . ; he will find himself in the supreme God where it is supremely good to be" (Augustine, *Confessions* 2.10.18, trans. Chadwick, 34). In fact, Augustine's *Confessions*, as a whole, can be said to be a description of Augustine's yearning for this "stable . . . enjoyment of [his] God" (7.17.23; trans. Chadwick, 127); he says of (or, rather, to) his God: "You are fullness and the inexhaustible treasure of incorruptible pleasure" (2.6.13; trans. Chadwick, 31). Elsewhere: "That is the authentic happy life, to set one's joy on you, grounded in you and caused by you" (10.22.32; trans. Chadwick, 198). Earlier in the same book, Augustine declares that his "fountain of delight" is found in God alone, for

"when I seek for you, my God, my quest is for the happy life" (10.19.29; trans. Chadwick, 196). This is also the triumphant note on which the *City of God* ends (22.30; trans. Dods, 1088), its "eternal felicity": "For what did [God] mean when he said, in the words of the prophet, 'I shall be their God, and they will be my people'? Did he not mean, 'I shall be the source of their satisfaction; I shall be everything that men can honorably desire: life, health, food, wealth, glory, honor, peace and every blessing'? For that is also the correct interpretation of the Apostle's words, 'so that God may be all in all.'" See also Burnaby, Amor Dei, and O'Donovan, *Problem of Self-Love*. Note also Gerald Bonner's discussion of desiderium in Augustine's theology in "Augustine and Mysticism," 113–19.

2. See Augustine, *On Christian Doctrine* 1.3–5, trans. Robertson, 9–11. See also O'Donovan, *Problem of Self-Love*; O'Donovan, "*Usus* and *fruitio*"; Canning, *Unity of Love*; Dupont, "Using or Enjoying Humans"; and O'Connor, "*Uti/Frui* Distinction"; and, for a more recent treatment of this question, Gregory, *Politics*, 319–50.

3. If study became a direct source of enjoyment, however, rather than used as a means toward the proper enjoyment of God, Augustine understood this to be a distortion of loves. Theology was to be enjoyed only insofar as it led to the *summum bonum*.

4. One needs to be mindful of false dichotomies when making this claim. In his seminal work *The Love of Learning and the Desire for God*, Jean Leclercq has pointed out that the goal of the monastics of the medieval period was to "enjoy God," while the emphasis of the "schools" shifted toward making proper distinctions in theology (191–202, 207–17, 222–28). At the same time, it would be unfair to claim that scholasticism was devoid of the enjoyment of God. See, for example, James A. Weisheipl's description of Thomas Aquinas as mystic and scholastic: "Mystics are rarely found today on university campuses. Perhaps that is why it comes as a surprise to learn that mysticism not only can survive academic life, but can even thrive on it. There is no reason why intellectuals cannot be saints and mystics" ("Mystic on Campus," 135). See also Constable, *Reformation of the Twelfth Century*, and Jaeger, *Envy of Angels*, for further nuances to Leclercq's argument. *Nonetheless, scholasticism's primary accent was no longer on sheer enjoyment*. According to Leclercq, this is what the scholastics needed to gain from monastic theology: the ability to delight in and adore the object of their study (*Love of Learning*, 222–28). Leclercq, of course, balances this out by reminding his reader of the limitations of monastic theology; the monastics needed the scholastics as well (207, 276).

5. For this shift in his thought, see Henry, *Path to Transcendence*, 118.

6. Augustine, *City of God* 22.30, 11.24, 20.21, trans. Dods, 867, 369, 744. See also Bonner, "Augustine and Mysticism," 119.

7. In some cases (e.g., with Guyon, as we shall see), the author argued that *desiderium* could be completely fulfilled.

8. While the tradition of interpreting the *Song of Songs* as the celebration of the individual's union with God emerged as early as Origen in the third century (see his *Commentary* and two *Homilies* on the Song), the medieval period experienced a boom in this approach. For detailed studies on medieval exegesis of the *Song*, see Turner, *Eros and Allegory*; Matter, *Voice of My Beloved*; Astell, *Song of Songs*; and Scheper, "Spiritual Marriage."

For an overview of its wider trajectory (beginning with the patristics), see Norris, *Song of Songs*. A helpful compilation of patristic commentaries can also be found in Wright and Oden, *Proverbs, Ecclesiastes*. See also Tanner, "History of Interpretation," 23–46. Certainly, this tradition continues well beyond the medieval period to authors such as Teresa of Avila, St. John of the Cross, and Madame Guyon.

9. In general, the language of "mystical union with Christ" needs to be differentiated from what the apostle Paul meant in his letters by "union with Christ." When engrafted into the vine, the believer attains "union" with Christ from the start, according to Paul. Most mystics, when referring to "union with Christ," speak of a different notion, or level and intensity, of union. Union with Christ is the goal, whether reached at the *eschaton* or after a trying period of "purgation" and "illumination" in this life.

10. Consider, for example, *The Soul's Journey toward God*, by Bonaventure, or Bernard of Clairvaux's writings on the *Song of Songs* (eighty-six sermons, in *Cantica canticorum*) and *On the Love of God*.

11. This generalization might be made of Protestant writers in particular. On the other hand, several writers of the Catholic Reformation renewed their primary emphasis on the enjoyment of God. See, for example, the *Interior Castle*, by Teresa of Avila (1515–82), the *Canticles* of St. John of the Cross (1542–92), and *Treatise on the Love of God*, by Francis de Sales (1567–1622). See also T. Koehler's important article "*Fruitio Dei*."

12. See, for example, Muller, *Post-Reformation Reformed Dogmatics*, 13–20.

13. See, for example, Bérulle, *Bérulle and the French School*. The explicit retrieval of this theme appears to have begun shortly after the Reformation conflict erupted, toward the second half of the sixteenth century, as well. See also note 11 above.

14. The sources that informed the Westminster Shorter Catechism (adopted by Parliament in 1647) remain a topic of exploration. Furthermore, it would be worthwhile to investigate other theological movements of the seventeenth century (both Protestant and Catholic) that made the *enjoyment of God* their primary goal.

15. A word search alone reveals that Calvin's *Institutes* focuses more on enjoying the "benefits of Christ" than on "enjoying God" per se.

16. Van Schurman would have had most training in the Heidelberg Catechism; the first statement of the Westminster Shorter Catechism, however, was universally accepted in the Reformed churches of Europe.

17. Cf. Guyon, *Moyen court*, 98: "La fin pour laquelle nous avons été créés est pour jouir de Dieu dès cette vie." Notably different, of course, is the emphasis on "this life." The actual phrase can be translated as "from this life on," rather than "forever," which might easily be taken as simply an eschatological marker. A similar phrase is found again later in the same treatise: "la fin pour laquelle elles ont été créés, qui est de jouir de Dieu" (125).

18. Ibid., 98.

19. See note 11 above.

20. This is admittedly truer of certain pockets of the church than others, and I am making the claim here about the dominant (or, rather, mainstream) theologies of Holland and France in particular.

21. See Prozesky, "Emergence of Dutch Pietism," for his discussion of Dutch Pietism as represented by Gisbertus Voetius, William Ames, and Jodocus van Lodensteyn (among the "first wave of Reformed Pietism," 32). Notably, Voetius was one of van Schurman's primary mentors. Prozesky argues that the "movement as a whole underwent gradual change with its early precisianism losing ground to devotional and on occasion mystical pursuits," yet he maintains that "moral rectitude" was of "paramount importance" from first to last (37).

22. Although Bossuet "won" the political battle, Fénelon's teaching may have reached a wide audience as well, even if imperceptibly (by virtue of being associated with Guyon's, it was largely suppressed).

23. The traditional itinerary of *purgatio, illuminatio, uniona* is well known in the history of Christian mysticism and dates back to Pseudo-Dionysius. See, for example, Louth, *Origins*, 63. Van Schurman and Guyon, however, intensify the use of these themes in their writing through their extreme, totalizing rhetoric.

24. Although there is growing scholarship on the violence of love in mystical theology (see, for example, McGinn, "Abyss of Love," 95–120), as well as the nature of finding pleasure *in* various forms of pain, some of the literature (e.g., Miller, "Mystical Masochism") likens this (wrongly in my estimation) to masochism. On the other hand, feminist theologians have offered important correctives to and qualifications of the imagery of submission to violence within Christian theology. See, for example, Brown, "For God So Loved the World?"; Fortune, "Transformation of Suffering"; Harrison and Heyward, "Pain and Pleasure"; and Redmond, "Christian

'Virtues'"; Imbens, *Christianity and Incest*; Brock, *Journeys by Heart* and "Losing Your Innocence"; and Miller, "Eroticized Violence."

25. The Quietist doctrine of "pure love" forbade the explicit desire for such "self-fulfillment." Love for God, *for God's own sake* (and with no regard for self-benefit) was central. Self-fulfillment, however, was an inevitable result in both van Schurman and Guyon's thought, because God's goodness and radical commitment to the individual were never to be doubted. This will be discussed further in chapters 5 and 6.

26. For example, there is only one chapter on "religion" in Merry Weisner's important volume *Women and Gender in Early Modern Europe*; other chapters in the volume touch on the subject of spirituality, though not as their main focus. Thankfully, Sylvia Brown's *Women, Gender, and Radical Religion in Early Modern Europe* contributes to this scarce list.

27. Bruneau, *Women Mystics*, 136. See also Gondal, *Madame Guyon*. Both of these works focus on Guyon's historical and political context rather than her theology. Research on van Schurman similarly focuses on her life rather than her theological contributions. Joyce Irwin has made significant strides in our current retrieval of van Schurman's life and thought, as have a few Dutch theologians (see Baar et al., *Choosing the Better Part*); much work remains to be done, however.

28. I am beginning work on a translation of the *Eukleria* for The Other Voice series, edited by Albert Rabil and Margaret King. This treatise includes van Schurman's autobiography and her defense of the Labadist movement, as well as the core of her spiritual theology. The first two chapters have recently been translated by Joyce Irwin in her collection *Anna Maria van Schurman*. The whole work was translated into German in 1783, and also into Dutch. The German translation may prove to be a valuable resource for my ongoing translation work. The Dutch translation, according to a few Dutch scholars, is not always accurate but may also be helpful to a lesser extent. I have translated various chapters of her *Eukleria*; my translation of Part I, chapters 19–24, is in Appendix C.

29. While several works have offered fresh insights into their lives and historical contexts, few have analyzed the complexity of their thought. Toward this end, I have worked on my own translation of key portions of the *Eukleria*, with the help of the keen eye of Janet Martin, a Latinist at Princeton University. A full English translation from the original Latin has not yet been completed or published, and a few Dutch scholars like van Veen have deemed the Dutch translation inaccurate. Unfortunately, much of the Dutch scholarship, while invaluable, is based on this Dutch translation rather than on the original. Chapters 1 and 2 of the *Eukleria* are translated in Irwin, *Anna Maria van Schurman*, and brief sections from later

chapters appear in Birch, *Anna van Schurman*. Chapters 3 through 9, however, are, for the most part, untranslated. In this book, Appendix C provides my own translation of the 1673 *Eukleria*'s concluding pages, and I offer my translations of other passages throughout chapter 2 of this work. I have also translated some of the unpublished letters she wrote to Johann Jakob Schütz from 1674 to 1675. These are housed at the University of Basel Library Archives, manuscript G2.II.33, fols. 2r–3v, 9r–12r, and 17–20 (letters 2, 4, and 8, respectively). (See Appendices A and B for my translations and the original Latin of letters 2 and 4.)

30. Thankfully, Joyce Irwin has been an important voice in rehabilitating Anna Maria van Schurman for the English-speaking world. See, for example, her translations of several of van Schurman's writings in Irwin, *Anna Maria van Schurman*. See also Baar et al., *Choosing the Better Part*, an important volume produced by Dutch scholars.

31. Dutch culture had long forgotten van Schurman's legacy, as evidenced by general lack of recognition when her name is mentioned in the Netherlands today. That she was the first woman admitted to study at the University of Utrecht (and the first woman to study at any Dutch university) has been generally unknown, as has the fact that she was chosen to commemorate the University of Utrecht's opening with her own eloquent Latin composition (see van Beek, *First Female University Student*). My visits to the Netherlands confirmed that this was true until 2007, when van Schurman publicly entered Dutch historical memory with the publication of several articles in Dutch newspapers, recognizing the four-hundredth anniversary of her birth. Thankfully, several Dutch scholars have begun retrieving van Schurman's works, as most notably demonstrated in de Baar et al., *Choosing the Better Part*.

32. Queen Christine of Sweden was among her many devotees, for example. Van Schurman's fame and influence will be further explored in chapters 2 and 3 of this work; see also in chapter 6.

33. Van Schurman, *Eukleria* [1673], chap. 2.II, 5, quoted in Irwin, *Anna Maria van Schurman*, 81. Given the context of van Schurman's time, the catechism was most likely the Heidelberg Catechism.

34. See van Beek, *First Female University Student*, 7 and 249. The next female to study at a Dutch university would be Aletta Jacobs over two centuries later.

35. Larsen's "'Star of Utrecht'" lists fifteen languages mastered by van Schurman. That book manuscript's introduction provides an in-depth overview of van Schurman's educational background and scholarly reputation, as well as the historical context of female erudites in early modern Europe in general.

36. See, for example, van Schurman, *Opuscula Hebraea*. See also Moore, "Anna Maria van Schurman" [1994], 191.

37. Irwin, "Anna Maria van Schurman: The Star of Utrecht," 68, quoting and translating from a work by Pierre Yvon, van Schurman's earliest biographer, entitled "Abrégé sincère de la vie et de la Conduite et des vrais sentimens de feu Mr. De Labadie," included in its entirety in Arnold, *Unparteyische Kirchen- und Ketzerhistorie* (Frankfurt, 1715), 2:1264ff.

38. While Labadism was primarily a Pietistic movement, a strong mystical bent also characterized its doctrine, as well as its way of life. Significantly, Pietism incorporated much of Catholic mystical thought into its own; Gottfried Arnold, one of its key leaders, for example, borrowed directly from Fénelon's writings—and Fénelon considered himself a disciple of Madame Guyon; see, for example, Erb, *Pietists*. Of course, Labadie was himself a former Jesuit. See Saxby, *Quest for the New Jerusalem*, as well as Certeau, *Mystic Fable*, 271–93.

39. On her continuing commitment to Calvinism, see, for example, Irwin, "Anna Maria van Schurman and Bourignon."

40. See, for example, Birch, *Anna van Schurman*, 110.

41. Van Beek, *First Female University Student*, 38–39. On the motto, see note 64 below, p. 224.

42. See Bruneau, *Women Mystics*, and De La Bedoyere, *Archbishop and the Lady*.

43. Whether or not she was, in the end, condemned for sounding "Protestant" or "Quietist" is difficult to determine from the records. See Bruneau, *Women Mystics*, and Knox, *Enthusiasm*, 344–52.

44. Even Madame Maintenon turned against Guyon, who had previously been her spiritual guide. The political machinations involved in this betrayal are described in Bruneau, *Women Mystics*. Guyon experienced multiple stages of trial before the authorities. Her second interrogation of 1694 led to her arrest in 1695, though without clear charges or a fair trial. This began her imprisonment, which lasted approximately eight years, first in Vincennes and then in the infamous Bastille.

45. At her confessor La Combe's request, Guyon began writing "an account of her spiritual life in 1682, which she would continue to work on until 1709; this eventually became *La vie de Mme. J.M.B. de la Mothe Guion*" ("Jeanne Marie Bouvier de La Motte Guyon /Madame Guyon [1648–1717]," September 2, 2012, http://archive.is/z4Ma). The cited Web article contains a helpful scholarly collection of early modern women's writings.

46. Guyon, *Vie*. Guyon speaks often of her "ailing, sickly, weak" husband.

47. See, for example, Bruneau, *Women Mystics*, and Gondal, *Madame Guyon*. Two important volumes have appeared in the past year: Guyon, *Jeanne Guyon: Selected Writings* and *Prison Narratives*. See also Ward, *Experimental Theology*.

48. See note 27. Susan St. Ville produced a very helpful, though unpublished, dissertation on Guyon's mystical language, "A Chaos without Confusion: A Study of the Mystical Discourse of Jeanne Guyon." Nancy Carol James's dissertation, "The Apophatic Mysticism of Madame Guyon," has been published as *The Conflict over the Heresy of "Pure Love" in Seventeenth-Century France: The Tumult over the Mysticism of Madame Guyon*; this book, while helpful, seems to be written for a more popular audience and works primarily with paraphrased English translations (or adaptations) rather than the French originals. See also James, *Pure Love*; while again written for a more popular audience, it includes an interesting chapter entitled "Guyon's Theology of the Holy Spirit."

49. Guyon is being rehabilitated by the Catholic world, by key scholars such as Marie-Louise Gondal; see, for example, her *Madame Guyon* for a definitive biography on Guyon. For centuries, Guyon's work had been neglected by her fellow Catholics, while Protestants eagerly appropriated her writings. Indeed, Guyon appeared to be a recalcitrant woman, unwilling to submit to the authority of the Catholic Church. Her emphasis on private devotion and unmediated confession, for example, sounded dangerously Protestant to her Catholic examiners.

50. Guyon, quoted in Upham, *Life, Religious Opinions*, 2.

51. Guyon, *Autobiography*, 81–82.

52. Guyon, *Madame Guyon's Spiritual Letters*, 128, 86.

53. See, for example, Miller, "Mystical Masochism"; Kristeva, *Tales of Love*, 297–317; Bruneau, "Mysticisme et psychose." See also Knox, *Enthusiasm*, 322–28.

54. Pierre Poiret, a Protestant publisher, did much to preserve the writings of Guyon. Her influence extended far beyond her lifetime, as well: John Wesley and Watchman Nee are among the numerous onlookers who appropriated her work in significant ways. See note 6 of chapter 4. See also Ward, *Experimental Theology*.

55. See Chevallier, "Madame Guyon et Pierre Poiret," 35–49. Notably, Pierre Poiret exchanged letters with Anna Maria van Schurman. This actual, even if indirect, connection between Guyon and van Schurman is another support of Ted Campbell's thesis, in *Religion of the Heart*, that cross-fertilization between the Protestant and Catholic worlds occurred in various shapes and forms. See also Knox, *Enthusiasm*, 398, for his discussion of the connection between Philip Spener and Pierre Poiret, yet another support of Wallmann's thesis, in *Philipp Jakob Spener*, 290–306),

that van Schurman influenced the genesis, even if only in part, of German Pietism through multiple vectors, particularly Schütz and Spener.

56. See Ward, *Experimental Theology*, 6–7, 11, 94–98 (for Wesley); Schopenhauer, *World as Will*, 384; Thulstrup, "Pietism," Barnett, *Kierkegaard*, and Dalrymple, "Ladder of Thorns" (for Kierkegaard); Pryce, "'Upon the Quakers,'" and Spencer, "Hannah Whitall Smith" (for early Quakers); Ward, *Early Evangelicalism*, 105–7, 129–32 (for Zinzendorf and Wesley); and Lee, "Madame Jeanne Guyon." Guyon also influenced A. W. Tozer and other thinkers indirectly through her spiritual disciple Fénelon; see Tozer, *Crucified Life*, e.g., 6–10 on the theme of spiritual perfection (which Fénelon would have learned from Guyon).

57. Guyon, quoted in Upham, *Life, Religious Opinions*, 23.

58. Guyon, *Madame Guyon's Spiritual Letters*, 54.

59. Anna Maria Van Schurman to Johann Jakob Schütz, August 1674, letter 2, p. 3, MS G2.II.33, fols. 2r–3v, University of Basel Library Archives. I am indebted to Joyce Irwin for her transcription of van Schurman's original handwriting and her generosity in sharing it with me. My translation of letters 2 and 4 can be found in Appendices A and B, respectively. This set of letters portrays only van Schurman's side of the correspondence, but one can easily surmise from them the general content of Schütz's letters.

60. Certainly, the problematic nature of her relentless pursuit of "self-annihilation" cannot be ignored. The dangers behind such an emphasis, however, can be more properly discerned only after her doctrinal loci have been carefully explored.

61. Van Schurman, *Eukleria* [1673].

62. Letters to Johannes Jacob Schütz, July 1674–February 1678, manuscript G2.II.33, fols. 2r–3v and fols. 9r–12r, University of Basel Library Archives.

63. See Wallmann, *Philipp Jakob Spener*, 290–306.

64. See chapter 4, note 6. Though this study occasionally alludes to her *Autobiography* (1709), her *"Short and Very Easy Method of Prayer* (1685), and other works, her commentary on the *Song of Songs* (*Commentaire au Cantique des cantiques de Salomon*) will be the central focus of analysis.

65. Particularly in bk. 3 of the *Institutes* ("On the Christian Life"), chaps. 7–8, Calvin addresses the importance of self-denial and bearing one's cross as a disciple of Christ. He even regards the "sum of the Christian life" as "the denial of ourselves" (bk. 3, chap. 7). His discussion of mortification and vivification can also be found in bk. 3, chap. 3.

66. For the complexities and problems of associating Quietism with Guyon, see the section "Guyon's Theological Synthesis" in chapter 6 below, as well as Pryce, "Exploration."

67. Although there is no evidence of van Schurman or Guyon reading each other's works, an interesting point of connection can be found in Pierre Poiret, who both corresponded with van Schurman (I am currently translating a series of unpublished letters between them) and preserved and published Guyon's works (Chevallier, "Madame Guyon et Pierre Poiret").

68. For the corrections by feminist theologians, see note 24 above.

CHAPTER 2

Throughout this book, biblical quotes are from the NRSV translation. Regarding the epigraph, cf. Mark 8:34–37 and Luke 9:23–25.

1. Anna Maria van Schurman to Johann Jakob Schütz, letter 2, 12/22 August 1674, MS G2.II.33, fols. 2r–3v, University of Basel Library Archives, p. 3. Thanks to Joyce Irwin for providing information on these unpublished letters.

2. See the Westminster Shorter Catechism of 1647 and the Heidelberg Catechism, as well as note 17 of chapter 1.

3. See also van Schurman's correspondence with Johann Jakob Schütz. The dialogue between Schütz and van Schurman around this issue will be further explored in the following chapter.

4. Wallmann argues persuasively in *Philipp Jakob Spener* that van Schurman influenced the genesis and development of Lutheran Pietism in nearby Germany (290–306), particularly through her influence on Schütz and Philipp Jakob Spener. Notably, Spener's *Pia desideria* was published in 1675, two years after van Schurman's *Eukleria*. Her correspondence with leading figures like Johann Jakob Schütz serves as another link to this important movement.

5. See Saxby, *Quest for the New Jerusalem*; Certeau, *Mystical Fable*, chap. 9.

6. See Baar and Rang, "Anna Maria van Schurman," 5.

7. Rivet to van Schurman, 1 March 1632, in Irwin, *Anna Maria van Schurman*, 41.

8. Quoted in Baar and Rang, "Anna Maria van Schurman," 7.

9. Jacob Thomasiu and Johannes Sauerbrei, *Diatribe academica de foeminarum eruditione* (1671). For the specific charge of spider-eating and what that implied, see Baar, "'Now as for the Faint Rumours,'" 7; see also Nicéron, *Mémoires*, 18.

10. Quoted in Baar and Rang, "Anna Maria van Schurman," 6–7.

11. Van Schurman, *Eukleria*, chap. 5, translated and quoted in Baar, "'Now as for the Faint Rumours,'" 92.

12. While the precise living arrangements of the Labadists are unclear (other than that single men and women lived on separate floors, and married couples in different quarters), we do know that they lived in shared community, following the pattern of Acts 2, i.e., "sharing all that they had in common" (see my translation of *Eukleria* [1763], chap. 9.XXIV, 205–6, in Appendix C). See also van Beek, *First Female University Student,* and Saxby, *Quest for the New Jerusalem.*

13. Although van Schurman's responsibilities shifted in part in 1638, she remained in the world of the academic elite. Her *Dissertatio* was published in 1641, and her scholarly trajectory continued for at least another decade.

14. See van Schurman, *Eukleria* [1673], chap. 5.I, 92.

15. Van Schurman, *Eukleria* [1673], chap. 2.XI, 26, trans. Irwin, 88. It is not clear from the context if she includes Voetius and Rivet among the "worldly theologians."

16. Van Schurman, *Eukleria* [1673], chap. 2.XI, 27, trans. Irwin, 88.

17. For an in-depth analysis of Labadie's own theological trajectory, see Saxby, *Quest for the New Jerusalem.* See also Certeau, *Mystic Fable,* chap. 9.

18. For a fuller analysis of the problematic nature of Labadie's ministry, both practical and theological, see Saxby, *Quest for the New Jerusalem.*

19. See Muller, *Post-Reformation Reformed Dogmatics,* 13–20, for more on the nature of Protestant scholasticism.

20. On the continuing influence of Calvinism on van Schurman, see Irwin, "Anna Maria van Schurman and Antoinette Bourignon."

21. See Baar and Rang, "Anna Maria van Schurman," 13. This portrait was finally dispelled (though with remaining ambiguities) by the newly authoritative biography of G. D. J. Schotel in 1853 (Baar and Rang, "Anna Maria van Schurman," 14).

22. Interestingly, the *Eukleria* itself can be said to be a masterpiece of erudition; van Schurman would unabashedly use all the powers at her disposal—even to refute those tools that she was at the moment employing. For her, intellectual sophistication was not inherently an ill; when used "purely" for "pure purposes," it also could be redeemed.

23. Van Schurman, *Eukleria* [1673], chap. 2.XV, 32, trans. Irwin, 91. The theme of "direct" revelation was astir in seventeenth-century Europe in other writers such as George Fox in England; a desire for direct contact

with the Divine (i.e., Bernard McGinn's definition of *mysticism*, the "immediate and direct consciousness of the presence of God"; *Foundations of Mysticism*, xvi–xvii, 262) was made explicit in their thought. Van Schurman is one representative of this growing trend of her time.

24. Van Schurman, *Eukleria* [1673], chap. 2.XIII, 29–30, quoted and translated in Clarke, "Anna Maria van Schurman," 22; see also Baar, "'Now as for the Faint Rumours,'" 87.

25. Baar, "'Now as for the Faint Rumours,'" 87.

26. O'Neill, "Schurman, Anna Maria," 557.

27. Irwin, "Anna Maria van Schurman: The Star of Utrecht," 81; also see van Schurman, *Eukleria* [1673], chap. 3.XVIII, 52.

28. Van Schurman, *Eukleria* [1673], chap. 2.XIV, 30, quoted and translated by Joyce Irwin in "Anna Maria van Schurman: Learned Woman of Utrecht," 179.

29. Van Schurman, *Eukleria* [1673], chap. 9.XXIV, 204, translation mine (and henceforth, unless indicated otherwise). What, then, qualifies as "excessive"? Van Schurman makes a significant qualification: intellectual pursuits are not inherently contrary to the "inmost knowledge" of God; the dangers of pride and reliance on "external" forms of knowledge, however, are all too readily present, and she found herself unable to contend with the risks of intellectual sophistication.

30. Van Schurman juxtaposes this "excessive desire to learn" (nimii sciendi desiderii, multiplicatarum scientiarum comprehensione) against "simplici & pura cognitione Christi crucifixi" (*Eukleria* [1673], chap. 9. XXIV, 204). Christ, then, is not to be "comprehended" (a term that in the Latin also connotes a grasping, seizing, or arrest) but rather "known" in the most inward parts, "simply and purely."

31. Ibid., chap. 3.V, 39 (italics mine). Van Schurman contrasts "tam arida ac superficialis de rebus divinis scientia" with "veram, intimam, ac salutarem Dei notitiam."

32. Ibid., chap. 3.XII, 46.

33. Ibid., chap. 2.XVI, 32, trans. Clarke, "Anna Maria van Schurman," 23.

34. Again, van Schurman may be presenting an unfair dichotomy between the work of the Holy Spirit and "learned" exegesis. She is aware of this false bifurcation, as described in note 29 above.

35. Van Schurman, *Eukleria*, [1673], chap. 3.XV, 50.

36. Ibid., chap. 2.XVI, 32. "Experienced" is my translation; "sensed" is Clarke's, "Anna Maria van Schurman," 23. Notably, this matches quite closely Bernard McGinn's definition of mysticism, which I have adopted for this work (the "immediate and direct consciousness of the presence of

God"; *Foundations of Mysticism*, xvi–xvii, 262). The debate over whether van Schurman was a mystic might be resolved, therefore, by this broader definition of mysticism.

37. *Eukleria* [1673], chap. 3.XV, 50, trans. Moore, "Anna Maria van Schurman" [1994], 225–26.

38. It appears that for van Schurman the term *Holy Spirit* is used synonymously for "the Spirit of Christ." The Holy Spirit illuminates scripture's inner meaning, and this is the equivalent of being taught directly by Christ, "the Master" (Luke 10:41–42).

39. Leclercq, in *Love of Learning*, for example, notes that monastic theology *needed* scholastic theology (276), and vice versa (222–28). One corrected the potential vices of the other, in mutual complementarity.

40. Again, van Schurman seems to have difficulty deciding where learning becomes "excessive."

41. Van Schurman, *Eukleria* [1673], chap. 4.I, 53: "Atqui, ut in caeteris rebus, res, et conceptus plurimum saepe differunt; ita que inter illas intellectu comprehensas veritates, in mente quasi deppictas, atque etiam amore quodam in corde receptas; et inter totalem mentis & cordis eversionem, conversionem & emendationem multum interesse quotidie addisco."

42. For a further discussion of "pure love," see van Schurman to Schütz, letter 4, 22 December 1674, MS G2.II.33, fols. 9r–12r, University of Basel Library Archives (hereafter "letter 4"), pp. 6–7. Van Schurman follows a long tradition, beginning with Augustine, that argues for the perfection of love through distillation or simplicity.

43. Van Schurman, *Eukleria* [1673], chap. 3.XIV, 48.

44. Ibid., chap. 3.XIV, 49–50.

45. Ibid., chap. 3.XIII, 48.

46. See Scheenstra, "On Anna Maria Van Schurman's 'Right Choice,'" 125. This state of abandonment also enables the individual to *return* to the finite world, with an appropriate love of self, others, and all creation *in God*.

47. These are also Augustinian terms, found prominently in his *Confessions* and *City of God*.

48. Admittedly, "pleasure seeking" is often seen as the antithesis of self-denial. Van Schurman's theology, however, presents the contrary.

49. Van Schurman to Schütz, letter 4, p. 13.

50. Van Schurman, *Eukleria* [1673], chap. 3.XV, 50; italics mine.

51. *Cognosco* and *notitia* come from the same Latin root.

52. See, for example, letter 4, p. 7: "Finally God himself becomes all things, [and] they themselves truly become nothing."

53. Van Schurman, *Eukleria* [1673], chap. 3.XII, 46–47. See also 55: "But therefore, to this extent, it is necessary that the Spirit of Christ be in us, that it may pray in us and for us and cause us to pray, and may *unite our mind and heart to God, and immerse [them] in his infinite ocean of divinity*" (italics mine). ("At ideo necesse est Spiritum Christi esse in nobis, ut in nobis & per nos precetur, & nos precari faciat; mentemque & cor nostrum Deo uniat, iusque infinito Divinitatis Oceano immergat.") For more on the image of the "ocean of divinity" prevalent within mystical literature, see McGinn, "Abyss of Love."

54. As in the above-cited quote from letter 4, "Finally God himself becomes all things, [and] they themselves truly become nothing" (7).

55. Translated and quoted in Baar, "'Now as for the Faint Rumours,'" 94; italics mine.

56. At the same time, the love of creature (including the love of self) is retrieved in the end, through a purified love. This dynamic will be discussed in the following chapter.

CHAPTER 3

1. Van Schurman, *Eukleria* [1673], chap. 9.XXIII, 20; see Appendix C for Latin original and for my translation of the treatise's final pages.

2. Schütz was a leading Pietist and a key representative of early Lutheran Pietism in Frankfurt. It has been argued that through her influence on Schütz van Schurman shaped the development of early Lutheran Pietism.

3. Anna Maria van Schurman to Johann Jakob Schütz, letter 4, 22 December 1674, MS G2.II.33, fols. 9r–12r, University of Basel Library Archives (hereafter "letter 4"). See my translation of this letter, side by side with the Latin original, in Appendix B.

4. Though we have only van Schurman's side of the correspondence, we can surmise the nature of his letters to her because she frequently repeats Schütz's questions. For example, she writes, "Here you raise the question worthy of the disciple of Christ, regarding the denial of one's own self: How far, indeed, should it be spurred on, as a general rule?" (ibid., p. 6).

5. Ibid., p. 8.

6. "To which I will respond, first, if we consider the words of the Lord concerning this argument with a simple eye, that they certainly put forward a most universal truth to disciples: that the followers of Christ must deny all things, except Himself" (ibid., p. 7).

7. Ibid., p. 10.

8. Ibid., pp. 8–9; italics mine. Van Schurman frequently speaks of "the denial of all things, including the self."

9. Ibid., p. 9.

10. Ibid.

11. Ibid., p. 11.

12. Ibid., p. 8.

13. Anna Maria van Schurman to Johann Jakob Schütz, letter 2, 12/22 August 1674, MS G2.II.33, fols. 2r–3v (hereafter "letter 2"), p. 3. See my English translation of this letter, side by side with the Latin original, in Appendix A.

14. Ibid., pp. 4–5.

15. It is important to note that Augustine taught the love of self, rather than self-hatred. A certain *type* of self-love is opposed, i.e., that which exalts self *over and against* God. Van Schurman also concludes in the direction of loving the self; she emphasizes, together with Bernard of Clairvaux, however, that self-love is the final step: after one has learned first to love all things (including the self) *in* God.

16. Letter 2, pp. 2–3.

17. It would be interesting to do a search on van Schurman's exposition of Gal. 2:20, if any can be found in her writings. It is not a prominent text in her *Eukleria*, though the sentiment and content are the same. Likewise, this particular theme resonates with Matt. 6:24: "No one can serve two masters. Either he will hate the one and love the other, or he will be devoted to the one and despise the other. You cannot serve both God and Money."

18. Letter 4, p. 10.

19. Letter 2, pp. 3–4.

20. Letter 4, p. 11.

21. Letter 2, p. 4. Van Schurman similarly employs images of battle in letter 4, p. 12: "For those whose hearts are cleansed through faith and renewed through the Spirit of God, the promises of the Gospel truly suffice and are safely applied when the people fight against the remnants of sin for the kingdom and the glory of their King, especially (as the Apostle says) to the point of blood."

22. 2 Cor. 10:5.

23. This passage from the *Eukleria* is translated and quoted in Baar, "'Now as for the Faint Rumours,'" 98.

24. Letter 2, p. 3.

25. Letter 4, pp. 11–12.

26. Ibid., p. 11.

27. Augustine was certainly one of the earlier champions of this teaching: the unruly self raises itself up against the knowledge of God. The Jansenists, among others within the Catholic tradition, would have agreed with this negative appraisal of human nature. Most strands of Catholic theology, however, are known for their higher anthropology. Nonetheless, many in the mystical tradition also stressed the importance of suppressing or "annihilating" this self. To name a few, one could point to Meister Eckhart, Marguerite Porete, and Mme. Jeanne Guyon. And Jean de Labadie himself was trained with the Jesuits in his early days. One cannot therefore point *simply* to van Schurman's Calvinism as the source of her stark portrayal of the self *against* God. In fact, the self is fully retrieved, after it has been "purified."

28. Van Schurman seems to share this view, as will become evident in the following section.

29. See letter 4, p. 13.

30. This hearkens back to Bernard of Clairvaux's "four degrees of love," in which the *manner* of love is purified such that former *objects* of love (i.e., the self, and others) are loved anew, with new purity of heart.

31. Letter 4, p. 7.

32. Ibid., p. 7.

33. Ibid., pp. 12, 7. In the phrase "the love of God," the ambiguity of the genitive (i.e., objective or subjective) is apt.

34. As she also states in this letter, "And so, I return to that first truth . . . that all things must be denied by the disciples of Christ, [all things] that are not God himself, *until they will have learned to love purely all things in God*" (ibid., pp. 8–9).

35. Ibid., pp. 12–13. Significantly, one can even love *oneself* "purely," then. Like Bernard of Clairvaux (see note 30 above), van Schurman makes the movement back to loving the self *in God*.

36. Stephen Pope, for example, has written a helpful article that elucidates this distinction in the thought of Thomas Aquinas. Keeping this distinction in mind will aid the reader of Thomas's work, as well as van Schurman's. See Pope, "Expressive Individualism," 386–90.

37. Letter 2, p. 5.

38. Letter 4, p. 6.

39. Ibid., pp. 6–7. In letter 2, van Schurman also writes that a powerful new work of the Spirit works self-denial in the elect, by a "certain violent wind." By it, the dead are "stirred up" and those "living for themselves destroyed."

40. Letter 4, p. 7. Van Schurman also writes that "the universal foundation of his grace is in the faithful, which unfolds itself through the whole course of their lives" (p. 12).

41. Ibid., p. 12.

42. This assumption is implicit in van Schurman's remarks in letter 4, quoted earlier, about those self-deceived people who "think that they have already been reawakened and [are] inhabitants of heaven, although they have not yet learned properly to die to the world and to themselves" (p. 11).

43. Van Schurman, *Eukleria* [1673], chap. 9.XXIII, 203.

44. There is a striking parallel in Guyon's discussion of self-annihilation, to be discussed in the following chapter.

45. Chalmers, "Expulsive Power."

46. Van Schurman, *Eukleria* [1673], chap. 3.XII, 46.

47. Letter 4, p. 7.

48. As n goes to infinity, $1/n$, $10/n$, and $2,000,000/n$ all converge to zero.

49. Letter 4, p. 7.

50. As in letter 4, p. 12, where she says that "the promises of the Gospel truly suffice and are safely applied when the people fight against the remnants of sin for the kingdom and the glory of their King, especially (as the Apostle says) to the point of blood." Van Schurman elaborates on the relation of acting and seeking to grace in far greater detail in her correspondence with Antoinette de Bourignon (mentioned also in letter 7 to Schütz). Chapter 5 of *Eukleria*'s Part II (in the 1685 edition) also addresses this question, although one cannot be certain that van Schurman penned this second treatise. Scholars are undecided as to whether this treatise can be properly attributed to van Schurman, but significant doubt has caused the majority to leave it to the side.

51. Letter 2, p. 1.

52. Ibid.

53. Ibid., p. 2. Van Schurman's reference to the Song of Songs is a traditional but important mystical trope. Her understanding of mystical union goes beyond that found in Calvin. See Calvin's *Institutes* and Dowey, *Knowledge of God*. (Interestingly, Reformed scholars debate whether Tamburello, in *Union with Christ*, portrayed Calvin himself as too much of a Bernardian.) See also Billings's important work, *Calvin, Participation*.

54. Letter 2, p. 1.

55. See, for example, Anna Maria van Schurman to Joseph Jakob Schütz, Wiewerti, 21/31 December 1676, letter 8, manuscript G2.II.33, fols. 17–20, University of Basel Library Archives, pp. 8–9. Notably, van Schurman seeks "communion with the faithful," whom she defines as those who are "dead to the world and to self, namely to pride and to self-love . . . and live unto Christ, not unto self" [Nos autem communionem cum illis fidelibus quaerimus, qui mundo et sibi, hoc est superbiae atque amori

proprio, quod ad eorum regnum, mortui sunt eoque Christo, non sibi vivunt] (fols. 18v–19r). The denial of self and the world is her ongoing criterion for "true Christianity." Chapter 5 of the *Eukleria* also focuses on Christ's union with his bride, the church who is his "mystic body."

56. Letter 2, pp. 2–3.

57. Letter 4, p. 7.

58. Again, van Schurman clearly means the *carnal* self that is to be denied. Using Calvin as her backdrop, she has the "mortification" of the "old man" and the vivification of the "new" in mind. She often fails to clarify the dignity of the *imago Dei*, however. Such totalizing language can be confusing and misleading, in the absence of important distinctions. The phrase "the false self," offered earlier in this chapter, may be more helpful for our context today. In chapter 6 I further distinguish between the "God-made self" and the "self-made self."

59. Translated and quoted in Irwin, "Anna Maria van Schurman: The Learned Maid of Utrecht," 181.

60. Van Schurman, *Eukleria* [1673], chap. 9.XXIV, 207.

61. Van Schurman, *Eukleria* [1673], chap. 2.XI, 25, trans. Irwin, 87.

62. Italics mine. Translated and quoted in Baar, "'Now as for the Faint Rumours,'" 98.

63. This topos—e.g., "I, a mere woman . . ."—riddles her earlier letters. See, for example, her letters to Rivet, in Irwin, *Anna Maria Schurman*, 39–56. In these earlier writings, van Schurman's words drip with the kind of modesty that was expected of women. See also Baar, "'Now as for the Faint Rumours,'" 100, and "Transgressing Gender Codes," 150.

64. See Irwin, *Anna Maria Schurman*, 1, for a description of van Schurman's apologetic rhetoric. Whereas Irwin argues that an "intensity of purpose and firmness of conviction" underlies "her apparent submissiveness," I posit that the shift in van Schurman's rhetoric reveals an actual, and not merely a supposed, change in her attitude.

65. Jean de Labadie and Pierre Yvon, leaders of the Labadist community, came to need her just as much as she needed them. She had assumed equality in the Labadist community and even become their theological spokesperson, humbly yet confidently holding her ground. The absence of a foreword (i.e., of male sponsorship) to the *Eukleria* is striking, especially as opposed to her earlier writings.

66. See Wallmann, *Philipp Jakob Spener*, 290–306. Schütz is but one example of the avenues through whom Spener was influenced. Knox also cites the connection between Pierre Poiret and Spener, for example (398).

67. Van Beek, *First Female University Student*.

68. Letter 4, p. 13. See the brief discussion of this passage in chapter 2 in the section "Self-Denial: The Key to Union with God."

CHAPTER 4

The chapter epigraph's translation of Guyon's *Commentaire au Cantique des cantiques de Salomon* is from Metcalf's translation (*Song of Songs of Solomon*, 101). Although Guenin-Lelle and Mourad provide the most recent and clear translation of Guyon's *Commentary*, I occasionally refer to previous translations (such as Metcalf's) that also preserve the meaning, due to certain phrases that they helpfully highlight. The epigraph to the section "Four Levels of Annihilation: Toward Union with God," is also from Metcalf's translation (*Song of Songs of Solomon*, 73).

1. For the tradition of *Song of Songs* interpretation, see note 8 of chapter 1.

2. The bride, according to Bernard of Clairvaux's *Commentary*, can refer to both the church and the individual believer, a view that originated from Origen's work. In St. John of the Cross's account, more attention is given to the union of the individual soul with Christ. As we shall see, Guyon focuses more upon the individual nature of the union as well; she concedes, however, that what is true of the individual is true of the church as a whole.

3. While St. John of the Cross also emphasizes annihilation in his *Canticles*, as does St. Francis de Sales in his *Treatise on the Love of God*, they do so with less intensity; their depictions of the bride are not as stark or "bloody" as Guyon's. It is possible that Guyon was familiar with Marguerite de Navarre's writings and her theory of annihilation, though I have not yet found clear evidence. Guyon's themes also overlap with that of Marguerite Porete, among others. See, for example, Schweitzer, "Von Marguerite von Porète"; Lichtmann, "Marguerite Porete"; Hollywood, "Suffering Transformed"; McGinn, "'Evil-Sounding.'"

4. He is also a "bridegroom of blood and a lover crucified" (Guyon, *Commentary*, trans. Guenin-Lelle and Mourad, Song 1:12, p. 112). See also Guyon's commentary on Exodus, specifically Exodus 4:25 ("Surely you are a bridegroom of blood to me"), Guyon, *Mystical Sense*, 196.

5. While it may be difficult to trace the exact source of her offense, we know that both her *Moyen court* and *Commentaire* elicited controversy and, ultimately, condemnation. The language is all the more problematic for modern readers, given its gendered depiction of the soul as bride who must undergo annihilation for the sake of the bridegroom.

6. For a number of reasons (which may or may not include her authorship of the Song of Songs commentary, in particular), interpreters such as Ronald Knox have relegated Guyon to the realm of the egomaniacal;

they find in her writings evidence of derangement and regard her mental state as off-kilter. Guyon was charged as a "madwoman" in her time as well as in subsequent eras; she was relegated to oblivion within the Catholic Church until recent decades, which have seen renewed interest in her and her work among Catholic scholars. After centuries of neglect, she has been reclaimed as a valid voice meriting careful attention. See especially Gondal, *Madame Guyon*, for a definitive biography on Guyon. Guyon's influence on the early Methodists in England, as well as the American Holiness movement, for example, has been widely documented. Her thought has also had enormous influence on important figures such as Søren Kierkegaard and Arthur Schopenhauer, that is, those whose reflections often focus on the perplexities of grave suffering. Less well known, however, is her current popularity among various movements in America, as well as in Europe and Asia (e.g., her *Moyen court* was translated into Chinese thanks to Watchman Nee's influence). Her books litter bookshelves in rather unexpected places (e.g., in the heartland of China) and are often the main textbooks for conferences on prayer and spirituality; her Song of Songs commentary alone has gone through multiple English translations and reprints, via a number of different publishers, and people continue to clamor for her work and ideas. A simple Web search reveals the breadth and popularity of this phenomenon. Just recently in her *Experimental Theology*, Ward has written (helpfully) on Guyon's reception in the States in particular. Guenin-Lelle and Mourad have also noted Guyon's strange "double reception history"—lauded by popular church circles and forgotten (or denigrated) by other streams of the church (as well as academia until recently), in their introduction to *Jeanne Guyon*, ix–xi.

7. Her writing in some respects mirrors the tumultuousness of her theology. In her *Spiritual Torrents* (*Les torrents spirituels*), for example, she describes the sheer speed and uncontrollability of the "waters" that overtake the soul.

8. "Let him kiss me with the kisses of his mouth" (Song 1:1).

9. Guyon, *Commentary*, trans. Guenin-Lelle and Mourad, Song 1:1, p. 100: "Le baiser que l'âme demande à son Dieu est l'union essentielle, ou la possession réelle, durable et permanente de son divin objet: c'est le mariage spirituel" (Guyon, *Commentaire*, Song 1:1, p. 205). A word study on *possession* would be fruitful here. Augustine, for example, uses this term frequently in his *Confessions*. Whether or not Guyon inherited her usage from him is a further question. It is important to note, however, that Augustine never used mystical readings of the Song in his own writings. It may seem peculiar that the kiss represents marriage, rather than any prior stage within the betrothal (unless, of course, it was commonplace that the

betrothed await marriage for this particular expression of love). The reasoning Guyon provides is that "God is all mouth" (*Commentary*, trans. Guenin-Lelle and Mourad, Song 1:1, p. 100; "Dieu est tout bouche," *Commentaire*, 1:1, 207). Therefore, the kiss symbolizes essential union. Guyon explains further, "It is necessary to know that God is all mouth, just as he is all word, and that the application of this divine mouth to the soul is perfect pleasure and the consummation of the marriage, by which the communication of God himself and his Word happens in this soul" (*Commentary*, trans. Guenin-Lelle and Mourad, Song 1:1, p. 100).

10. See note 9 of chapter 1 for various understandings of "union with Christ."

11. Guyon, *Moyen court*, 136–37: "All are called to . . . enjoy God both in this life and in the next." This theme first appears in her *Moyen court* and is reiterated throughout her *Commentaire*. See also *Moyen court*, 82: "The end for which we were created, is to enjoy God even in this life; yet alas, this is least in the thoughts of most men. . . . When possessing God who is the sovereign good, we possess the kingdom of God, which is the height of felicity, and the very end for which we were created." "In this life" marks a significant difference from the Westminster Catechism, which asserts that "the chief end for which [humanity] was created is to . . . enjoy [God] forever," emphasizing the eschaton.

12. Guyon, *Song of Songs*, trans. Whitaker House, Song 1:2 and 6:3 [Whitaker House translation follows the Anglican numbering in chaps. 1 and 6, as compared to the Vulgate numbering in Guyon's original and in Guenin-Lelle and Mourad's translation], pp. 11 and 153. This idea may have come from Teresa of Avila, for whom spiritual betrothal is lower than mystical marriage.

13. Guyon, *Song of Songs*, trans. Whitaker House, Song 6:5, pp. 161–62. Guyon offers little guidance in her commentary on how to become the betrothed of Christ; her commentary is instead a guide to moving from being the betrothed to being the bride. "Mais hélas qu'il y a encore de chemin à faire et qu'il y a bien à souffrir, avant que cette union tant désirée soit accordée et consommé!" (Guyon, *Commentaire*, Song 6:4 [discrepancy is due to the difference between Guyon's Vulgate and Whitaker's Anglican numberings for Song's chap. 6], p 277).

14. Guyon, *Commentary*, trans. Guenin-Lelle and Mourad, Song 6:4, pp. 157–58, and 1:1, p. 100. Guyon does not indicate at this point who any of these "spiritual writers" are. She does cite a wide range of authors and some of their works, however, elsewhere in her *Song of Songs* and her later *Justifications*—even if simply to lend credence to her own claims. Among them are St. John Climacus, Bernard of Clairvaux, Thomas à Kempis

(*Imitation of Christ*), Teresa of Avila, John of the Cross, St. Francis de Sales, and John of St. Samson (*Contemplations*). See also Guenin-Lelle and Mourad, introduction to *Jeanne Guyon*, 18–30, especially 25, where Guyon's most often cited authors are listed in order of frequency.

15. Guyon, *Commentary*, trans. Guenin-Lelle and Mourad, Song 1:1, pp. 100–101.

16. Guyon, *Song of Songs*, trans. Whitaker House, Song 1:2, p. 11: "la possession réelle, durable et permanente de son divin objet" (Guyon, *Commentaire*, Song 1.1 [discrepancy is due to the difference between Guyon's Vulgate and Whitaker's Anglican numberings for Song's chap. 1], p. 205). Interestingly, Guyon writes that either union may be transitory *or* permanent. Immediately, a question arises. How is it that the union of the powers is said to be potentially permanent? If the soul remains in this state permanently, is the transition into essential union thereby precluded? Rather than assuming that the union of the powers must cease, she seems to be envisioning various kinds of unions layered upon each other; in other words, the essential union is a deeper level of union, "added to" (so to speak) the betrothal, the more "superficial" union (trans. Whitaker House, Song 1:2, p. 12). The distinguishing factor, then, must be, not the permanent or transitory nature of the union, but the "possession" of its beloved. Also, see note 9 above regarding the term *possession*.

17. Guyon, *Song of Songs*, trans. Whitaker House, Song 1:2, p. 13.

18. Guyon, *Commentary*, trans. Guenin-Lelle and Mourad, Song 1:1, p. 99. The idea of three forms of activity in the soul goes back to Augustine (*De Trinitate* 10.11.17), but Guyon's usage of "faculties" of the soul originates from Peter Lombard's interpretation of Augustine (*Sentences* 1.3.2).

19. Guyon writes of a "suspension or an absorption of the senses" (*Commentary*, trans. Guenin-Lelle and Mourad, Song 2:5, p. 118).

20. Guyon, *Commentary*, trans. Guenin-Lelle and Mourad, Song 1:1, p. 100: "Lorsqu'elle se fait sentir dans la seule volonté, par une amoureuse jouissance, . . . c'est l'union d'amour, attribuée au Saint-Esprit" (Guyon, *Commentaire*, 206). Guyon follows the Augustinian tradition here in assigning different members of the Trinity to these different faculties. The Father is associated with the memory, the Word (or Son) with understanding, and the Holy Spirit with the will.

21. Guyon, *Commentary*, trans. Guenin-Lelle and Mourad, Song 1:1, p. 100: "la plus parfaite de toutes, parce qu'elle approche plus que nulle autre de l'union essentielle; et que c'est principalement par elle que l'âme y arrive" (Guyon, *Commentaire*, 206).

22. Guyon, *Commentary*, trans. Guenin-Lelle and Mourad, Song 1:1, pp. 99–101.

23. Ibid., Song 1:1, p. 100.

24. "Sa parfaite jouissance, qui n'est autre que l'union essentielle" (Guyon, *Commentaire*, 229): "[the soul's] perfect joy, which is none other than essential union" (*Commentary*, trans. Guenin-Lelle and Mourad, Song 2:6, p. 118).

25. According to Guyon, the bride of Christ can experience essential blessedness here and now, even without sight (*Song of Songs*, trans. Whitaker House, Song 1:2a, p. 15). This is a departure from traditional theology (e.g., Augustine, Aquinas, and so on). "Puisque l'on est heureux dès que l'on possède le bien souverain, et que l'on peut en jouir et le posséder sans le voir. L'on en jouit ici dans la nuit de la foi, où l'on a le bonheur de la jouissance sans avoir le plaisir de la vue: au lieu que, dans l'autre vie, l'on aura la claire vision de Dieu avec le bonheur de le posséder. Mais cet aveuglement n'empêche ni la vraie possession, ni la très réelle jouissance de l'objet, ni la consommation du mariage divin" (Guyon, *Commentaire*, 207).

26. All of the quotes in this paragraph are from Guyon, *Song of Songs*, trans. Guenin-Lelle and Mourad, Song 1:1, p. 102.

27. Guyon, *Commentary*, trans. Guenin-Lelle and Mourad, Song 1:1, p. 102. The word *sinking* is Metcalf's translation and can also be found in the Whitaker edition, *Song of Songs*, which relies largely on the Metcalf translation. For a further study on the theme of the "sinking" of the soul, see McGinn, "Abyss of Love." "Or cela se fait lorsque l'âme perd sa proper consistence, pour ne subsister qu'en Dieu: ce qui se doit entendre mystiquement, par la perte de toute propriété et par un récoulement amoureux et parfait de l'âme en Dieu" (Guyon, *Commentaire*, 209).

28. Guyon, *Song of Songs*, trans. Whitaker House, Song 1:2a, p. 18. "Mais c'est comme une goutte d'eau qui perd sa consistance sensible: lorsqu'elle est mise dans une cuve de vin, où elle est changée sensiblement en vin; quoique son être et sa matière en soient toujours distincts, et qu'un Ange pût, si Dieu le voulait, en faire la division. De même cette âme put être toujours séparée de son Dieu, quoique la chose soit très difficile" (Guyon, *Commentaire*, Song 1.1, p. 209).

29. Guyon, *Song of Songs*, trans. Metcalf, Song 1:1, p. 29. "Elle est très propre à être unie, mêlée et transformée en son Dieu" (Guyon, *Commentaire*, 209).

30. For a further study of the language of the "ocean of divinity," see McGinn, "Abyss of Love."

31. Guyon, *Song of Songs*, trans. Metcalf, Song 6:4, p. 102.

32. Guyon, *Song of Songs*, trans. Metcalf, Song 1:1, p. 29: "et non pas selon le dépouillement réel de la subsistance intime" (Guyon, *Commentaire*, 209).

33. *Sacrifice, renunciation, suffering,* and *submission* are among the many terms that Guyon employs to describe the process the soul must undergo to be united to her lover. This language sounds rather dysfunctional, reminding the modern reader of abusive lovers. Indeed, God appears as the ultra-sadist in this depiction. Various authors have discussed—and some have questioned—the "cruelty" of divine love and its violent nature (e.g., McGinn, "Abyss of Love"). Feminist theologians, in particular, have argued against the kind of worldview that Guyon forwards, offering important qualifications and questions. Among others, see Brown, "For God So Loved the World?"; Fortune, "Transformation of Suffering"; Harrison and Heyward, "Pain and Pleasure"; Redmond, "Christian 'Virtues'"; Imbens, *Christianity and Incest*; Brock, *Journeys by Heart* and "Losing Your Innocence"; and Miller, "Eroticized Violence" and "Mystical Masochism."

34. See Daeschler, "Anéantissement," for a history of the term.

35. See, for example, her comments on Song 3:8, 4:9, 6:4, and 7:13. In the next chapter, I will discuss the question of *who* performs the stripping action: God, the self, or both? In other words, who is the primary agent?

36. Guyon, *Commentary*, trans. Guenin-Lelle and Mourad, Song 1:1, p. 100. As already discussed, one difference between the union of the powers and the essential union is that the latter unites the entire person into God's own unity. The distinction between the three members of the Trinity is removed, as is the disunity of the individual. The united soul is united to God in God's unity. What this means to Guyon is not entirely clear, yet she feels free to employ this language. Another difference is that intermediary means of union (in the first union) are replaced by an "immediate operation" of union (in the essential union); again, what this means has not been elucidated and is simply stated. What follows in Guyon's commentary is another way of explaining the soul's advance from betrothal to marriage—or perhaps the manner in which intermediary operations become "immediate" ones. Her language remains unclear here. It may be that she notes tradition in the opening pages of her Song of Songs Commentary, only to then develop her own thought.

37. "This going out is very different from the one spoken about above [comment on Song 1:7] and much more advanced, because the first one was a departure from natural satisfactions, in order to be able to please the Beloved, but this one a departure from the possession of the self, so as to be possessed only by God, and so that, no longer noticing herself within her, she only finds herself within him. This is a transporting of the creature to its origin, such as will be described later" (Guyon, *Commentary*, trans. Guenin-Lelle and Mourad, Song 2:10, p. 121): ". . . et que, ne s'apercevant plus en elle, elle ne se trouve plus qu'en lui" (Guyon, *Commentaire*, 233).

38. Thus far, this might sound similar enough to the union of the powers, where "understanding" and "memory" are absorbed into God, by a profound "self-forgetfulness," as explained above. However, the soul has reached a new level, a more advanced stage in which she is being called out from self, and back into her "Original."

39. Guyon, *Song of Songs*, trans. Whitaker House, Song 3:1, p. 79. This particular quotation comes from her *Justifications*, vol. 2, p. 57 (the footnotes quoting the *Justifications* appear in Metcalf's translation and also in the Whitaker House translation, which borrows in large part from Metcalf). See note 41 below.

40. In her *Moyen court*, Guyon makes repeated reference to "finding the Kingdom of God" within. The influence of Teresa of Avila can arguably be found here, as Guyon is said to have read Teresa and to have been familiar with her *Interior Castle*. A further discussion of this "center of the soul" as the particular residence of God would be helpful, although it lies outside the scope of this project. This tradition can certainly be traced back to Augustine, who writes about accessing the *imago Dei* within. One might, furthermore, find resonance with Meister Eckhart's discussion of the "ground" of the soul.

41. The *Justifications* is Guyon's three-volume work, written in 1694 as a defense of her earlier writings, including her *Commentary on the Song of Songs*. Arguably with the help of Fénelon, she appeals to orthodox mystics, citing accepted thinkers to demonstrate that her thought is aligned with church teaching. At some point, sections from the *Justifications* were added to Guyon's *Commentary on the Song of Songs* as footnotes. They do not appear in the 1790 Paris edition, so it is unclear when they were added or by whom. Metcalf simply states in the introduction to his English translation that they "have been added," and they often serve to shed light on otherwise opaque material.

42. Guyon, *Song of Songs*, trans. Metcalf, Song 3:1, p. 60; this particular quote comes from her *Justifications*, vol. 2, p. 57.

43. For more on the "abyss of God," see McGinn, "Abyss of Love." See also the language of van Schurman along these lines, in chapter 2, the section "The Importance of Nothingness: 'Immersed in the Measureless Ocean of Divinity.'"

44. See McGinn, "Problem of Mystical Union." In this essay, McGinn demonstrates that Tauler and Suso made the same distinction in qualifying Eckhart's language of annihilation.

45. Guyon employs various terms to describe the lure of self-perception. The soul "sees" itself, has "regard" for itself, and pays "attention" to itself. The key issue here is that of *attending to* self. Self-attention

prevents the soul from *attending to* God and focusing one's mind and affections upon him. Simone Weil develops this theme further in her writings on the spiritual life.

46. Guyon, *Song of Songs*, trans. Whitaker House, Song 3:1, p. 79. In the early stages, one must turn inward to devote oneself to the destruction of interior passions, for example. One is to focus on the interior, rather than only on the active life or the exterior, for God dwells within (Guyon, *Song of Songs*, trans. Whitaker House, Song 1:6–7, pp. 29–30). Later on, however, the soul must turn toward her lover (who also remains without), rather than contemplate the self or sink deeper within herself. As Guyon puts it, "Those self-reflections, which were useful in the beginning, become exceedingly injurious at the end" (*Song of Songs*, trans. Whitaker House, Song 3:1, p. 78). This shift away from introversion and introspection applies even to the confession of sin, as found in Guyon's *Moyen court*. This move was certainly deemed problematic by her religious superiors.

47. Guyon, *Justifications*, vol. 2, p. 57 (italics mine), inserted into her commentary on Song of Songs 3:1 (Guyon, *Song of Songs*, trans. Whitaker House, Song 3.1, p. 78).

48. The soul is still at the betrothal stage at this point in the commentary, yet Guyon calls this soul the "bride," even if proleptically.

49. As Augustine put it, "My weight is my love" (*Pondus meum amor meus*); in the case of Guyon, one might say, "My gaze is my love."

50. Guyon, *Song of Songs*, trans. Whitaker House, Song 4:9, p. 106 (italics mine): "Parce que votre amour pur et droit, qui vous tenait appliquée uniquement à moi, ne vous permettait pas de vous regarder vous-même, ni vos propres intérêts: mais seulement de m'envisager avec amour, ainsi que votre souverain objet" (Guyon, *Commentaire*, 255).

51. Guyon, *Song of Songs*, trans. Whitaker House, Song 2:15, pp. 70–71.

52. Guyon, *Song of Songs*, trans. Whitaker House, Song 4:9, pp. 106–7: "Mais hélas! dira cette Amante affligée, comment vous aurais-je regardé, puisque je ne sais où vous être? Elle ne sait pas que son regard est devenu si épuré que, étant toujours direct et sans réflexion, elle ne connaît pas son regard et ne s'aperçoit pas qu'elle ne cesse point de voir" (Guyon, *Commentaire*, 255).

53. Perhaps this provides some clue into the "immediate" (versus mediated) nature of the essential union.

54. Guyon, *Song of Songs*, trans. Whitaker House, Song 4:9, p. 107. Note that this dynamic is very similar to that described by Anna Maria van Schurman in the closing pages of her *Eukleria*.

55. Guyon, *Commentary*, trans. Guenin-Lelle and Mourad, Song 3:7–3:8, pp. 129–30.

56. "As self-praise is what keeps the soul in darkness, and is the cause of all her melancholy nights, the divine attributes are armed against it, that it may not usurp that which belongs only to God" (Guyon, *Song of Songs*, trans. Whitaker House, Song 3:8, p. 89).

57. Guyon, *Commentary*, trans. Guenin-Lelle and Mourad, Song 3:8, p. 129: "All holding swords, and most expert in war: every man's sword upon his thigh, because of fears in the night."

58. As we shall see, self-righteousness becomes the greatest obstacle to union with God and must be extricated decisively through the "final renunciation," yet to come. The battle has only begun; but God does not leave the soul to its own devices, in this dark, dejected state. She explains that these armed men fight to rid the soul of her self-attachments. The sword that destroys the secret presumption of the soul is the "Word of God, deep, searching, and effectual." And this word is "most intimate and penetrating" and "efficient." The second person of the Trinity, the "uncreated Word," is at work here, reducing "to ashes all who oppose its passage." His incarnation served, in fact, to bring human presumption to naught. As Guyon puts it: "[The divine Word] entered into the abasement of the creature to destroy its elevation, and into its weakness to knock down its strength; and it took the form of the sinner to strike down self-righteousness. It does the same in the soul—it abases it, it weakens it, it covers it with misery" (Guyon, *Commentary*, trans. Guenin-Lelle and Mourad, Song 3:8, p. 130).

59. When the soul learns to do this, she will have become less attached to herself. Self-reliance hinders union with God, for the soul clings to, and relies upon, the self rather than God. Regarding the self as nothing, and God as everything, however, prepares the soul for her marriage.

60. See Levinas, "Useless Suffering," Thompson, *Art of Suffering*, and Ward, "Suffering and Incarnation," for further challenges to the general notion of suffering.

61. Guyon, *Song of Songs*, trans. Whitaker House, Song 3:8, p. 88. "They are all armed because it is necessary that the soul be destroyed in all these things to be admitted into Solomon's bed and thus to be the spouse so that the marriage takes place and is consummated" (*Commentary*, trans. Guenin-Lelle and Mourad, p. 130). "Ils sont tous armés, parce qu'il faut que l'âme soit détruite en toutes ces choses, pour être admise dans le lit de Salomon, pour être épouse et afin que le mariage s'achève et se consomme" (Guyon, *Commentaire*, 244).

62. Guyon, *Song of Songs*, trans. Whitaker House, Song 1:16, p. 50: "l'auteur et le centre de tous biens" (Guyon, *Commentaire*, 1:15, 224).

63. She is clothed with God's beauty, not her own, and must return praise to God. The bride attributes all (praise, glory, pleasure) to her bridegroom, because *"nothing belongs to us*—no praise, no glory, and no

pleasure—everything must be referred to Him who is the Author and Center of every good" (Guyon, *Song of Songs*, trans. Whitaker House, Song 1:16, p. 50). Later, however, the bride comes to *share* in the very attributes of God, as we shall see.

64. Augustine, for example, portrayed the infection of sin (*viscum*) as an invisible glue whose viscosity was used to trap birds.

65. Guyon, *Commentary*, trans. Guenin-Lelle and Mourad, Song 2:1 (*"I am the flower of the field, and the lily of the valleys"*), 115. "Je suis, dites-vous, moi-même la fleur du champ, une fleur que vous ne recueillerez pas dans le repos du lit, mais dans le champ de combat, de travail et de souffrance. Je suis le lis des vallées, qui ne croît que dans les âmes anéanties. Ainsi si vous voulez que je vous tire de votre terre, et que je prenne vie en vous, il faut que vous soyez dans le dernier anéantissement: et si vous voulez me trouver, il faut que vous entriez dans le combat et dans la souffrance" (Guyon, *Commentaire*, 226).

66. See note 64 above. This *viscum* keeps the individual mired in self and sin.

67. Guyon, *Song of Songs*, trans. Metcalf, Song 2:12, p. 55: "The Spouse . . . must now be pruned, cut down, stripped and destroyed."

68. Ibid., 46. "Il ne l'est pas encore comme un Epoux, que je doive embrasser dans son lit nuptial; mais seulement comme un bouquet de croix, de peines et de mortifications. Comme un Epoux de sang et un Amant crucifié, qui veut éprouver ma fidélité, en me donnant une bonne part à ses souffrances, car c'est alors ce qu'il donne à l'âme" (Guyon, *Commentaire*, 222). Cf. Guyon, *Commentaire*, 255: "Pour marquer néanmoins l'avancement de cette Ame, déjà héroïque, elle ne dit pas mon Bien-aimé me donnera le bouquet de la Croix, mais il sera lui-même ce bouquet, car toutes mes Croix seront celles de mon Bien-aimé."

69. Guyon, *Song of Songs*, trans. Whitaker House, Song 5:2, p. 118.

70. In her *Autobiography*, the slander and misunderstanding of others is an oft-repeated theme. Guyon explains the torment that she endured at the hand of her mother-in-law, for example: she longed for quiet, prayer, and contemplation, which apparently elicited the rage of her family (even during the early years of her spiritual journey). Later on, she would be slandered for impropriety in her relations with Father La Combe, and other allegations would be leveled at her without any evidence.

71. Guyon, *Song of Songs*, trans. Whitaker House, Song 5:3, p. 122.

72. Guyon, *Song of Songs*, trans. Metcalf, Song 5:3, p. 83 n., from *Justifications*, vol. 2, p. 201.

73. It would be fruitful to do a study of Guyon's usage of Gal. 2:20 ("I have been crucified with Christ, it is no longer I who live, but Christ

who lives in me"). Her corpus is immense, and tracing her references to this text is beyond the scope of this project.

74. Ibid., 85. See also the comment on Song 1:7, "It is therefore necessary that the creature who aspires to the divine union, being well persuaded of the all of God and of its own nothingness, go forth from itself, having only scorn and hatred for self, so as to keep all its esteem and its love for God; and in the same way, it will be admitted into his union. This going forth from the self, by the continual renunciation of self-interest, is the interior exercise that the celestial Lover counsels to the souls who sigh after the kiss of his mouth" (Guyon, *Commentary*, trans. Guenin-Lelle and Mourad, 109).

75. *Song of Songs*, trans. Whitaker House, Song 5:7, p. 138. Note the resonance here with van Schurman's teaching on "becoming nothing."

76. Ibid., 90; *Song of Songs*, trans. Metcalf, Song 5:6, p. 88. Guyon's use of neo-Platonic imagery is striking, most likely inherited from northern European mystics like Ruysbroec and his followers.

77. *Song of Songs*, trans. Metcalf, Song 5:7, p. 90.

78. Guyon, *Vie*, 128. Note again the resonance with van Schurman's emphasis on God being "All" and the self "nothing." It would be fruitful also to compare Guyon with Marguerite de Navarre's teaching on annihilation of the self and merging with "le Tout," though outside the scope of this project (see also note 3 above).

79. Guyon, *Song of Songs*, trans. Whitaker House, Song 1:2a, p. 12.

80. Guyon, *Song of Songs*, trans. Metcalf, Song 7:11, p. 115.

81. Guyon, *Commentary*, trans. Guenin-Lelle and Mourad, Song 6:4, p. 156.

82. Ibid., Song 6:5, p. 159. Regarding this fusion, cf. Bernard of Clairvaux's fourth degree of love and Anna Maria's discussion of returning to the "love of self" once one's love has been purified. Similarly here, the soul's gaze has been purified. Guyon, however, continues: "But all this must be hidden and covered from her view, so that, like a seraphim, she must have veiled eyes, in order no longer to see anything or seek anything in this life. That is, she is not to want to see anything or to look for any discovery by herself, which she cannot do without infidelity. But that does not prevent God from making her discover and understand whatever he pleases. Only the heart remains uncovered because it cannot love too much" (Guyon, *Song of Songs*, trans. Guenin-Lelle and Mourad, Song 6:4, 156).

83. Ibid., Song 6:4, pp. 156–57: "Ici l'Ame ne doit plus et ne peut plus faire de distinction de Dieu et d'elle: Dieu est elle et elle est Dieu, depuis que, par la consommation du mariage, elle est recoulée en Dieu et se trouve perdue en lui, sans pouvoir se distinguer ni se retrouver; la vraie

consommation du mariage fait le mélange de l'âme avec son Dieu, si grand et si intime qu'elle ne peut plus se distinguir ni se voir" (Guyon, *Commentaire*, 276–77). See note 92 below on the possible wordplay between *l'âme* and *l'esprit*.

84. Guyon, *Song of Songs*, trans. Whitaker House, Song 1:2a, p. 18. "C'est comme une goutte d'eau qui perd sa consistance sensible: lorsqu'elle est mise dans une cuve de vin, où elle est changée sensiblement en vin; quoique son être et sa matière en soient toujours distinct" (Guyon, *Commentaire*, Song 1:1, p. 209). The "drop of water falling into a cup of wine" is a traditional image, going back to Bernard of Clairvaux, *De diligendo Deo* 10.

85. *Song of Songs*, trans. Whitaker House, Song 1:2a, 18: "Un Ange pût, si Dieu le voulait, en faire la division. De même cette âme put être toujours séparée de son Dieu, quoique la chose soit très difficile" (Guyon, *Commentaire*, Song 1:1, p. 209).

86. Guyon, *Song of Songs*, my own translation for "fusion that divinizes," the remainder trans. Whitaker House, Song 6:5, 161. "C'est ce mélange qui divinise, pour ainsi parler, les actions de cette créature, arrivée à un état aussi haut et sublime que celui-ci: parce qu'elle partent d'un principe tout divin, à cause de l'unité qui vient d'être liée entre Dieu et cette Ame fondue et recoulée en lui, Dieu devenant le principe des actions et des paroles de cette Ame, quoiqu'elle leur donne aussi le jour et les produise au-dehors" (Guyon, *Commentaire*, Song 6:4, p. 277).

87. Guyon, *Song of Songs*, trans. Whitaker House, Song 7:13, pp. 189–90: "Unité admirable! Tout est commun à l'Epoux et à l'Epouse. Comme elle n'a plus rien qui soit à elle, elle se rend aussi communs tous les biens de son Epoux: elle n'a plus de biens, ni d'intérêts que les siens, . . . mon Bien-aimé, lui dit-elle, tout ce que J'ai est à vous, et tout ce que vous avez est à moi. Je suis tellement dénuée et dépouillée de tout que je vous ai gardé, donné réservé de toutes sortes de fruits, de toutes manières d'actions et de productions quelles qu'elles soient, sans en excepter aucune. Je vous ai donné toutes mes œuvres, tant les vieilles que vous avez opérées en moi, dès le commencement, que les nouvelles que vous opérez à tout moment par moi-même. De plus, je n'ai rien que je ne vous aie donné; mon âme, avec toutes ses puissances et ses opérations; mon corps avec ses sens et tout ce qu'il peut faire. Je vous ai tout consacré, et comme vous me les avez donnés à garder, m'en conservant l'usage, je les garde tous pour vous; de sorte que, et quant à la propriété et quant à l'usage tout est à vous" (Guyon, *Commentaire*, 292).

88. Guyon, *Song of Songs*, trans. Whitaker House, Song 6.5, p. 161.

89. Ibid., Song 7:11, p. 187.

90. Ibid. Perhaps one can remain distinct, even while transformed "into" another. Transformation does not necessarily imply confusion; one can "become" that which one loves—and yet remain distinct. Other passages, however, suggest indistinction, and therein lies the problem.

91. Guyon, *Song of Songs*, trans. Metcalf, Song 6:4, p. 101.

92. Ibid. It is possible that Guyon is employing wordplay here, substituting the feminine *âme* for the masculine *esprit* (from John 4:24, "Dieu est esprit," which becomes "Dieu est elle [*âme*]" in Guyon). (Thanks go to Anne Larsen who pointed this out to me.)

93. See Knox, *Enthusiasm*; Gondal, *Madame Guyon*. Even popular websites, like "The Mindless Mysticism of Madame Guyon" (www.pfo .org/mguyon.htm), seek to counter the following that Guyon has among lay Christians today.

94. Guyon, *Song of Songs*, trans. Whitaker House, Song 6:5, p. 162. "Mais la consommation du mariage ne se fait que lorsque l'Ame est tellement fondue, anéantie et désappropriée qu'elle peut toute, sans réserve, s'écouler en son Dieu. Alors se fait cet admirable mélange de la créature avec son créateur qui les réduit en unité, pour ainsi parler, quoique avec une disproportion infinie: telle qu'est celle d'une goutte d'eau avec la mer: en ce que quoiqu'elle soit devenue mer, toutefois elle est toujours une petite gouttelette, bien qu'elle soit proportionée en qualité d'eau avec toute la mer et propre à être mélangée, et ne faire plus qu'une mer avec elle" (Guyon, *Commentaire*, Song 6:4, 277).

95. Her *Spiritual Torrents* (1682) describes the impetuousness with which the soul loses herself and is joined to God.

96. She does, in fact, make it a point to note that mystical theology, at times, necessarily defies human reason.

97. See Certeau, "Mystic Speech."

98. Kristeva, *Tales of Love*, 297–317.

99. See also St. Ville, "Chaos without Confusion," 9–11, 44, and 85–90.

100. See, for example, the opening lines of *Moyen court.*

CHAPTER 5

1. Guyon states in her *Justifications* that "it is the approach of the fire that blackens the wood, and not its removal." She explains that the bride is "rendered dark-complexioned by the excess of the love that intends to perfect her in Himself, by cleansing her of everything opposed to His own purity" (*Justifications*, vol. 2, p. 274, inserted as a note to Guyon's commentary in *Song of Songs*, trans. Metcalf, Song 1:5, p. 35).

2. Guyon, *Song of Songs*, trans. Whitaker House, Song 8:5, pp. 200–201.

3. For example, Guyon appeals to a stirring passage from St. Francis de Sales's *Treatise on the Love of God* (9.15) that uses this medical imagery (*Song of Songs*, trans. Whitaker House, Song 8:14, pp. 218–19). Earlier on, Guyon writes, "Thy *breasts*, O God, from which Thou nourishest souls in their beginnings, are so sweet and pleasant, that they render Thy children . . . stronger than the stoutest men who are drinkers of *wine*. They are *so fragrant* that, by their charming *perfume*, they attract those souls that are happy enough to perceive it; they are also like a *precious ointment* that heals every interior wound" (*Song of Songs*, trans. Metcalf, Song 1:1, p. 30). Further, in her commentary on chap. 1, she also speaks of "the *ointment* Thou hast already poured forth to heal the evil that sin has caused in our powers, and to purify our senses from the corruption that has there entered" (Song 1:3, p. 31).

4. Guyon, *Song of Songs*, trans. Metcalf, Song 8:5, p. 122.

5. Ibid., Song 4:7, p. 72: "She would now be ready for permanent union, if there were not still within her remains of her former harsh, unyielding, bounded and limited nature, which stands in the way of her happiness. It is not a fault in her nor is it even offensive in the sight of God; it is simply a natural defect, derived from Adam, which her Bridegroom will insensibly take away": "Elle serait par là disposée à l'union permanente, si sa qualité encore dure et rétrécie, bornée et limitée n'empêchait ce bonheur. Cette qualité n'est pas une tache qui soit en elle, ni rien qui offense Dieu: c'est seulement un défaut de sa nature, prise en Adam, que son Epoux détruira insensiblement" (Guyon, *Commentaire*, Song 4:3, p. 252).

6. Guyon, *Song of Songs*, trans. Metcalf, Song 4:1, p. 69. "For her faults are no longer flagrant sins, nor scarcely offences; but rather defects in her still hard and contracted nature, which suffers incredible pain in being so enlarged that it may be lost in God": "Car ses fautes ne sont plus des péchés notables ni presque des offenses, mais des défauts qui sont dans sa nature encore dure et rétrécie, laquelle a une peine incroyable à être étendue pour se perdre en Dieu" (Guyon, *Commentaire*, Song 4:1, p. 249).

7. Guyon, *Song of Songs*, trans. Whitaker House, Song 6:3, p. 153: "Elle ne peut s'empêcher d'exprimer son contentement par ces paroles: *Je suis toute à mon Bien-aimé et mon Bien-aimé est tout à moi.* O avantage inexplicable! Je n'en peux dire autre chose, si ce n'est que je suis toute sans réserve à mon Bien-aimé, et que je le possède sans obstacle, sans empêchement et sans restriction" (Guyon, *Commentaire*, Song 6:2 [discrepancy is due to the difference between Guyon's Vulgate and Whitaker's Anglican numberings for Song's chap. 6], 274).

8. Cf. van Schurman's discussion of this very theme in chapter 2's section "The Importance of Nothingness: 'Immersed in the Measureless Ocean of Divinity.'"

9. Interestingly, the self is not always equated with the soul in Guyon's usage. It is the "self" that needs to be annihilated, not the soul (*l'âme*) per se. *Self* carries with it negative overtones, such as self-love, self-regard, and so on. *Soul* is often used in more neutral terms; for example, it is the soul that longs for God, runs after the Bridegroom, and is united to God in marriage. At the same time, Guyon also writes of the "soul" needing to be freed from vestiges of self-love (see note 10 below for an example). Again, ambiguity of terms remains in Guyon's treatise. In the end, both the soul and the self (however interchangeably at times these terms are used) need to be cleansed from excessive preoccupation with "self," and this is what leads to radical "self-annihilation." See also the discussion in chapter 4's section "Four Levels of Annihilation: Toward Union with God" for ways in which the soul is said to be "stripped" and "skinned" or "pillaged," toward this end. In softer terms, the soul is also "lost," "melted," and "sunk" or "submerged" into the "ocean of divinity."

10. Guyon, *Song of Songs*, trans. Whitaker House, Song 6:3, pp. 152–53: "The moment the soul is wholly freed from self-praise, she is all ready to be received into the nuptial couch of the Bridegroom. She is no sooner introduced there than, tasting the chaste and holy delights of the kiss of His mouth, which she desired at first (see Song of Songs 1:2a), and which she now enjoys in that essential union that has been bestowed upon her, she cannot refrain from expressing her joy in these words: *I am my beloved's, and my beloved is mine!* Oh, wonderful gain! I can describe it no further than that I am unreservedly given up to my Beloved, and that I possess Him without obstacle, hindrance, or restraint!": "Sitôt que l'Ame est entièrement désappropriée, elle est toute disposée pour être reçue dans le lit nuptial de l'Epoux, ou elle n'est pas plutôt introduite que, goûtant les sacrées et chastes délices du baiser de la bouche qu'elle avait désiré d'abord, et qu'elle possède à présent par l'union essentielle dont elle vient d'être gratifiée, elle ne peut s'empêcher d'exprimer son contentement par ces paroles: *Je suis toute à mon Bien-aimé et mon Bien-aimé est tout à moi.* O avantage inexplicable! Je n'en peux dire autre chose, si ce n'est que je suis toute sans réserve à mon Bien-aimé, et que je le possède sans obstacle, sans empêchement et sans restriction" (Guyon, *Commentaire*, Song 6:2, p. 274).

11. Guyon, *Song of Songs*, trans. Metcalf, Song 6:8, pp. 106–7.

12. Guyon, *Song of Songs*, trans. Whitaker House, Song 6:3, p. 153: "Vous êtes si fort à votre Bien-aimé que rien ne vous empêche de vous perdre en lui; depuis que vous avez été toute fondue par la chaleur de son

amour, vous avez été disposée à vous écouler en lui, comme dans votre fin" (Guyon, *Commentaire*, Song 6:2, p. 274). Francis de Sales spoke in similar terms in his *Treatise on the Love of God* (which Guyon is careful to cite in her *Justifications*, footnoted later in Metcalf's translation of her commentary on the Song of Songs, and incorporated into the text of the Whitaker edition): the soul "[comes] forth from self and the confinement of nature to follow Him who has called her," melting "into her Beloved" (Guyon, *Song of Songs*, trans. Metcalf, Song 6:2, pp. 98–99). She leaves "herself behind forever, not only to be united to her Beloved, but to be wholly mingled and made one with him" (*Song of Songs*, trans. Whitaker House, Song 6:3, p. 154, citing from St. Francis de Sales's *Treatise on the Love of God* [6.12]). Guyon cites earlier in that same passage from St. Francis de Sales's *Treatise on the Love of God* (6.12): "But how is this holy melting of the soul into its Beloved accomplished? . . . Like melted balsam, deprived of consistency and solidity, it runs and flows into that which it loves. It does not dart itself by a sudden effort, nor does it cling and clasp as though it would by force become united, but it only flows gently along like a limpid and liquid thing, into the Divinity it adores. . . . So the soul, which though loving, was yet dwelling in self, issues forth in this holy and blessed stream, quitting itself forever, not only to be united to its Beloved, but to be wholly mingled and made one with Him" (Guyon, *Song of Songs*, Song 6:2, pp. 98–99).

13. Guyon, *Commentary*, trans. Guenin-Lelle and Mourad, Song 6:2, p. 155.

14. At worst, perhaps Creation itself was a sort of fall from one's original source, akin to neo-Platonic emanations; an investigation into potential neo-Platonic influences upon Guyon's thought might be a worthwhile enterprise. At the same time, Guyon would never say that the act of creation itself lacked in perfection.

15. Guyon, *Song of Songs*, trans. Whitaker House, Song 1:8, p. 40. See also Certeau, "Mystic Speech," 95, and St. Ville, "Chaos without Confusion," 83–84, for a discussion of the "nothing" versus the "all."

16. Alternately, one may argue that the infection of sin is eradicated first, then followed by the soul's creaturely limitations. Nonetheless, the soul's creatureliness cannot be separated from its infection even from the start; but once the infection is addressed its creatureliness poses its own problem.

17. Admittedly, Guyon would say that there are various seasons in the soul's journey toward God. In the initial stages, she needs to confront sin within. In the final stages, however, she reaches a near perfection—and is limited only by her created narrowness. The manner in which the disease was corrected along the way is not entirely clear (i.e., apart from annihila-

tion); Guyon presents the disease of sin as dark and irrevocable, requiring annihilation. At the same time, the "host of defects" that the soul uncovers in herself turns out to be an asset; Guyon says the soul is more pleasing to the groom when she recognizes the defects that scar her spiritual appearance. A series of annihilations is therefore necessary. First, sin must be destroyed; then, one's created limitedness is also swallowed up in a (further) annihilation.

A contradiction seems to arise in Guyon's thought: she allows for the state of perfection later on, yet she holds that the self needs to remain suppressed. Is this only by virtue of its created nature? She avers that the soul's sinful tendencies can re-emerge at any point.

18. See note 9 above on Guyon's ambiguous interchanging of the terms *self* and *soul*.

19. Guyon writes also in her *Moyen court* that those who devote themselves to Christ "leave themselves to be moved and led by the spirit of grace, who will conduct them to the end for which they were created, which is, to enjoy God. . . . This union cannot be made in the soul by any activity of its own, since God does not communicate himself to the soul, but in proportion as its passive capacity is enlarged."

20. As we have seen earlier, Guyon explains: "The Bridegroom here calls her by the name of *Spouse*, and invites her to hasten in permitting herself to be destroyed and annihilated, and receive the spiritual union. He calls her to her wedding and coronation" (*Song of Songs*, trans. Metcalf, Song 4:8, p. 73). The invitation and call of the Bridegroom are key, and her response is simply to "come" and "permit" herself to be destroyed.

21. Admittedly, one may not have the right to "require" consistency of Guyon. She was anything but systematic, and she herself admits that her own categories defy categorization. See also chapter 4's section "Transgressive Language" for a discussion of the strategy of deliberate "transgressions" of boundaries in meaning.

22. The term *self-annihilation*, which we have been using thus far, is also rendered problematic by the question of agency. At first glance, *self-annihilation* seems to suggest that the soul annihilates herself, i.e., if we take the verb for this noun to be an active one. We might, on the other hand, interpret the term to mean, simply, "annihilation of the self," without explicit reference to the agent behind the annihilating force. Because of the latter case, we will allow the term to remain ambiguous. See also the opening section of chapter 6.

23. Guyon, *Song of Songs*, trans. Whitaker House, Song 2:5, p. 7. Cf. *Commentary*, trans. Guenin-Lelle and Mourad, Song 2:5, pp. 117–18, "He gives it a single grace to prepare it for the sufferings that must follow."

24. Guyon, *Song of Songs*, trans. Metcalf, Song 2:4, pp. 48–49: "La bien-aimée du Roi, sortant du doux entretien qu'elle vient d'avoir avec lui, paraît à ses compagnes comme ivre et toute hors de soi. Elle l'était bien en effet; puisque, ayant bu du plus excellent vin de l'Epoux, elle ne pouvait du moins qu'elle ne fût embrasée de la plus forte ardeur. Aussi l'était-elle de telle sorte, que s'en apercevant fort bien elle-même, elle prie ses compagnes de ne pas s'étonner de la voir dans un état si extraordinaire. Mon ivresse, leur dit-elle, m'est tout à fait pardonnable, puisque mon Roi m'a fait entrer dans ces divins celliers. C'est là qu'il a ordonné en moi la charité. . . . J'ai bu si abondamment de son vin pur et fort qu'il a ordonné en moi la charité" (Guyon, *Commentaire*, Song 2:3 [*sic*; typo for 2:4], p. 227).

25. Guyon, *Song of Songs*, trans. Metcalf, Song 2:3, p. 49.

26. Ibid. Cf. the Bernardian elements of van Schurman's theology of "pure love" in chapter 3's section "Purifying One's Loves."

27. Cf. Augustine, on the idea that God, as the highest good, should be the object of the soul's desire and enjoyment (*fruitio*) and that created things should be used (*usus*) as a means toward achieving that good, in *On Christian Doctrine* 1.3–5, trans. Robertson, 9–11.

28. Guyon, *Song of Songs*, trans. Metcalf, Song 2.4, p. 49.

29. Ibid., Song 8:7 ("Many waters cannot quench love, neither can the floods drown it"), p. 123: "Si les plus grandes eaux des afflictions, des contradictions, des misères, pauvretés et traverses n'ont pu éteindre la charité, dans une telle Ame, il ne faut pas croire que les fleuves de l'abandon à la providence le puissent faire: puisque ce sont eux qui la conservent" (Guyon, *Commentaire*, Song 8:7, p. 298).

30. Guyon, *Song of Songs*, trans. Whitaker House, Song 1:13, p. 46.

31. Guyon, *Song of Songs*, trans. Metcalf, Song 5:12, p. 93.

32. This seems to imply that those who do not experience suffering are doomed to forfeit union with God. They can never be made "fit" for the spiritual marriage—a difficult claim indeed. Guyon, *Song of Songs*, trans. Metcalf (modified), Song 5:3, p. 83, quoting from *Justifications*, vol. 2, p. 201.

33. Guyon, *Song of Songs*, trans. Whitaker House, Song 5:3, p. 121.

34. What this "removal" looks like is unclear in Guyon's commentary on the Song of Songs; perhaps it involves making compromises or somehow avoiding difficult circumstances.

35. Guyon, *Song of Songs*, trans. Whitaker House, Song 5:4, p. 129.

36. Ibid., Song 5.4, pp. 130–31.

37. Ibid., Song 5.4, p. 132.

38. Strangely, Guyon takes this one step further. She speaks of a "thirst" for the cross (as opposed to "desire"). While she does not inflict suffering upon herself, the soul "thirsts" for it.

39. Guyon, *Song of Songs*, trans. Metcalf, Song 8:4, p. 120.

40. *Song of Songs*, trans. Whitaker House, Song 7:12, p. 188. This theme was crucial to Ruysbroec and his followers (including some in France).

41. Guyon, *Autobiography*, 120.

42. Although Guyon has distinguished the "union of the powers" from the "essential union," the essential union nonetheless involves a submerging of the soul's "powers" into God. Union no longer occurs by intermediary means, and one is no longer united to the distinct members of the Trinity; it nonetheless involves an absorption of the faculties into the very unity of God.

43. Guyon, *Song of Songs*, trans. Whitaker House, Song 6.6, pp. 163–64 (italics mine): "L'Epoux redit à son Epouse ce qu'il lui avait dit autrefois, pour lui faire voir qu'elle a présentement très réellement et en libre usage ce qu'elle n'avait alors qu'en germe. Ses dents sont ses puissances, qui sont tellement redevenues innocentes, pures et nettes qu'elles sont parfaitement lavées. Les brebis auxquelles elles ressemblent ne sont plus tondues comme les premières, parce que la facilité de l'usage des puissances est rendue d'une manière admirable et sans confusion. . . . Elles ne son plus stériles, ayant une double fécondité: l'une de faire beaucoup plus qu'elles ne faisaient auparavant et l'autre, de le faire mieux" (Guyon, *Commentaire*, Song 6:5, pp. 278–79).

44. *Song of Songs*, trans. Whitaker House, Song 8:12, p. 207.

45. See McGinn, "Two Female Apostolic Mystics."

46. Guyon, *Song of Songs*, trans. Whitaker House, Song 6:5, p. 163: "si net et si vide de toutes pensées" (Guyon, *Commentaire*, Song 6:4, p. 278).

47. Guyon, *Song of Songs*, trans. Whitaker House, Song 7:4, pp. 179–80.

48. Knox has plenty to say about the megalomaniac nature of her *Autobiography*; others, like Henri Bremond, however, take her words at face value, favoring them over even Bossuet's. Upham, on the other hand, allows for some exaggeration, while holding on to the kernel contained within.

Guyon does not appear to use the term *mystical death* as discretely or as concretely as mystics like Catherine of Siena and Teresa of Avila. For Guyon, the annihilation of the self seems to be more of an ongoing process, occurring at multiple levels. There may certainly be critical moments of death, but they seem to be less pronounced in her autobiography than in accounts of Catherine of Siena's life, for example.

49. See Guyon, *Song of Songs*, trans. Whitaker House, Song 6:1, p. 150 (which is the equivalent of *Commentary*, trans. Guenin-Lelle and Mourad, Song 5:17, p. 153); and Guyon, *Song of Songs*, trans. Whitaker House, Song 8:13, p. 210.

50. Guyon, *Song of Songs*, trans. Whitaker House, Song 7:2, p. 178.

51. Guyon, *Justifications*, vol. 1, p. 114, inserted as a note to Guyon's commentary in *Song of Songs*, trans. Metcalf, Song 7:12, p. 116. See n. 41 of chapter 4.

52. For a treatment of Guyon as apostolic bride, see McGinn, "Two Female Apostolic Mystics."

53. Guyon, *Song of Songs*, trans. Whitaker House, Song 7:12, p. 188–89.

54. It may be that she added her footnote on the "active-passive" state in response to charges against her of Quietism.

55. "It is no longer herself nor her fruits that she contemplates, but she sees everything in God" (*Song of Songs*, trans. Whitaker House, Song 7:12, p. 189).

56. Ibid., Song 1:8, p. 37.

57. Guyon, *Song of Songs*, trans. Metcalf, Song 8:14, p. 128; see also *Song of Songs*, trans. Whitaker House, Song 7:12, p. 189.

58. Guyon, *Song of Songs*, trans. Whitaker House, Song 8:14, p. 212.

59. Guyon speaks frequently of "inconceivable happiness" (e.g., *Song of Songs*, trans. Metcalf, Song 2:16, p. 58; see also the quotation given in note 10 of this chapter).

60. "*Draw me,* says she, into the most interior chambers of my soul, that my powers and senses may all run to Thee by this deeper though less perceptible course. *Draw me,* O Divine Lover! *and we will run after Thee* by recollection which causes us to perceive the divine force by which Thou drawest us towards Thee. In running, we will be guided by a certain *odor,* perceived by virtue of Thine attraction which is the smell of the *ointment* Thou hast already poured forth to heal the evil that sin has caused in our powers, and to purify our senses from the corruption that has there entered. We will even outrun this odor to reach Thee, the center of our bliss. This excellent *perfume* gives rise to the prayer of recollection; because the senses as well as the powers all *run after* its odor, which causes them to taste with delight *that the Lord is good* (Psalm 34:8)" (Guyon, *Song of Songs*, trans. Metcalf, Song 1:3, p. 31).

61. Ibid., Song 1:1, 2, p. 30.

62. Ibid., Song 1:3, p. 31. "Cette jeune Amante prie l'Epoux de la tirer par le centre de son âme, comme si elle n'était point satisfaite de la douceur de ce baume répandu dans ses puissances: car elle pénètre déjà par la grâce de son Epoux, qui l'attire toujours plus fortement qu'il y a une jouissance de lui-même, et plus noble et plus intime que ce qu'elle goûte à présent. C'est ce qui la porte à faire cette demande à son Epoux" (Guyon, *Commentaire*, Song 1:3, p. 211).

63. Guyon, *Song of Songs*, trans. Metcalf, Song 1:2, p. 31. Guyon notes that some of these young souls depart from the path as a result of this immature desire: "Those who leave Him, and permit themselves to be guilty of offences against Him, are such as sought Him only for his delights; not for Himself; when He takes these away, they seek their pleasure elsewhere." On the other hand, "A soul that has enjoyed God in the unspeakable degree, has acquired too refined a taste to be pleased any longer with earthly things" (Song 1:7, p. 38, Metcalf's footnote quoting Guyon's *Justifications*, vol. 1, p. 417).

64. Ibid., Song 1:3, p. 32.

65. She has not yet understood the seeming "cruelty" of his "love," to again leave so suddenly. (At this stage, the soul has not yet reached the marriage.) Without this seeming absence of the divine, however, the "soul would never depart from self, and consequently would never be lost in God." The soul's lover only *seems* to have disappeared (Guyon, *Song of Songs*, trans. Whitaker House, Song 2:9, p. 64). In reality, God is hidden only to test her: he never "removes his look from her, protecting her more carefully than ever, being more closely united to her than ever before by the new union [of the powers] that has just taken place" (Song 2:9, p. 64).

66. Guyon, *Song of Songs*, trans. Metcalf, Song 1:3, p. 32. This is, of course, a common theme that Guyon may have picked up from John of the Cross, among others.

67. Ibid., Song 1:7, p. 40, Metcalf footnoting from Guyon, *Justifications*, vol. 1, p. 417.

68. Ibid., 37. At this juncture, Quietistic elements are clearly evident. This constitutes a departure from classical formulations of this theme of self-surrender.

69. Guyon, *Song of Songs*, trans. Whitaker House, Song 1:13, pp. 45–46; italics mine. "Lorsque l'Epouse, ou plutôt l'Amante (car elle n'est pas encore l'Epouse), a trouvé l'Epoux, elle est si transportée de joie qu'elle voudrait d'abord s'unir à lui. Mais l'union de jouissance continuelle n'est pas encore arrivé. Il est à moi, dit-elle, je ne peux douter qu'il ne se donne à moi dans ce moment, puisque je le sens; mais il est à moi comme un bouquet de myrrhe. Il ne l'est pas encore comme un Epoux, que je doive embrasser dans son lit nuptial; mais seulement comme un bouquet de croix, de peines et de mortifications. Comme un Epoux de sang et un Amant crucifié, qui veut éprouver ma fidélité, en me donnant une bonne part à ses souffrances" (Guyon, *Commentaire*, Song 1:12 [discrepancy is due to the difference between Guyon's Vulgate and Whitaker's Anglican numberings for Song's chap. 1], p. 222).

70. See Heb. 12:2. See also Guyon, *Song of Songs*, trans. Metcalf, Song 4:15, p. 78: "souls who are sincerely desirous of entering into the interior kingdom, and are willing to endure its toils in the hope of enjoying its fruits." Later on, Guyon writes of the need to suffer with Christ (through "crosses, reproaches, and destruction"), *in order to reign with Him* (2 Tim. 2:12) (*Song of Songs*, trans. Whitaker House, Song 3:10, pp. 93–94).

71. Whereas the glory mentioned by Paul is often interpreted as eschatological, Guyon's assertion is that it is attainable in this life. The annihilation of the soul is necessary, however, for this glory to be revealed.

72. Guyon, *Song of Songs*, trans. Metcalf, Song 3:5, p. 64.

73. Ibid., Song 8:5, p. 121.

74. Ibid., Song 6:2, pp. 97–98; italics mine.

75. As Guyon writes in her *Moyen court*: "None can be ignorant, that the sovereign good is God; that essential happiness consists in the union with God; that the saints are more or less glorified, according as this union is more or less perfect" (136).

76. In addition, the soul's essential happiness is found in God's own blessedness—in a God who is "infinitely perfect & forever blessed" (Guyon, *Song of Songs*, trans. Whitaker House, Song 8:14, pp. 214–15). This is one significant point at which Quietism fails, or at the very least certain interpretations of Quietism.

77. As in Latin, for example, there is a grammatical distinction; two kinds of *ut* clauses exist: result *or* purpose clauses (and not both concomitantly). The manner in which one interprets the *ut* makes an enormous difference in the meaning of a sentence.

78. Guyon, *Song of Songs*, trans. Whitaker House, Song 1:8, p. 37.

79. Guyon, *Song of Songs*, trans. Metcalf, Song 3:9, p. 67.

80. Ibid., Song 4:8, p. 73.

81. Guyon uses the analogy of Abraham's sacrifice of Isaac (Gen. 22) in her other writings, e.g., in her Genesis commentary.

82. Job 13:15. See also the proclamation of Daniel's friends of old: "Even if he does not deliver . . ." (Dan. 3:17–18).

83. Guyon, *Commentary*, trans. Guenin-Lelle and Mourad, Song 6:2, p. 155.

84. Guyon, *Autobiography*, 147; italics mine.

85. Guyon, *Song of Songs*, trans. Metcalf, Song 8:5, p. 121: "Who is this that cometh up from the wilderness, replete with delights, leaning upon the arm of her beloved?": "L'Ame monte peu à peu du désert: car son soi-même est un désert, depuis qu'elle l'a abandonné. Ce n'est plus seulement le désert de la foi, mais c'est le désert d'elle-même. Elle regorge toute de délices; parce qu'elle en est comblée et si pleine que comme un bassin

trop rempli des eaux de sa source, elle surabonde de tous côtés, pour en faire part aux autres. Elle n'est plus appuyée sur elle-même; c'est pourquoi elle ne craint plus l'abondance de ses délices. Elle n'a plus de peur d'être renversée, puisque son Bien-aimé, qui les répand dans son sein, les porte lui-même, avec elle, souffrant qu'elle marche appuyée sure lui" (Guyon, *Commentaire*, Song 8:5, pp. 296–97).

86. *Song of Songs*, trans. Whitaker House, Song 8:14, pp. 212–14. See also *Song of Songs*, trans. Metcalf, Song 8:14, p. 129, footnote from *Justifications*, vol. 1, p. 180: "Desire is ever the child of Love; if my love be in God alone, and for himself alone, without respect to self, my desires will be in him alone, and equally pure of selfish motive."

87. *Song of Songs*, trans. Whitaker House, Song 8:14, p. 215: "He is the author of its desires as well as of all its other actions, without any aid from the soul and even without its knowledge—unless he reveals it to the soul directly or through the words that it is led to address to others."

88. Ibid., Song 8:14, p. 215.

89. Ibid., Song 8:14, p. 216.

90. Ibid., Song 8:14, p. 217: "It is [God] who prays and grants his own petitions."

91. Ibid., Song 8:14, p. 213.

92. Ibid., Song 8:14, p. 215.

93. Ibid., Song 8:14, pp. 215–16.

94. The soul is to become the "beverage of God," characterized by a melted heart, soft and yielding (Guyon, *Song of Songs*, trans. Metcalf, Song 7:9, pp. 114–15): The "interior of the soul, which is the best wine, for it is perfectly fluid and runs into God without being hindered by any obstacle in its own consistence . . . is a wine for God's drinking, for He receives the soul into Himself, changing and transforming her *into* Him; He makes her His pleasure and delight. He *forms* and *reforms* her, causing her more and more to disappear and to be more and more wonderfully transformed in Him. It is truly worthy to be the beverage of God, for she alone is capable of making it, and it is also worthy of the soul, since that is its sovereign good and final end" (italics mine).

95. Guyon, *Song of Songs*, trans. Whitaker House, Song 8:14, p. 220. See also note 12 of this chapter for Francis de Sales's usage of this imagery.

96. Guyon, *Song of Songs*, trans. Metcalf, Song 7:6, p. 112; cf. the image of the mirror as used by Augustine in his *De Trinitate*, with reference to the *imago Dei* within the soul. St. Ville also discusses the usage of the "mirror" in Guyon's writing in "Chaos without Confusion."

97. See the above section "Whence the Violence?"

98. Interestingly, any discussion of Christ's wrestling in the Garden is absent from Guyon's narrative. On the other hand, the soul's wrestling process serves a *different* purpose from Christ's—to overcome enmity between the soul and God (which the God-man never knew).

99. In fact, one may liken this blurring of wills to the Apollinarian heresy, thereby accounting for (at least, by analogy) the disappearance (or disregarding) of Christ's human will.

100. I am grateful to Bernard McGinn for helping me to see this distinction and nuancing my reading of Guyon on this point.

101. Guyon, *Song of Songs*, trans. Metcalf, Song 8:12, p. 131.

102. Again, see the discussion on the Chalcedonian problem in chapter 4's section "Transgressive Language."

103. As a result, her union with God is far less lively than Christ's own union with the Father. If not that, then the perfection of Christ's union is demeaned.

104. Guyon writes that the bride is often concealed "in the secret recesses of a living sepulcher" (*Song of Songs*, trans. Whitaker House, Song 6:7, p. 166).

105. Guyon, *Song of Songs*, trans. Metcalf, Song 8:4, p. 120.

106. If she were to slip out of her abandoned state, however, she would lose not only her perfection but also, according to some translations, her very salvation (Guyon, *Song of Songs*, trans. Metcalf, Song 8:6, p. 123). Metcalf and Whitaker interpret the original French to mean that the soul would head immediately to hell at this point, but Guenin-Lelle and Mourad's later translation indicates that the soul would be "as if in hell" (Guyon, *Commentary*, trans. Guenin-Lelle and Mourad, p. 174, comment on Song 8:6, "Put me as a seal upon your heart . . . for love is strong as death, jealousy as hard as hell"). This latter translation is more faithful to the original: "Il la veut tellement toute pour lui que, si par une infidélité autant difficile que funeste, elle venait à se retirer de sa dépendance, elle serait dès ce moment rejetée de lui, comme dans un enfer, par l'excès de son indignation" (Guyon, *Commentaire*, Song 8:6, p. 298).

107. This phrase originates from Miles, *Desire and Delight*, chap. 4, and "Textual Harassment."

108. Certeau, "Mystic Speech" and *Mystic Fable*; cf. St. Ville, "Chaos without Confusion," 77–80, 85–90. For challenges to using the phrase *mystical experience*, see McGinn, "Mystical Consciousness."

109. The long tradition of apophatic mysticism stretches back to Pseudo-Dionysius and extends to *The Cloud of Unknowing*, and so forth. See Turner, *Darkness of God*.

110. See, for example, Leclercq, *Love of Learning*, 222–28, 207, 276, and Weisheipl, "Mystic on Campus."

111. See, for example, Ward, *Experimental Theology.*

CHAPTER 6

1. In advancing this view, van Schurman holds to her Calvinist convictions. Guyon too sounds surprisingly Reformed in her low anthropology and her emphasis on the primacy of grace. Whether or not the Jansenists or the Huguenots influenced Guyon is a question that remains unexplored. Though she does not cite them in her *Justifications* and appeals rather to the classics (like the writings of St. John of the Cross and Francis de Sales, among others), it is difficult to ascertain the different trends "in the air" that she might have unwittingly picked up. See Guenin-Lelle and Mourad, introduction to *Jeanne Guyon*, 18–30, for the various theological influences on Guyon's thought.

2. Taylor, in *Sources of the Self*, for example, traces the modern notion of the "self" to the Enlightenment. For an illuminating discussion of the "mystical self" in Bernard of Clairvaux, Meister Eckhart, and John of the Cross, see McGinn, "Reflections on the Mystical Self."

3. Guyon gives a qualified endorsement of ascetic mortifications in her *Short and Very Easy Method of Prayer* (chap. 10), as well as in her *Vie* (pt. 1, chap. 11). However, it is clear from her *Commentary on the Song of Songs* that her focus is not on physical deprivation but on reorientation of one's will and mind-set.

4. Admittedly, Guyon's imagery is more violent, as we will discuss.

5. In his *Confessions*, Augustine writes of God's "merciful chastisement" and "severe mercy" (trans. Chadwick, 25, 150).

6. Thanks go to my colleague Gerald L. Sittser for this particular distinction and terminology.

7. Augustine also showed the value he placed on the integrity of creation by differentiating between "use" (*usus*) and "enjoyment" (*fruitio*) in his later works. See note 2 of chapter 1 above.

8. See also note 6 of chapter 4; note 56 of chapter 1.

9. Schopenhauer, *World as Will*, 384.

10. Van Schurman, *Eukleria* [1673], 204–6 (see Appendix C for my translation).

11. See, for example, van Schurman's letters to Johannes Jacob Schütz, July 1674–February 1678, manuscript G2.II.33, particularly fols. 2r–3v and

fols. 9r–12r, Archives at the University of Basel Library. Her correspondence with Antoinette de Bourignon displays a similar attitude; see letter
3 (3 March 1668) and letter 4 (6 April 1668) from de Bourignon to van
Schurman, Royal Library, The Hague, MS 78 C 44, fols. 2r–5v, published
in Bourignon, *Le Tombeau de la Fausse Théologie*. See also Irwin, "Anna
Maria van Schurman and Antoinette Bourignon"; Albrecht, "Konfessionsprofil und Frauen"; Baar, "Transgressing Gender Codes"; and Saxby,
Quest for the New Jerusalem.

12. See, for example, my translation of pp. 6–7 of letter 2 (van Schurman to Schütz), in Appendix A.

13. This may be due, in part, to the legacy of Augustine, who argued
that the *summum bonum* alone was to be enjoyed and that creation should
be *used* to enhance that supreme enjoyment. See notes 1 and 2 of chapter 1.

14. A suspicion of "learnedness" is, again, nothing new. It is an ancient
theme that has found multiple variations throughout the history of the
church. Its origin might even be found in the apostle Paul's words regarding the "foolishness" of "human wisdom" (1 Cor. 1:25, 3:19).

15. Though Leclercq speaks primarily of the medieval period, he also
directs his comments to present-day monastics (*Love of Learning*, 276; and
191–202, 207–17, 222–28). See also Weisheipl, "Mystic on Campus"; Constable, *Reformation of the Twelfth Century*; Jaeger, *Envy of Angels*.

16. Guyon writes that the ignominy associated with bearing one's
cross is worse than the actual cross itself. According to her account, she
endured slander of multiple kinds, including an accusation of immoral conduct with her confessor, Father La Combe. None of the charges against her
were substantiated.

17. Comment on Song of Songs 6:2.

18. Bruneau, *Women Mystics*, 125.

19. Father La Combe encountered trouble with the authorities for
sounding too sympathetic to Protestant doctrine and was imprisoned until
his dying breath. First banished to the Bastille in 1687, and then to the
castle of Lourdes until 1715, he was said to have gone insane during his
long confinement. (He developed dementia during that time and tragically
lost his coherency.)

20. Guenin-Lelle and Mourad, preface to *Jeanne Guyon*, xi.

21. See, for example, Hirsh, "Back in Analysis," 292–93 n. 40, as well
as Miller, "Mystical Masochism"; Kristeva, "Pure Silence"; Bruneau, "Mysticisme et psychose"; Knox, *Enthusiasm*, 322–28. Bruneau, among others,
has argued against "psychosis" in Guyon's life (see *Women Mystics*), *contra*
Balsama, "Madame Guyon."

22. See Pryce, "Exploration," for a further analysis of the Quietist elements of Guyon's theology.

23. Muller, *Post-Reformation Reformed Dogmatics,* 17–18.

24. It may have been, in fact, the bridging nature of the Jansenists' theology that won them harsh opposition from both sides. On the other hand, Campbell, in *Religion of the Heart,* argues that while Jansenists were insistent on their anti-Protestant stance, demonstrating not a little anti-Protestant animosity (see, for example, Kolakowsi, *God Owes Us Nothing,* and Sedgwick, *Jansenism in Seventeenth-Century France*), significant cross-fertilization was occurring between Catholic and Protestant thought, namely between Jansenism and French Calvinism, as well as between Quietism and Pietism, where Catholic mysticism and Protestant spirituality found ultimate resonance. Guyon and van Schurman appear to be vivid illustrations of such cross-fertilization.

25. Guyon's connection to the Protestant world, through her publisher, Pierre Poiret, is notable. Interestingly, Poiret (a Dutch Protestant) also exchanged letters with van Schurman, indicating an actual point of connection between these two women. See Chevallier, "Madame Guyon et Pierre Poiret." Admittedly, Poiret probably did not influence Guyon's thought, as he served primarily to publicize her work; nonetheless, this point of contact is illustrative of Campbell's argument that cross-fertilization between the Catholic and Protestant world occurred during this period. See also Tamburello, *Union with Christ.*

26. Irwin, "Anna Maria van Schurman: The Star of Utrecht," 81; also see van Schurman, *Eukleria* [1673], chap. 3.XVIII, 52.

27. Ibid. Interestingly, van Schurman continued to do that, even after joining the Labadist movement. For example, we find her debating Antoinette de Bourignon on the nature of grace and salvation, engaging in finely tuned theological distinctions in the second part of her *Eukleria* (1685 edition, 113–65) and in letters exchanged with Bourignon, cited in note 11 above. In these exchanges, she attempted to convince Bourignon of the priority of grace, even as Bourignon tried to convince her of the error of her ways.

28. Van Schurman, *Eukleria* [1673], 3.V, 39.

29. See, for example, Tamburello, *Union with Christ,* Dowey, *Knowledge of God,* and Billings, *Calvin, Participation.*

30. One must be wary of artificial dichotomies and false caricatures, such as the claim that Voetius's Pietism was "nothing but" harsh, rigorous moralizing. At the same time, various scholars have attempted to demonstrate that his version of Pietism focused more on rules for "godly living" than it did on joy-filled intimacy with Christ. See, e.g., Prozetsky, "Emergence of Dutch Pietism."

31. See Wallmann, *Philipp Jakob Spener* (297–306).

32. See Prozesky, "Emergence of Dutch Pietism," on mysticism in Pietist thought.

33. See, for example, her language of "immersion" into the "infinite ocean of divinity" in *Eukleria* [1673], chap. 3.XII, 46, 55.

34. The exact source of doctrinal dissension is yet unclear. The original reports criticize her lifestyle and her decision to leave the Academy in order to join Labadie's commune more than they specifically analyze her new "doctrine." Her theology, however, was certainly influenced by her leader, Labadie, who had been trained as a Jesuit and would have been familiar with mystical texts. See, for example, Labadie's *Manuel de pieté*, upon which much of the format of van Schurman's *Eukleria* is patterned, and Saxby, *Quest for the New Jerusalem*.

35. Scholarship on Labadie's mystical influences is still lacking, though research has begun on his *Manuel de pieté*. Though I have had illuminating conversations on this subject with Dutch scholars, we have yet to investigate the full extent of van Schurman's (direct and indirect) mystical sources. Because of his widespread reception, Jan van Ruysbroec's thought may have been an influence upon van Schurman, though I have yet to explore these streams of influence. See Mommaers and De Paepe, *Jan van Ruusbroec*. See also Prozesky, "Emergence of Dutch Pietism."

36. As mentioned earlier, the definition of *mysticism* that I have adopted throughout this work is Bernard McGinn's: the "immediate and direct consciousness of the presence of God" (*Foundations of Mysticism*, xvi–xvii, 262; see notes 23 and 36 of chapter 2). See Tamburello, *Union with Christ*, note 40 below, and note 53 of chapter 3, as well as Calvin's *Institutes* (bk. 3, chap. 3) on mortification and vivification.

37. See, for example, Van Schurman, *Eukleria* [1673], chap. 3.XII, 46 and 55. See also van Schurman to Schütz, 12/22 August 1674, letter 2, MS G2.II.33, fols. 2r–v), pp. 2–3, for her language of being "intoxicated" in the wine cellars of the divine lover.

38. See note 65 of chapter 1.

39. Van Schurman cites Calvin frequently throughout her *Eukleria*, even as she borrows from other traditions via Labadie.

40. See Appendices A and B for her exchanges with Schütz that touch on these themes. Also see Tamburello, *Union with Christ*. Whether Calvin wrote about "union with Christ" in the manner in which the mystics like Bernard did is still debated.

41. See, for example, her exchange with Schütz, examined in chapter 3's section "An Essential Practice or the 'Crown of Perfection'?"

42. Bonhoffer, *Cost of Discipleship*, 99.

43. Nonetheless, in her *Justifications*, Guyon claimed that she remained orthodox.

44. Her influence on John Wesley and the Methodist movement, as well as the early Quakers and Moravians, has previously been noted.

45. Nonetheless, she was probably influenced by the teachings of figures like Francis de Sales, Jane de Chantal, Catherine of Genoa, John of the Cross, and Teresa of Avila, even if only transmitted orally. See notes 40 and 14 of chapter 4. See also Guenin-Lelle and Mourad, introduction to *Jeanne Guyon*, 21–30.

46. Despite Guyon's lack of formal education, she was extremely literate; she read and memorized large portions of scripture, at least according to her own account, and she was certainly a prolific writer.

47. This, of course, was a standard mystical trope, which Guyon employs liberally.

48. De La Bedoyere, *Archbishop and the Lady*.

49. Of course, she *had* to argue this if she wanted to escape the miserable fate of the heterodox. Given that she was writing upon the heels of the Quietist controversy in Rome, all were on edge against these "novel ideas."

50. On Teresa de Avila, see note 12 of chapter 5; on de Sales, see note 40 of chapter 4.

51. LeBrun, "Quiétisme."

52. On the other hand, the controversy from Rome had been well known in France, and Molinos's ideas would have been in circulation.

53. Guyon qualifies in her *Justifications* that the most perfect kind of passivity is "active passivity" and quotes Francis de Sales to prove her point. Whether this later "footnote" was specifically in response to the charges of Quietism is difficult to determine. Her accent, however, does seem to fall more heavily on passivity, even more so than on "active-passivity" (see chapter 5's section "Perfect Passivity: The Active-Passive State").

54. The extent of Guyon's "Quietism" is today a subject of debate, but that question is not the focus of this volume. See Pryce, "Exploration," for further discussion of this very theme. On the question of Guyon's heterodoxy, see also Knox, *Enthusiasm*, 322–28, 344–52; Balsama, "Madame Guyon." From my point of view, if one were to label Guyon's thought Quietist, one would have to do the same with Job's proclamation, "Though he slay me, I will praise him" (Job 13:15) or with the cry of Daniel's three friends, "If our God whom we serve is able to deliver us . . . , let him deliver us. *But even if he does not*, let it be known, O king, that we will not serve your gods" (Daniel 3:17–18). To be fair, Guyon might properly be called a "semi-Quietist" because of her emphasis on passivity and holy indifference.

55. See chapter 5 above, the section "Whence the Violence? Guyon's Theological Anthropology," for a discussion of this theme. On the Catholic

side, a more detailed exploration of potential cross-currents between Jansenism and Guyon's theological framework would illuminate further her anthropology and its often hidden sources. Interestingly, Jansenism does not make it into the index page of Guenin-Lelle and Mourad's important volume, *Jeanne Guyon: Selected Writings*, but I suspect that connections may be discovered by further research. (See note 24 above, for example.)

56. For example, van Schurman writes to Schütz that "finally God himself becomes all things, [and] they themselves truly become nothing" (22 December 1674, letter 4, MS G2.II.33, fol. 10v, p. 7), and Guyon speaks of "the all of God and [the soul's] own nothingness" in her commentary to the Song of Songs 1:8 (Guyon, *Song of Songs* [1997], 40).

57. We know that Protestants warmly embraced Guyon, and van Schurman was in frequent correspondence with Catholics in France (e.g., with Antoinette de Bourignon, one of Guyon's forerunners), so there seems to have been some measure of inter-religious traffic between these two pivotal figures. See note 24 above.

58. Guyon, *Moyen court*, 98, and again on 125: "la fin pour laquelle elles ont été créés, qui est de jouir de Dieu." Whether Guyon had access to some version of the Westminster Shorter Catechism (through either oral or written transmission) is still undetermined. We do know that she shared many conversations with Protestant followers in her later years, most notably with Pierre Poiret, with whom Anna Maria van Schurman had also corresponded.

59. Catholics and Calvinists certainly disputed the nature of grace, faith, justification, and the sacraments. What van Schurman and Guyon held in common is therefore instructive.

60. Phil. 3:7–10.

61. Kristeva, *Tales of Love*, 185; see also 297–317.

62. "The house of my soul is too small for you to come to it. May it be enlarged by you. It is in ruins: restore it" (*Confessiones* 1.5.6; [Chadwick, *Confessions*, 6]). For van Schurman and Guyon, the denial, or annihilation, of the self paradoxically serves this purpose; it leads to the expansion of the soul, to be newly filled by the infinite.

63. Matt. 16:24; Mark 8:34–37; Luke 9:23–24.

64. Van Beek, *First Female University Student*, 38–39. Van Beek explains that van Schurman wrote a poem (in German) on this motto of hers, possibly after receiving a marriage proposal that she declined as part of her promise of chastity. Van Schurman wrote this poem in Gothic lettering over a paper-cutting labyrinth composed of hearts and crosses, which is shown on the front cover of this book.

65. Guyon, *Autobiography*, 147; italics mine.

Bibliography

PRIMARY SOURCES BY GUYON

Original-Language Editions

Guyon, Jeanne. *Commentaire au Cantique des cantiques de Salomon.* In *Les torrents et Commentaire au Cantique des cantiques de Salomon, 1683–1684*, edited by Claude Moralie. Grenoble: Jérôme Millon, 1992.

———. *Les justifications de Madame J. M. B. de la Mothe Guyon.* 3 vols. Paris: Dutoit, 1791.

———. *Le Moyen court et autres écrits spirituels: Une simplicité subversive, 1685.* Edited by Marie-Louise Gondal. Grenoble: Jérôme Millon, 1995.

———. *Les torrents spirituels.* In *Les opuscules spirituals de Madame J. M. B. de la Mothe Guion*, edited by Pierre Poiret. Cologne, 1720.

———. *La Vie de Mme J. M. B. de la Mothe Guion écrite par elle-même, qui contient toutes les experiences de la vie intérieure, depuis ses commencemens jusqu'à la plus haute consummation, avec toutes les directions relatives.* Edited by Jean-Philippe Dutoit. 3 vols. Paris: Libraires associés, 1790.

Translations

Guyon, Jeanne. *Autobiography of Madame Guyon, in Two Parts.* Chicago: Moody Press, 1988.

————. *The Book of Exodus: A Study of Exodus from the Viewpoint of the Deeper Christian Life*. Jacksonville, FL: Seedsowers, 2002.

————. *Commentary on the Song of Songs of Solomon*. In *Jeanne Guyon: Selected Writings*, translated by Dianne Guenin-Lelle and Ronney Mourad, 99–180. Mahwah, NJ: Paulist Press, 2012.

————. *Experiencing the Depths of Jesus Christ*. Translation of *Moyen court et très facile pour l'oraison*. Goleta, CA: Christian Books, 1975.

————. *Jeanne Guyon: Selected Writings*. Translated by Dianne Guenin-Lelle and Ronney Mourad. Mahwah, NJ: Paulist Press, 2012.

————. *Madame Guyon's Spiritual Letters*. Augusta, ME: Christian Books Publishing House, 1982.

————. *The Mystical Sense of the Sacred Scriptures with Explanations and Reflections Regarding the Interior Life (Genesis–Deuteronomy)*. Translated by Thomas Watson Duncan. Philadelphia: George W. McCalla, 1913.

————. *The Prison Narratives of Jeanne Guyon*. Translated by Ronney Mourad and Dianne Guenin-Lelle. New York: Oxford University Press, 2012.

————. *Song of Songs*. Translation of *Commentaire au Cantique des cantiques de Salomon* [no translator's name given, but appears to have borrowed much from the Metcalf translation]. New Kensington, PA: Whitaker House, 1997.

————. *The Song of Songs of Solomon: With Explanations and Reflections Having Reference to the Interior Life*. Translation of *Commentaire au Cantique des cantiques de Salomon* by James W. Metcalf. New York: A. W. Dennett, 1879.

————. *The Song of the Bride*. Sargent, GA: SeedSowers, 1990. Translation of *Commentaire au Cantique des cantiques de Salomon*.

PRIMARY SOURCES BY VAN SCHURMAN

Original-Language Editions

Van Schurman, Anna Maria. *Amica Dissertatio inter Annam Mariam Schurmanniam et Andr. Rivetum de capacitate ingenii muliebris ad scientias*. Paris, 1638. Translated into English as *The Learned Maid, Or, Whether a Maid May Be a Scholar?* (Leiden, 1639).

————. *Eukleria seu Melioris Partis Electio. Tractatus Brevem Vitae ejus Delineationem exhibens. Luc 10:41,42. Unum necessarium. Maria optimam partem elegit.* Altona, 1673.

————. *Eukleria seu Melioris Partis Electio. Pars secunda, Historiam vitae ejus usque ad mortem persequens. Luc. 10:41,42 Unum necessarium Maria optimam partem elegit.* Amstelodami, 1685.

————. *Opuscula Hebraea, Graeca, Latina, Gallica. Prosaica & Metrica.* Lugduni Batavororum, 1648.

————. *Pensées d'A. M. de Schurman sur la Reformation necessaire à présent à L'Eglise de Christ.* Amsterdam, 1669.

Translations

Van Schurman, Anna Maria. *Eukleria* (chapters 1 and 2). In *Anna Maria van Schurman: Whether a Christian Woman Should Be Educated and Other Writings from Her Intellectual Circle*, edited and translated by Joyce L. Irwin, 73–94. Chicago: University of Chicago Press, 1998.

————. *Whether a Christian Woman Should Be Educated.* In *Anna Maria van Schurman: Whether a Christian Woman Should Be Educated and Other Writings from Her Intellectual Circle*, edited and translated by Joyce L. Irwin. Chicago: University of Chicago Press, 1998.

OTHER SOURCES

Albrecht, R. "Konfessionsprofil und Frauen: Anna Maria van Schurman (1607–1678) und Antoinette Bourignon (1616–1680)." *Jahrbuch der Gesellschaft für Niedersächsische Kirchengeschichte* 96 (1998): 61–75.

Andersen, Jenny. "Anna Maria van Schurman." In *Reading Early Women: An Anthology of Texts in Manuscript and Print, 1500–1700*, edited by Helen Ostovich and Elizabeth Sauer, 168–89. London: Routledge, 2003.

Armogathe, Jean Robert. *Le quiétisme.* Paris: Presses Universitaires de France, 1973.

Arnold, Gottfried. *Unparteyische Kirchen- und Ketzerhistorie.* Vol. 2. Frankfort, 1715.

Astell, Ann W. *The Song of Songs in the Middle Ages.* Ithaca, NY: Cornell University Press, 1995.

Augustine. *The City of God.* Translated by Marcus Dods. New York: Modern Library, 1950.

———. *Confessions.* Translated by Henry Chadwick. Oxford: Oxford University Press, 1991.

———. *On Christian Doctrine.* Translated by D. W. Robertson Jr. Upper Saddle River, NJ: Prentice-Hall, 1958.

Baar, Mirjam de. "'Now as for the Faint Rumours of Fame Attached to My Name . . .': The *Eukleria* as Autobiography." In *Choosing the Better Part: Anna Maria van Schurman (1607–1678),* edited by Mirjam de Baar, Machteld Löwensteyn, Marit Monteiro, and A. Agnes Sneller, translated by Lynne Richards, 87–103. Dordrecht: Kluwer Academic Publishers, 1996.

———. "Transgressing Gender Codes: Anna Maria van Schurman and Antoinette Bourignon as Contrasting Examples." In *Women of the Golden Age: An International Debate on Women in Seventeenth-Century Holland, England and Italy,* edited by Els Kloek, Nicole Teeuwen, and Marijke Huisman, 143–52. Hilversum: Verloren, 1994.

———. "Verleid of verkozen? Anna Maria van Schurman en het huiszezin van Jean de Labadie." In *Op zoek naar vrouwen in ketterij en sekte: Een bronnenonderzoek,* edited by Dorothée van Paassen and Anke Passenier, 116–41. Kampen: Kok, 1993.

Baar, Mirjam de, Machteld Löwensteyn, Marit Monteiro, and A. Agnes Sneller, eds. *Choosing the Better Part: Anna Maria van Schurman (1607–1678).* Translated by Lynne Richards. Dordrecht: Kluwer Academic Publishers, 1996. Originally published as *Een uitzonderlijk geleerde vrouw* (Zutphen: Walburg Pers, 1992).

Baar, Mirjam de, and Brita Rang. "Anna Maria van Schurman: A Historical Survey of Her Reception since the Seventeenth Century." In *Choosing the Better Part: Anna Maria van Schurman (1607–1678),* edited by Mirjam de Baar, Machteld Löwensteyn, Marit Monteiro, and A. Agnes Sneller, translated by Lynne Richards, 1–22. Dordrecht: Kluwer Academic Publishers, 1996.

Balsama, George Daniel. "The Controversy over French Quietism during the Reign of Louis XIV: Doctrine and Politics, 1686–1700." PhD diss., Brown University, 1970.

———. "Madame Guyon: Heterodox." *Church History* 42 (September 1973): 350–65.

Barnett, Christopher. *Kierkegaard, Pietism, and Holiness.* Burlington, VT: Ashgate Publishing, 2011.

Beaude, Joseph, et al. *Madame Guyon.* Grenoble: Jérôme Millon, 1997. Proceedings of the conference "Recontres autour de la vie et l'oeuvre de Madame Guyon," 1996, Thonon-les-Bains, France.

Becker-Cantarino, Barbara. "Erwäahlung des bessern Teils: Zur Problematik von Selbstbild und Fremild in Anna Maria van Schurmans 'Eukleria.'" In *Autobiographien von Frauen: Beiträge zu ihrer Geschichte,* edited by Magdalene Heuser, 24–48. Tübingen: Niemeyer, 1996.

Bérulle, Pierre. *Bérulle and the French School: Selected Writings.* Edited by William M. Thompson. Translated by Lowell M. Glendon. New York: Paulist Press, 1989.

Billings, Todd. *Calvin, Participation, and the Gift: The Activity of Believers in Union with Christ.* New York: Oxford University Press, 2008.

Birch, Una. *Anna van Schurman: Artist, Scholar, Saint.* London: Longmans, Green, 1909.

Bonhoffer, Dietrich. *The Cost of Discipleship.* New York: Macmillan, 1963.

Bonner, Gerald. "Augustine and Mysticism." In *Augustine: Mystic and Mystagogue,* edited by Frederick Van Fleteren, Joseph C. Schnaubelt, and Joseph Reino. New York: P. Lang, 1994.

Bourignon, A. *Le Tombeau de la Fausse Théologie.* Amsterdam, 1671.

Bossuet, J. B. *Quakerism a-la-mode, or, A History of Quietism.* London: J. Harris & A. Bell, 1698.

Brandes, Ute. "Anna Maria van Schurman." In *Women Writers in German-Speaking Countries,* edited by Elke P. Frederiksen and Elizabeth G. Ametsbichler. Westport, CT: Greenwood Press, 1998.

Bremond, Henri. *A Literary History of Religious Thought in France.* 3 vols. New York: Macmillan, 1936.

Briggs, Robin. *Early Modern France, 1560–1715.* 2nd ed. New York: Oxford University Press, 1998.

Brock, Rita. *Journeys by Heart: A Christology of Erotic Power.* New York: Crossroad, 1988.

———. "Losing Your Innocence but Not Your Hope." In *Reconstructing the Christ Symbol,* edited by Maryanne Stevens, 30–53. Mahwah, NJ: Paulist Press, 1993.

Brown, Joanne, and Carol R. Bohn. "For God So Loved the World?" In *Christianity, Patriarchy, and Abuse: A Feminist Critique,* edited by Joanne Brown and Carol R. Bohn, 1–30. Cleveland, OH: Pilgrim Press, 1989.

Brown, Sylvia. *Women, Gender, and Radical Religion in Early Modern Europe.* Boston: Brill Academic Publishers, 2007.

Bruneau, Marie-Florie. "Mysticisme et psychose: L'autobiographie de Jeanne Guyon." PhD diss., University of California, Berkeley, 1981.
———. Women Mystics Confront the Modern World. Albany: SUNY Press, 1988.
Bulckaert, Barbara. "L'éducation de la femme dans la correspondence d'Anna Maria van Schurman et André Rivet." In La femme lettrée à la Renaissance: Actes du colloque international, edited by Michel Bastianensen, 197–209. Leuven: Peeters, 1997.
Burnaby, John. Amor Dei: A Study of the Religion of St. Augustine. 1947. Reprint, Norwich: Canterbury Press, 1991.
Bynum, Caroline Walker. Holy Feast and Holy Fast: The Religious Significance of Food to Medieval Women. Berkeley: University of California Press, 1987.
Calvin, John. The Institutes of the Christian Religion. Edited by John T. McNeill. Translated by Ford Lewis Battles. Philadelphia: Westminster Press, 1960.
Cameron, Euan, ed. Early Modern Europe. New York: Oxford University Press, 1999.
Campbell, Ted. The Religion of the Heart: A Study of European Religious Life in the Seventeenth and Eighteenth Centuries. Columbia: University of South Carolina Press, 1991.
Canning, Raymond. The Unity of Love for God and Neighbour in St. Augustine. Heverlee-Leuven: Augustinian Historical Institute, 1993.
Certeau, Michel de. "Crise sociale et réformisme spirituel au début du XVIIe siècle: Une nouvelle spiritualité chez les Jésuites français." Revue d'Ascetique et de Mystique 41 (1965): 339–86.
———. The Mystic Fable: The Sixteenth and Seventeenth Centuries. Translated by Michael B. Smith. Chicago: University of Chicago Press, 1992. Originally published as La fable mystique, XVIe–XVIIe siècle (Paris: Éditions Gallimard, 1982).
———. "Mystic Speech." In Heterologies: Discourse on the Other, translated by Brian Massumi. Theory and History of Literature 17. Minneapolis: University of Minnesota Press, 1986.
Chalmers, Thomas. "The Expulsive Power of a New Affection." In Sermons and Discourses, 2:271–78. New York: Thomas Carter, 1844.
Chau, Carolyn. "'What Could Possibly Be Given?': Towards an Explanation of Kenosis as Forgiveness—Continuing the Conversation between Coakley, Hampson, and Papanikolaou." Modern Theology 28 (January 2012): 1–24.

Chevallier, Marjolaine. "Madame Guyon et Pierre Poiret." In *Madame Guyon*, edited by Joseph Beaude et al., 35–49. Grenoble: Jérôme Millon, 1997.

———. "Quel ministère pour une femme? L'exemple d'Antoinette Bourignon (1616–1680) et de Jeanne-Marie Guyon (1647–1717)." *Positions Luthériennes* 47, no. 2 (April 1999): 199–214.

———. "Sur les marges de la spiritualité chrétienne du Grand Siècle en France." Paper presented at Princeton Theological Seminary, 2000.

Clarke, Desmond. "Anna Maria van Schurman and the 'Unum Necessarium.'" Unpublished paper, August 18, 1999.

Coakley, Sarah. *Powers and Submissions: Spirituality, Philosophy and Gender*. Malden, MA: Blackwell, 2002.

Constable, Giles. *The Reformation of the Twelfth Century*. Cambridge: Cambridge University Press, 1998.

Dalrymple, Timothy. "The Ladder of Thorns: Soren Kierkegaard on the Varieties of Suffering." PhD diss., Harvard University, 2009.

Davis, Natalie Zemon. "City Women and Religious Change." Ch. 3 in *Society and Culture in Early Modern France*. Stanford, CA: Stanford University Press, 1975.

De La Bedoyere, Michael. *The Archbishop and the Lady: The Story of Fénelon and Madame Guyon*. London: Collins, 1956.

Deyon, Solange. "'S'il est nécessaire que les filles soint sçavantes,' un manifeste Féministe au XVIIe siècle." In *De l'humanisme aux Lumières, Bayle et le protestantisme,* edited by Michelle Magdelaine and Maria-Cristina Pitassi. Oxford: Voltaire Foundation, 1996.

Douma, Anna Margaretha Hendrika. *Anna Maria van Schurman en de Studie der Vrouw*. Amsterdam: H. J. Paris, 1924.

Dowey, Edward A., Jr. *The Knowledge of God in Calvin's Theology*. Grand Rapids, MI: Eerdmans, 1994.

Dumas, François Ribadeau. *Fénelon et les saintes folies de Madame Guyon*. Geneva: Editions du Mont-Blanc, 1968.

Dupont, Anthony. "Using or Enjoying Humans: *Uti* and *Frui* in Augustine." *Augustiniana* 54 (2004): 475–506.

Erb, Peter C., ed. *Pietists: Selected Writings*. New York: Paulist Press, 1983.

Fénelon, François de Salignac de la Mothe. *The Archbishop of Cambray's Dissertation on Pure Love, with an Account of the Life and Writings of the Lady, for Whose Sake the Archbishop was Banish'd from Court; and the Grievous Persecutions She Suffer'd in France for her Religion.* 1735. Reprint, Germantown, PA: Christopher Sowr, 1750.

Fortune, Marie M. "The Transformation of Suffering: A Biblical and Theological Perspective." In *Violence against Women and Children: A Christian Theological Sourcebook*, edited by Carol J. Adams and Marie M. Fortune, 85–90. New York: Continuum, 1995.

Ghijsen, H. C. M. "Anna Maria van Schurman, 1607–1678." *De Gids* 90, no. 1 (1926): 380–402, and no. 2 (1926): 105–28.

Göbel, M. *Geschichte des christlichen Lebens in der rheinisch-westphälischen evangelischen Kirche*. Vol. 2. Coblens, 1852.

Gondal, Marie-Louise. *Madame Guyon (1648–1717): Un nouveau visage*. Paris: Éditions Beauchesne, 1989.

Gregory, Eric. *Politics and the Order of Love: An Augustinian Ethic of Democratic Citizenship*. Chicago: University of Chicago Press, 2008.

Guenin-Lelle, Dianne, and Ronney Mourad. Introduction to *Jeanne Guyon: Selected Writings*, edited and translated by Dianne Guenin-Lelle and Ronney Mourad. Mahwah, NJ: Paulist Press, 2012.

Guerrier, Louis. *Madame Guyon: Sa vie, sa doctrine, et son influence, d'après les écrits originaus et des documents inédits*. Paris: Librairie académique, Didier, 1881.

Harrison, Beverly Wildung, and Carter Heyward. "Pain and Pleasure: Avoiding the Confusions of Christian Tradition in Feminist Theory." In *Sexuality and the Sacred: Sources for Theological Reflection*, edited by James Nelson and Sandra P. Longfellow, 131–48. Louisville, KY: Westminster/John Knox Press, 1994.

Henry, Paul. *The Path to Transcendence: From Philosophy to Mysticism in Saint Augustine*. Translated by Francis F. Burch. Pittsburgh, PA: Pickwick Press, 1981. Originally published as *La vision d'Ostie: Sa place dans la vie et l'oeuvre de saint Augustin* (Paris: J. Vrin, 1938).

Heppe, Heinrich. *Geschichte der Quietistischen Mystik in der Katholischen Kirche*. Berlin: Wilhelm Hertz, 1875.

———. *Geschichte des Pietismus und der Mystik in der Reformirten Kirche, namentlich der Niederlande*. Leiden, 1879.

Hirsh, Elizabeth. "Back in Analysis: How to Do Things with Irigaray." In *Engaging with Irigaray: Feminist Philosophy and Modern European Thought*, edited by Carolyn Burke, Naomi Schor, and Margaret Whitford, 285–316. New York: Columbia University Press, 1994.

Holloway, Mark. *Heavens on Earth: Utopian Communities in America, 1680–1880*. Mineola, NY: Dover Publications, 1996.

Hollywood, Amy. "Suffering Transformed: Marguerite Porete, Meister Eckhart, and the Problem of Women's Spirituality." In *Meister Eck-*

hart and the Beguine Mystics: Hadewijch of Brabant, Mechthild of Magdeburg, and Marguerite Porete, edited by Bernard McGinn, 87–113. New York: Continuum, 1994.

Imbens, Annie. *Christianity and Incest*. Translated by Patricia McVey. Minneapolis: Fortress Press, 1992.

Irwin, Joyce. "Anna Maria van Schurman and Antoinette Bourignon: Contrasting Examples of Seventeenth-Century Pietism." *Church History* 60 (September 1991): 301–15.

———. "Anna Maria van Schurman: Eine Gelehrte zwischen Humanismus und Pietismus." In *Geschichte der Mädchen- und Frauenbildung*, edited by Elke Kleinau, 309–24. Frankfurt: Campus-Verlag, 1996.

———. "Anna Maria van Schurman: From Feminism to Pietism." *Church History* 46 (March 1977): 48–62.

———. "Anna Maria van Schurman: The Learned Maid of Utrecht." In *Women Writers of the Seventeenth Century*, edited by Katharina M. Wilson and Frank J. Warnke, 164–85. Athens: University of Georgia Press, 1989.

———. "Anna Maria van Schurman: The Star of Utrecht." In *Female Scholars: A Tradition of Learned Women before 1800*, edited by J. R. Brink, 68–85. Montreal: Eden Press Women's Publications, 1980.

———, ed. and trans. *Anna Maria van Schurman: Whether a Christian Woman Should Be Educated and Other Writings from Her Intellectual Circle*. Chicago: University of Chicago Press, 1998.

———. "From Orthodoxy to Pietism: The Self-Reflections of Anna Maria van Schurman." *Covenant Quarterly* 38 (February 1980): 3–12.

Jaeger, Stephen. *The Envy of Angels: Cathedral Schools and Social Ideals in Medieval Europe, 950–1200*. Philadelphia: University of Pennsylvania Press, 2000.

James, Nancy Carol. "The Apophatic Mysticism of Madame Guyon." PhD diss., University of Virginia, 1998.

———. *The Conflict over the Heresy of Pure Love in Seventeenth-Century France: The Tumult over the Mysticism of Madame Guyon*. Lewiston, NY: Edwin Mellen, 2008.

———. *The Pure Love of Madame Guyon: The Great Conflict in King Louis XIV's Court*. Lanham, MD: University Press of America, 2007.

Jantzen, Grace. *Power, Gender, and Christian Mysticism*. Cambridge: Cambridge University Press, 1995.

Johnson, William Stacy, and John Leith, eds. *Reformed Reader: A Sourcebook in Christian Theology*. Vol. 1. *Classical Beginnings, 1519–1799*. Louisville, KY: Westminster/John Knox Press, 1993.

Knox, Ronald A. *Enthusiasm: A Chapter in the History of Religion*. 1950. Reprint, Notre Dame, IN: University of Notre Dame Press, 1994.

Koehler, T. "Fruitio Dei." In *Dictionnaire de spiritualité: Ascétique et mystique doctrine et histoire*, 5:1546–69. Paris: Beauchesne, 1964.

Kolakowski, Leszek. *Chrétiens sans Église: La conscience religieuse et le lien confessionnel au XVIIe siècle*. Translated by Anna Posner. Paris: Gallimard, 1969.

———. "Dutch Seventeenth-Century Neo-denominationalism and *Religio rationalis*." In *The Two Eyes of Spinoza and Other Essays on Philosophers*, edited by Zbigniew Janowski and translated by Agnieszka Kolakowska. South Bend, IN: St. Augustine's Press, 2004.

———. *God Owes Us Nothing: A Brief Remark on Pascal's Religion and on the Spirit of Jansenism*. Chicago: University of Chicago Press, 1995.

———. "The Mystical Heresy and the Rationalist Heresy in Dutch Calvinism at the End of the Seventeenth Century." In *The Two Eyes of Spinoza and Other Essays on Philosophers*, edited by Zbigniew Janowski and translated by Agnieszka Kolakowska. South Bend, IN: St. Augustine's Press, 2004.

Kristeva, Julia. *Tales of Love*. Translated by Leon S. Roudiez. New York: Columbia University Press, 1987. Originally published as *Histoires d'amour* (Paris: Denoël, 1983).

Labadie, Jean de. *Manuel de Pieté, contenant quelques Devoirs et Actes religieux et Chrétiens vers Dieu. Pour L'usage familier de l'Eglise Françoise-Walone de Middelbourg*. Middelbourg, 1668.

———. *La reformation de l'Eglise par le pastorat. Continuë en deus letres pastorales de Jean de Labadie, ministre de Jesus Christ. Ecrites à quelques siens intimes amis & pasteurs zélez. Premiere letre*. Middelbourg, 1667.

Larsen, Anne. "'The Star of Utrecht' Anna Maria van Schurman: The Educational Vision and Transnational Reception of a Savante." Unpublished manuscript.

Le Brun, Jacques. "Le Quiètisme entre la modernité et l'archaïsme." In *Modernité et non-conformisme en France*, edited by M. Yardeni, 86–99. Leiden: Brill Academic Publishers, 1983.

Leclercq, Jean. *The Love of Learning and the Desire for God: A Study of Monastic Culture*. Translated by Catharine Misrahi. New York: Fordham University Press, 1982. Originally published as *L'amour des lettres et le désir de Dieu* (Paris: Éditions du Cerf, 1957).

Lee, Bo Karen. "Madame Jeanne Guyon (1648–1717), A Short and Very Easy Method of Prayer." In *Christian Spirituality: The Classics*, edited by Arthur Holder, 257–68. New York: Routledge, 2009.

Levinas, Emmanual. "Useless Suffering." In *Entre Nous: On Thinking-of-the-Other*, translated by Michael B. Smith and Barbara Harshav, 91–101. London: The Athlone Press, 1998.

Lichtmann, Maria. "Marguerite Porete and Meister Eckhart: *The Mirror for Simple Souls* Mirrored." In *Meister Eckhart and the Beguine Mystics: Hadewijch of Brabant, Mechthild of Magdeburg, and Marguerite Porete*, edited by Bernard McGinn, 65–86. New York: Continuum, 1994.

Lindberg, Carter, ed. *The Pietist Theologians: An Introduction to Theology in the Seventeenth and Eighteenth Centuries*. Malden, MA: Blackwell, 2005.

Linde, S. van der. "Anna Maria van Schurman en haar Eucleria." *Theologia Reformata* 21 (1978): 117–45.

Lough, John. *An Introduction to Seventeenth-Century France*. New York: David McKay, 1954.

Louth, Andrew. *The Origins of the Christian Mystical Tradition: From Plato to Denys*. 1981. Reprint, Oxford: Clarendon Press, 1999.

Mallet-Joris, Françoise. *Jeanne Guyon*. Paris: Flammarion, 1978.

Matter, E. Ann. *The Voice of My Beloved: The Song of Songs in Western Medieval Christianity*. Philadelphia: University of Pennsylvania Press, 1990.

McGinn, Bernard. "The Abyss of Love: The Language of Mystical Union among Medieval Women." In *The Joy of Learning and the Love of God: Studies in Honor of Jean LeClerq*, edited by E. Rozanne Elder, 95–120. Kalamazoo, MI: Cistercian Publications, 1995.

———. "'Evil-Sounding, Rash, and Suspect of Heresy': Tensions between Mysticism and Magisterium in the History of the Church." *Catholic Historical Review* 90, no. 2 (April 2004): 193–212.

———. *The Foundations of Mysticism*. The Presence of God: A History of Western Christian Mysticism 1. New York: Crossroad, 1991.

———. "Love, Knowledge, and *Unio Mystica* in the Western Christian Tradition." In *Mystical Union and Monotheistic Faith*, edited by Moshe Idel and Bernard McGinn, 59–86. New York: Macmillan, 1989.

———. "Mystical Consciousness: A Modest Proposal." *Spiritus* 8, no. 1 (2008): 44–63.

———. "The Problem of Mystical Union in Eckhart, Seuse, and Tauler." In *Meister Eckhart in Erfurt*, edited by Andreas Speer and Lydia Wegener, 538–53. Berlin: Walter de Gruyter, 2005.

———. "Reflections on the Mystical Self." In *Cahiers Parisiens/Parisian Notebooks*, vol. 3, ed. Robert Morrissey, 110–31. Paris: University of Chicago Center Press in Paris, 2007.

———. "Three Forms of Negativity in Christian Mysticism." In *Knowing the Unknowable*, edited by John Bowker, 99–121. New York: I. B. Taurus, 2009.

———. "Two Female Apostolic Mystics: Catherine of Siena and Madame Jeanne Guyon." In *How the West Was Won: Essays on Literary Imagination, the Canon, and the Christian Middle Ages for Burcht Pranger*, edited by Willemien Otten, Arjo Vanderjagt, and Hent de Vries, 313–27. Leiden: Brill, 2010.

McGinn, Bernard, ed. *Meister Eckhart and the Beguine Mystics: Hadewijch of Brabant, Mechthild of Magdeburg, and Marguerite Porete.* New York: Continuum, 1994.

Mercedes, Anna. *Power For: Feminism and Christ's Self-Giving.* London: T and T Clark International, 2011.

Mihailescu, Calin Andrei. "High Nights: Post-Tridentine Mystical Literature (Spain, France, England, Germany, Italy)." PhD diss., University of Toronto, 1992.

Miles, Margaret. *Desire and Delight: A New Reading of Augustine's Confessions.* New York: Crossroad, 1992.

———. "Textual Harassment: Desire and the Female Body." In *The Good Body: Asceticism in Contemporary Culture*, edited by Mary G. Winkler and Letha B. Cole. New Haven, CT: Yale University Press, 1994.

Miller, Julie B. "Eroticized Violence in Medieval Women's Mystical Literature: A Call for a Feminist Critique." *Journal of Feminist Studies in Religion* 15, no. 2 (1999): 25–49.

———. "Mystical Masochism and the Spiritual Status Quo: The Limitations of Appropriation." In *The Eclectic Edition*, edited by Phil Lampe and Julie B. Miller. San Antonio, TX: University of the Incarnate Word, 2004.

Mommaers, P., and N. De Paepe, eds. *Jan van Ruusbroec: The Sources, Content and Sequels of His Mysticism.* Leuven: Leuven University Press, 1984.

Moore, Cornelia Niekus. "Anna Maria van Schurman (1607–1678)." *Canadian Journal of Netherlandic Studies* 11, no. 2 (1990): 138–61.

———. "Anna Maria van Schurman." In *Women Writing in Dutch*, edited by K. Aercke. New York: Garland, 1994.

Mülhaupt, Erwin. "Anna Maria von Schürmann, eine Rheinländerin zwischen zwei Frauenleitbildern." *Monatshefte für evangelische Kirchengeschichtte des Rheinlandes* 19 (1970): 149–61.

Muller, Richard A. *Post-Reformation Reformed Dogmatics*. Vol. 1. *Prolegomena to Theology*. Grand Rapids, MI: Baker Book House, 1987.

Nicéron, Jean-Pierre. *Mémoires pour servir l'histoire des hommes illustres dans la Republic des Lettres: Avec un catalogue raisonné de leurs ouvrage*. Vol. 33. Paris, 1736.

Norris, Richard A., Jr., ed. and trans. *The Song of Songs: Interpreted by Early Christian and Medieval Commentators*. The Church's Bible. Grand Rapids, MI: Wm. B. Eerdmans, 2003.

O'Connor, William Riordan. "The *Uti/Frui* Distinction in Augustine's Ethics." *Augustinian Studies* 14 (1983): 45–62.

O'Donovan, Oliver. *The Problem of Self-Love in St. Augustine*. New Haven, CT: Yale University Press, 1980.

———. "*Usus* and *fruitio* in Augustine, *De doctrina Christiana* I." *Journal of Theological Studies* 33 (1981): 361–97.

O'Neill, Eileen. "Schurman, Anna Maria (1607–78)." In *Routledge Encyclopedia of Philosophy*, vol. 8, 556–59. London: Routledge, 1998.

Paige, Nicholas Dugan. "Being Interior: French Catholic Autobiographies and the Genesis of a Literary Mentality, 1596–1709 (Jeanne Guyon, Antoinette Bourignon, Jean Joseph Surin)." PhD diss., University of Pennsylvania, 1996.

Patrick, Laude. *Approches du quiétisme: Deux etudes. Suivies du Moyen court et très facile pour l'oraison de Madame Guyon (texte de l'édition de 1685)*. Paris: Papers on French Seventeenth Century Literature, 1991.

Pope, Stephen. "Expressive Individualism and True Self-Love: A Thomistic Perspective." *Journal of Religion* 71 (1991): 384–99.

Prozesky, Martin H. "The Emergence of Dutch Pietism." *Journal of Ecclesiastical History* 28, no. 1 (January 1977): 29–37.

Pryce, Rosemary Elaine. "An Exploration of the Theology of Quietism: Its Historiography, Representation and Significance in the Christian Mystical and Quaker Conditions." M.Phil. thesis, University of Birmingham, 2014.

———. "'Upon the Quakers and the Quietists': Quietism, Power, and Authority in Late Seventeenth-Century France, and Its Relation to Quaker History and Theology." *Quaker Studies* 14, no. 2 (March 2010): 212–23.

Randall, Catharine. "'Loosening the Stays': Madame Guyon's Quietist Opposition to Absolutism." *Mystics Quarterly* 26, no. 1 (March 2000): 15–22.

Rang, Brita. "In Distanz zur Moderne: Die gelehrte Anna Maria van Schurman." In *Gelehrsamkeit und kulturelle Emanzipation*, edited by Angelika Ebrecht, 23–47. Stuttgart: Metzler, 1996.

Redmond, Sheila A. "Christian 'Virtues' and Recovery from Child Sexual Abuse." In *Christianity, Patriarchy, and Abuse: A Feminist Critique*, edited by Joanne C. Brown and Carol R. Bohn, 70–88. Cleveland, OH: Pilgrim Press, 1989.

Roothaan, Angela, and Caroline van Eck. "Anna Maria van Schurman's verhouding tot de wetenschap in haar vroege en late werk." *Algemeen Nederlands Tijdschrift voor Wijsbegeerte* 82 (1990): 194–211.

Saxby, Trevor J. *The Quest for the New Jerusalem: Jean de Labadie and the Labadists*. Dordrecht: Martinus Nijhoff, 1987.

Schama, Simon. *The Embarrassment of Riches: An Interpretation of Dutch Culture in the Golden Age*. New York: Alfred A. Knopf, 1987.

Scheenstra, Erica. "On Anna Maria van Schurman's 'Right Choice.'" In *Choosing the Better Part: Anna Maria van Schurman (1607–1678)*, edited by Mirjam de Baar, Machteld Löwensteyn, Marit Monteiro, and A. Agnes Sneller, translated by Lynne Richards, 117–32. Dordrecht: Kluwer Academic Publishers, 1996.

Scheper, George Louis. "The Spiritual Marriage: The Exegetic History and Literary Impact of the Song of Songs in the Middle Ages." PhD diss., Princeton University, 1971.

Schopenhauer, Arthur. *The World as Will and Representation*. Edited by Judith Norman, Alistair Welchman, and Christopher Janaway. Cambridge: Cambridge University Press, 2010.

Schotel, G. D. J. *Anna Maria van Schurman*. Hertogenbosch: Gebroeders Muller, 1853.

Schweitzer, Franz-Josef. "Von Marguerite von Porète (d. 1310) bis Mme Guyon (d. 1717): Frauenmystik im Konflikt mit der Kirche." In *Frauenmystik im Mittelalter*, edited by P. Dinzelbacher and D. Bauer, 256–74. Ostfildern: Schwabenverlag, 1985.

Sedgwick, Alexander. *Jansenism in Seventeenth-Century France: Voices from the Wilderness*. Charlottesville: University Press of Virginia, 1977.

Smet, Ingrid A. R. "In the Name of the Father: Feminist Voices in the Republic of Letters (A. Tarabotti, A. M. van Schurman, M. de Gournay)." In *La femme lettrée à la Renaissance: Actes du Colloque international*

Bruxelles, 27–29 mars 1996, edited by Michel Bastiaensen, 177–96. Louvain: Peeters, 1997.

Sneller, A. Agnes. "Een geleerde vrous: Anna Maria van Schurman als literaire persoon." *Literatuur* No. 6 (1986): 339–50.

Spencer, Carole Dale. "Hannah Whitall Smith and the Evolution of Quakerism: An Orthodox Heretic in an Age of Controversy." *Quaker Studies* 18, no. 1 (September 2013): 7–22.

St. Ville, Susan Monica. "A Chaos without Confusion: A Study of the Mystical Discourse of Jeanne Guyon." PhD diss., University of Chicago, 1996.

Tamburello, Dennis E. *Union with Christ: John Calvin and the Mysticism of St. Bernard.* Louisville, KY: Westminster John Knox Press, 1994.

Tanner, J. Paul. "The History of Interpretation of the Song of Songs." *Bibliotheca Sacra* 154, no. 613 (1997): 23–46.

Taylor, Charles. *Sources of the Self: The Making of the Modern Identity.* Cambridge, MA: Harvard University Press, 1989.

Thomasiu, Jacob, and Johannes Sauerbrei. *Diatribe academica de foeminarum eruditione.* Leipzig: Hahnius, 1671.

Thompson, Ann. *The Art of Suffering and the Impact of Seventeenth-Century Anti-Providential Thought.* Burlington, VT: Ashgate Publishing, 2003.

Thulstrup, Marie Mikulová. "Pietism." In *Kierkegaard and Great Traditions*, vol. 6 of *Bibliotheca Kierkegaardiana*, edited by Niels Thulstrup and M. Mikulová Thulstrup. Copenhagen: C. A. Reitzels, 1981.

Tozer, A. W. *The Crucified Life.* Ventura, CA: Regal, 2011.

Tschackert, Paul. *Anna Maria van Schürmann.* Gotha, 1876.

Turner, Denys. *The Darkness of God: Negativity in Christian Mysticism.* Cambridge: Cambridge University Press, 1995.

———. *Eros and Allegory: Medieval Exegesis of the Song of Songs.* Kalamazoo, MI: Cistercian Publications, 1995.

Upham, Thomas C. *Life, Religious Opinions and Experience of Madame de la Mothe Guyon.* London: H. R. Allenson, 1905.

Van Beek, Pieta. "De geleerdste van allen: Anna Maria van Schurman." In *Met en zonder lauwerkrans: Schrijvende vrouwen uit de vroegmoderne tijd 1550–1850*, edited by Riet Schenkeveld-van der Dussen, Piet Couttenier, Karel Porteman, and Lia van Gemert, 206–10. Amsterdam: Amsterdam University Press, 1997.

———. *The First Female University Student: Anna Maria van Schurman (1636).* Utrecht: Igitur, 2010.

———. "One Tongue Is Enough for a Woman: The Correspondence in Greek between Anna Maria van Schurman and Bathsua Makin." *Dutch Crossing* 19 (1995): 22–48.

———. "Sol iustitiae illustra nos: De 'femme savante' Anna Maria van Schurman en de universiteit van Utrecht." *Akroterion* 40: 145–62.

———. *"Verbastert Christendom"*: *Nederlandse gedichten van Anna Maria van Schurman.* Houten: Den Hertog, 1992.

———. "Een vrouwenrepubliek der Letteren: Anna Maria van Schurman en haar network van geleerde vrouwen." *Tydskrif vir Nederlands en Afrikaans* 3 (1996): 36–49.

Van der Kooi, Cornelius. *As In a Mirror: John Calvin and Karl Barth on Knowing God. A Diptych.* Translated by Donald Mader. Leiden: Brill, 2005. Originally published as *Als in een Spiegel* (Kampen: Kok, 2002).

Wallmann, Johannes. "Labadismus und Pietismus: Die Einflüsse des niederländischen Pietismus auf die Entstehung des Pietismus in Deutschland." In *Pietismus und Reveil*, edited by J. van den Berg and J. P. van Dooren, 141–68. Leiden: Brill, 1978.

———. *Philipp Jakob Spener und die Anfänge des Pietismus.* Tübingen: J. C. B. Mohr (Paul Siebeck), 1986.

Ward, Graham. "Suffering and Incarnation." In *Suffering Religion*, edited by Robert Gibbs and Elliot R. Wolfson, 163–80. New York: Routledge, 2002.

Ward, Patricia A. *Experimental Theology in America: Madame Guyon, Fénelon, and Their Readers.* Waco, TX: Baylor University Press, 2012.

Ward, W. R. *Early Evangelicalism: A Global Intellectual History, 1670–1789.* New York: Cambridge University Press, 2006.

Weisheipl, James A. "Mystic on Campus: Friar Thomas." In *An Introduction to the Medieval Mystics of Europe*, edited by Paul Szarmach. Albany: State University of New York Press, 1984.

Weisner, Merry E. *Women and Gender in Early Modern Europe.* Cambridge: Cambridge University Press, 2000.

Wright, J. Robert, and Thomas Oden, eds. *Proverbs, Ecclesiastes, Song of Solomon.* Ancient Christian Commentary on Scripture 9. Downers Grove, IL: InterVarsity Press, 2005.

Index

mystical tradition and, 57
Teresa of Avila on, 179n8
tradition of interpretation as
individual's union with God,
179n8
soul
annihilation as precondition to loss
of the self into immensity of
God's own being, 63
center of, 63, 201n40
as distinguished from self in Guyon,
83, 209n9
indistinct from God in consummation of spiritual marriage, 74–75
infection from sin vs. creatureliness,
85, 210n16
mystical death, 97–98
purging of evil quality to allow
union with God, 82
union of the three traditional
faculties with members of the
Trinity, 60–61, 198n18
Spener, Philipp Jakob, 12
influenced by van Schurman, 120,
186n4, 194n66
spiritual betrothal, 60–61
distinguished from spiritual
marriage, 200n36, 213n42
Teresa of Avila on, 197n12
as union of the powers, 59
spiritual itinerary as concern of van
Schurman and Guyon, 13
spiritual marriage, 61–63
consummation of, 74–80
as essential union, 59–60, 75
joy of seeing attained only in next
life, 62
spiritual practices of Guyon as model
of resistance, 116
St. Ville, Susan, 80
submission
as theme in Guyon's thought, 11
use of term by Guyon, 200n33
suffering. *See also* sacrifice in Guyon's
thought
for the sake of the Beloved, 115–16
as theme in Guyon's thought, 11

types of, 116
use of term by Guyon, 200n33
summum bonum
Augustine on, 1–2, 220n13
shared vision of, 125–26
surrender of the self to God and, 127

Teresa of Avila
on enjoyment of God, 179n11
influence on Guyon, 123, 124,
197n12, 198n14, 201n40, 223n45
on *Song of Songs,* 179n8
theological anthropology
of Guyon, 81–85, 124, 219n1
higher anthropology in Catholic
thought, 192n27
of van Schurman, 41–43
theology
Jansenist, 221n24
mutual need of monastic and
scholastic, 189n39
similarities between Guyon and van
Schurman, 124–25
viewed as science by van Schurman
in *Dissertio,* 23
theology of Guyon, 122–25
challenges in, 115–17
theology of van Schurman, 119–22
ineffectiveness of her early, 19–20
and inner transformation, 120
limitations in, 113–15
shift in, 24
Thomas à Kempis, 123, 197n14
Thomas Aquinas as mystic and
scholastic, 178n4
torrents spirituels, Les (Guyon), 10,
196n6
Treatise on the Love of God (Francis
de Sales), 195n3, 208n3, 210n12

understanding, effectiveness after
consummation of spiritual
marriage, 92
union, essential. *See* essential union;
spiritual marriage
union of love as union of will with the
Holy Spirit, 61

BO KAREN LEE

is associate professor of spirituality and historical theology at Princeton Theological Seminary.

Milton Keynes UK
Ingram Content Group UK Ltd.
UKHW022246080824
446652UK00021B/433